The COURTESAN, the MAHATMA & the ITALIAN BRAHMIN

TALES FROM INDIAN HISTORY
MANU S. PILLAI

ILLUSTRATIONS BY PRIYA KURIYAN

cntxt

First published by Context an imprint of Westland Publications Private Limited in 2019

1st Floor, A Block, East Wing, Plot No. 40, SP Infocity, Dr MGR Salai, Perungudi, Kandanchavadi, Chennai 600096

Westland, the Westland logo, Context and the Context logo are the trademarks of Westland Publications Private Limited, or its affiliates.

Copyright © Manu S. Pillai, 2019
Illustrations Copyright © Priya Kuriyan, 2019

Manu S. Pillai asserts the moral right to be identified as the author of this work.

ISBN: 9789388689786

10 9 8 7 6 5 4 3 2 1

The views and opinions expressed in this work are the author's own and the facts are as reported by him, and the publisher is in no way liable for the same.

A number of essays in this collection were published in a shorter format in the author's column Medium Rare in *Mint Lounge*. Other essays were first published in *The Hindu*, *Hindustan Times*, *Open*, *The News Minute* and *Mathrubhumi*.

All rights reserved

Typeset by SÜRYA, New Delhi

Printed at Thomson Press (India) Ltd

No part of this book may be reproduced, or stored in a retrieval system, or transmitted in any form or by any means, electronic, mechanical, photocopying, recording, or otherwise, without express written permission of the publisher.

MIX
Paper
FSC FSC® C010615

For Achu

CONTENTS

INTRODUCTION   XIII

PART ONE: BEFORE THE RAJ

THE ITALIAN BRAHMIN OF MADURAI	3
A MARATHA PRINCE'S MORALITY PLAY	7
A MUSLIM DEITY IN A HINDU TEMPLE	12
THE TALE OF TWO SHAKUNTALAS	18
A DALIT AT THE TEMPLE DOOR	23
THE WORLD OF SHIVAJI MAHARAJ	29
BASAVA, WOMEN AND THE LINGAYAT TRADITION	37
'JODHABAI': MORE THAN AKBAR'S WIFE	44
A WEAVER AND HIS MESSAGE	49
A CITY FOR A COURTESAN?	53
WHAT IF VIJAYANAGAR HAD SURVIVED?	58
SULTANS AND RAJAHS: TEXTS AND TRADITIONS	62
DARA SHUKOH: POET AMONG WARRIORS	69
THE LOST BEGUM OF AHMEDNAGAR	74
THE STORY OF THE *KAMASUTRA*	78

SULTANS AND PADSHAHS: FOREIGNNESS IN INDIANNESS	83
MEENAKSHI: FIRST A WARRIOR	87
THE WOMAN WHO HAD NO REASON FOR SHAME	92
ALAUDDIN KHILJI: RULING BY THE SWORD	98
THE COURTESAN WHO BECAME A PRINCESS	103
MEERABAI: A DIFFERENT KIND OF VALOUR	109
THE AKBAR OF THE DECCAN	114
JAHANGIR: THE ENDEARING ECCENTRIC	119
VARARUCHI'S CHILDREN AND THE MAPPILAS OF MALABAR	124
THE WOMAN WITH NO BREASTS	131

PART TWO: STORIES FROM THE RAJ

WHAT IF THERE WAS NO BRITISH RAJ?	143
ROWDY BOB: THE VICTOR OF PLASSEY	148
THE BLOODY MONSOON OF VELLORE	155
WILLIAM JONES: INDIA'S BRIDGE TO THE WEST	160
THE GENTLEMAN REFORMER OF BENGAL	167
THE COLONIAL STATE AND INDIA'S GODS	173
WHEN A TEMPLE WAS BESIEGED IN AYODHYA	178
A FORGOTTEN INDIAN QUEEN IN PARIS	184
THE STORY OF WAJID ALI SHAH	189
VICTORIA MAHARANI AND INDIA	194
THE ABSENT QUEEN OF LAKSHADWEEP	199
THE ENGINEER AND HIS RICE BOWL	204
THE MAN BEHIND MODERN HINDI	209
THE RAILWAYS AND INDIA	215
THE PHULES AND THEIR FIGHT	219

THE AMMACHIES OF TRAVANCORE	226
MACAULAY: THE IMPERIALIST WE LOVE TO HATE	233
FOOTBALL AND NATIONALISM IN INDIA	240
MANUBAI: THE RANI BEFORE THE BATTLE	245
POWER, PREJUDICE AND CURZON	250
WHEN SAVARKAR JUMPED SHIP	255
SAVARKAR'S THWARTED 'RACIAL DREAM'	260
THE CHAMPION OF TUTICORIN	264
THE COMPLICATED V.K. KRISHNA MENON	271
THE SEAMSTRESS AND THE MATHEMATICIAN	276
AN UNSENTIMENTAL MAN OF ACTION	281
THE RESURRECTION OF BALAMANI	286
THE GRAMOPHONE QUEEN OF INDIA	291
A BRAHMIN WOMAN OF SCANDAL	296
'I'M A NAGA FIRST, A NAGA SECOND, AND A NAGA LAST'	300
THE MONK FOR EVERY INDIAN	305
THE PHOTOGRAPHER–PRINCE OF JAIPUR	310
PERIYAR IN THE AGE OF 'ANTI-NATIONALS'	317
ANNIE BESANT: AN INCONVENIENT WOMAN	321
WHAT IF THE MAHATMA HAD LIVED?	326

PART THREE: AFTERWORD

AN ESSAY FOR OUR TIMES	339
SOURCES AND FURTHER READING	353
AUTHOR'S NOTE & ACKNOWLEDGEMENTS	381

INTRODUCTION

We live in times when history is polarising. It has become to some an instrument of vengeance, for grievances imagined or real. Others remind us to draw wisdom from the past, not fury and rage, seeing in its chronicles a mosaic of experience to nourish our minds and recall, without veneration, the confident glories of our ancestors. The collection you hold tells stories from India's countless yesterdays and of several of its men and women. It is an offering that seeks to reflect the fascinating, layered, splendidly complex universe that is Indian history at a time when life itself is projected in tedious shades of black and white. There is much in our past to enrich us, and a great deal that can explain who we are and what choices must be made as we confront grave crossroads in our own times. But, in the end, each reader must draw her own conclusions—this book seeks only to light the way, and to reiterate the importance of that age-old principle: context.

Manu S. Pillai
May 2019

PART ONE

BEFORE THE RAJ

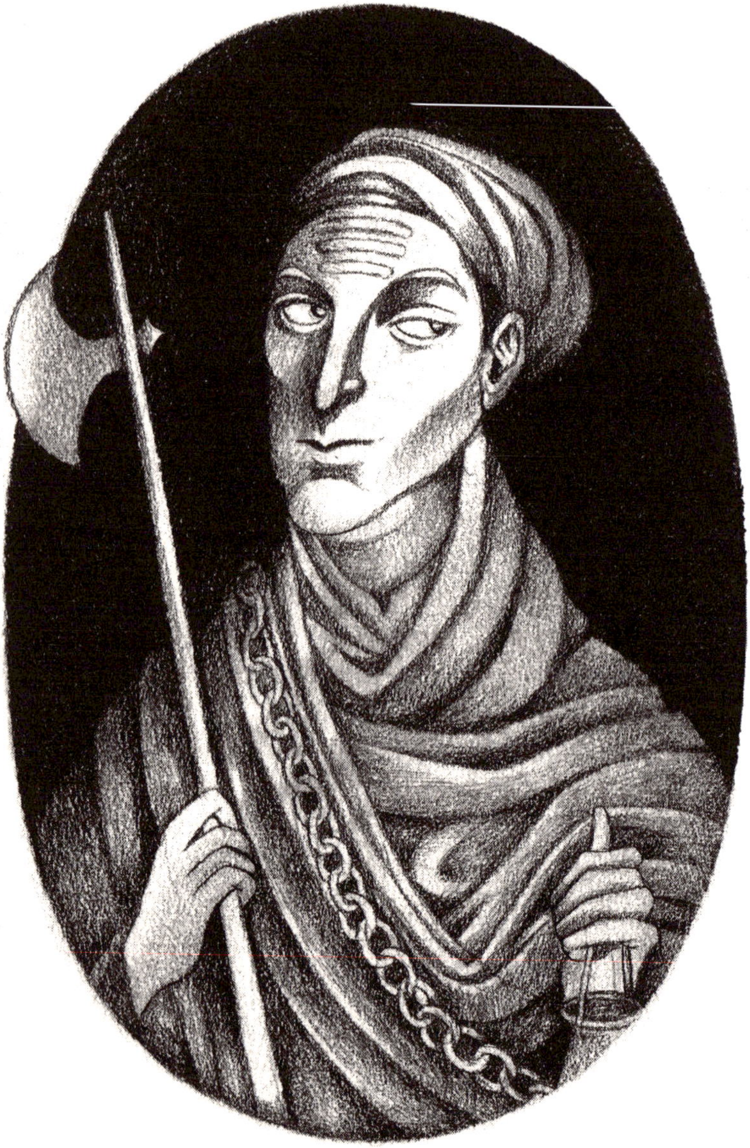

THE ITALIAN BRAHMIN OF MADURAI

In 1623, a venerated sanyasi arrived at the court of the *poligar* (governor) of Sendamangalam, in Tamil Nadu. On the face of it, he was like other divines of his time: One acolyte held up a cadjan parasol, while another carried the tiger skin on which the holy man reposed. Yet another cradled his books, and a fourth a vessel with sanctified water to be sprinkled wherever the party made a halt. Ramachandra Nayaka, lord of Sendamangalam, received them warmly and washed the guru's feet with reverence. In the conversation that followed, a grant of land and other favours were discussed so that the sanyasi might establish a branch of his mission at this important urban centre. After spending a respectable amount of time in the area, the visitors carried on with their travels, going to Salem, where too the provincial administrator received the old man with deference. He was assigned lodgings in 'the finest quarter of the town', and received also a promise of that coveted thing: the governor's official friendship.

When Roberto de Nobili was born in Montepulciano, Italy, in 1577, nobody in his family could have guessed that the boy would spend most of his life oceans away, in the dusty plains of the Indian peninsula, dressed as a sanyasi. The de Nobilis were a military set—they claimed descent from the Holy Roman emperor Otto III, and were related to cardinals, saints, and even a pope or two. As the eldest son of his house, Roberto was expected to carry on the line, but by adolescence he had already quarrelled with his parents and announced his desire to serve the Catholic church. He fled in disguise to Naples and obtained a theological education before setting sail, in 1604, for India. The journey was not smooth—the *Sao Jacinto* was shipwrecked and months were lost in Mozambique. But at last de Nobili arrived in Goa, and quickly thereafter moved to Cochin. And then, to put an even greater distance between himself and the furiously violent government of the Portuguese, the Italian Jesuit orchestrated a transfer to the Christian mission in Madurai—a mission that in fifteen years had made a grand total of zero conversions.

As a missionary, de Nobili's objectives were hardly original. 'I long most keenly,' he declared, 'to travel about these vast spaces, staff in hand, and to win their innumerable peoples for Christ Our Lord.' But what made this particular servant of god stand out was the manner in which he went about collecting his sheep. Soon after he arrived in Madurai in 1606, de Nobili grasped what his colleague, a Portuguese soldier-turned-padre, thirty-six years his senior, had failed to see. European missionaries were dismissed as unclean *parangis* (a variant of the word firangi) who ate beef, kept no caste distinctions, and reaped most converts from 'polluted' communities. Their message, then, was tainted as one for the inferior orders. The older man had no qualms about dealing with the low, given his own working-class origins; de Nobili, however, with his exalted family credentials, his sophisticated education, and a desire to make the gospel attractive to more than the peasantry, decided on a new way going forward. As he announced to a superior with a flourish, 'I will become a Hindu to save the Hindus'.

What followed was a fascinating social experiment. De Nobili acquired a staggering knowledge not only of Tamil, but also Telugu and Sanskrit—a brahmin convert even gave him access to the Vedas, though prejudice prevented him from seeing in them anything beyond 'ridiculous legends and stories'. Soon, de Nobili began to live like a 'native': The Jesuit's cassock was discarded for the ochre garb of a sanyasi, and only food cooked by brahmins was served on his plantain leaf. He began to keep a self-righteous distance from his colleague, establishing a veritable caste system between them—indeed, in 1619, when summoned by angry seniors to Goa to explain himself, de Nobili refused even to eat with them. A new church was constructed (a coconut ceremoniously smashed at its founding) and here, seating was on the basis of status, so that low-born converts had to wait by the threshold while the high-born sat in the front. Meanwhile, de Nobili preached the Bible to the brahmins as a kind of lost Veda, all the time also building up connections with the high and mighty of the land.

Shrewd as this inculturative strategy was, it was also successful. Many brahmins converted, as did a brother of Ramachandra Nayaka of Sendamangalam. In 1610, the Madurai mission had sixty converts, but by the time he died, de Nobili's flock numbered four thousand. The process was not altogether devoid of problems, though. The Italian's high-handedness provoked complaints from his colleague, and in

Goa he was firmly told to suspend his controversial methods. Not only did de Nobili cheerfully disregard such censure, he made more enemies by going behind Goa's back, leveraging connections in Rome and getting, in 1623, Pope Gregory XV himself to declare support for the Madurai mission. In Madurai, meanwhile, brahmins were not ignorant of de Nobili's strategy, and while he was treated well in general by local grandees, a conservative backlash meant there were also times when he had to bear the brunt of their wrath—as in 1640, when he was thrown into prison for a spell.

De Nobili's style provoked a debate about how Eastern peoples ought to be converted (just as his memory still provokes right-wing ire in India). He claimed that the tuft on the head (*kudumi*) and the sacred thread were merely social symbols and converts could continue wearing them. His opponents, however, argued that conversion meant conversion into a European frame, in spirit as well as its outer manifestations. In the end, as it happened, they were the ones who succeeded when it came to church politics, and de Nobili's aristocratic overconfidence led to his downfall: In 1646, he was transferred out of Madurai, and died, blind and distressed, ten years later in Mylapore. It was a lonely end for a clever man with an insatiable zeal. And though his successes lingered, some of them still visible in Tamil Catholicism (such as the car festival of Our Lady of Velankanni, replete with Hindu cultural influences), the taint he had tried so hard to expel came back soon enough to haunt the missionaries: They were parangis, defiled folk, and theirs was a faith only for the poor and weak.

A MARATHA PRINCE'S MORALITY PLAY

In 1684, a twelve-year-old Maratha boy was installed as ruler in Tamil Thanjavur, not long after the region's older Nayaka dynasty folded out of history. The event was emblematic of India in this bustling age, with Tamil Nadu alone attracting Afghan horsemen, Bundela Rajputs, Telugu warriors, and other varieties of adventurers. Our adolescent prince, Shahuji Bhonsle, however, came from a family that was of especial significance for the country. Ten years earlier, his half-uncle, the celebrated Shivaji, had crowned himself king of the Marathas, and theirs was a clan that would seek power over distant reaches of the subcontinent in the years to come. Shahuji, too, was a king worthy of his elaborate titles, but even as he tackled matters of state and deployed armies in the field, he cultivated a reputation as a patron of the arts. Going out of his way to attract as many as forty-six men of letters to his court, he conferred on them an endowed agraharam (settlement), named (with typical princely modesty) after himself.

Interestingly, Shahuji, whose reign lasted till 1712, was also a poet—his *Panchabhasha Vilasa Natakam* reflects the plurality of influences that surrounded him, featuring Tamil, Telugu, Marathi, Sanskrit, and even Hindi verses. He was obsessed with Shiva of the Thiruvarur temple, and many were the plays and songs composed with his blessings that eulogised this deity. Some credit him as the composer of the *Thyagesa Kuravanji* dance drama, centred on the adoration of the lord by a woman. The theme and story are fairly conventional and fit into the larger tradition of Bhakti literature. What is perhaps remarkable—and has been described by scholars as 'a work of extreme, deliberately outrageous provocation'—is another play from his time: the *Sati Dana Suramu* (Take My Wife). While some suggest it might have been composed by one of his court poets, the text itself names Shahuji as its creator, adding casually that he composed it 'to outlast the sun, moon, and stars'.

The *Sati Dana Suramu* is a tremendously entertaining parody of social conventions—one that holds up a mirror to tedious notions of India's past that cast everything as pious and monotonously proper. The setting is the Vishnu temple in Mannargudi, where a brahmin ('Morobhatlu the Magnificent') arrives with his disciple for a popular festival. What upsets this pilgrimage—and, by extension, the correct order of things—is the brahmin's infatuation with a woman he unexpectedly encounters. Not only is his pupil scandalised by this sudden outburst of lust ('My teacher has gone crazy'), but the woman comes from the other end of society: she is an untouchable. When the student warns his guru to protect his reputation, the teacher retorts that greater men had succumbed to lust and survived. When the disciple suggests that females are demons, the older man responds: 'She's no demon, she's a *woman*.' When the frustrated pupil pleads that his guru focus on the 'Vedas and Puranas and Sastras' and their promise of eternal bliss, the brahmin distractedly sniffs that he has 'no use for insipid, eternal bliss'.

Soon, the brahmin approaches the woman, declaring cockily, 'Your charm has reduced me to ashes.' The lady, somewhat taken aback by this unsolicited declaration of love, is polite and reminds her interlocutor of the rules of caste and tradition. 'We eat beef, we drink liquor … Don't talk to me,' she says. Morobhatlu does not care. 'We drink cow's milk,' he replies, 'but you eat the whole cow. You must be more pure.' Clearly startled, the lady decides to lecture him on the impermanence of desire, the permanence of dharma, and other pious philosophical principles, hoping this will make him go away. She also reminds him that she is married, and that it would be best for everyone concerned if he stopped 'this incoherent prattle'. But Morobhatlu is immovable. 'We brahmins have made up all the rules, and invented religion. There is no better dharma than satisfying a brahmin's need,' he giggles. Perhaps, he adds, she could look upon the act as simple charity. 'Give me your loins,' he coyly suggests, 'like offering [a brahmin] land.'

In the end, the woman's husband arrives and, after an initial attempt to beat up his wife's high-born stalker, this untouchable too demands, 'Haven't you read the Sastras?' Irony, in fact, is writ across the composition, where the low-born out-brahmin the brahmin—and so is brilliant comic effect. When the woman's husband reminds Morobhatlu about the godly path, the brahmin responds: 'Final freedom is that state of no pain, no pleasure, no qualities, nothing—or so some idiot said. But when a ravishing young woman ... is free from her clothes—that's freedom for me.'

At long last, then, the husband agrees to present his wife to the brahmin, only for the latter to belatedly heed his pupil's voice ('Have a little detachment; think of the subtle meaning of Vedic words'). In the course of events that follow, the husband is upset, the wife is bewildered, and finally Shiva arrives and liberates everybody from this hilarious, singular quandary. (A little too hilarious, perhaps, for later commentators, who argued that much of the literary patronage extended by Shahuji was for 'vulgar' texts such as this one.)

The *Sati Dana Suramu* is, on the face of it, a simple parody. But viewed in its context, Shahuji, we find, was

The Courtesan, the Mahatma & the Italian Brahmin

making a comment on society itself. As the scholar Sanjay Subrahmanyam notes, 'the play was written ... for public performance' at a major festival, which means its irreverence was consumed by large numbers of pilgrims and locals. Not only does it combine on one stage brahmins and untouchables, it also cleverly exalts Shiva (Shahuji's preferred deity), who swoops in to save the day at a site associated with Vishnu. Questions are raised on ethics and morality, on lust and the role of women. But the larger point Shahuji seemed to make—and make with much mirth and laughter—was that asking questions and turning some tables was not such a bad idea after all. As this Maratha prince in Tamil country asks us at the end of his Sanskrit–Telugu production: 'You, who have seen this play, decide for yourselves and tell us: Who, among these four, is the best?'

A MUSLIM DEITY IN A HINDU TEMPLE

India is a palimpsest of the most curious tales. And very often, seemingly incongruous elements from the realm of fable and myth lend an ironic congruence to the concrete world of men. All through history, a generous fabrication of mythology has helped politics navigate the awkward corners in which its protagonists land themselves. Shivaji is a case in point. The Maratha warrior had emerged as a real force in the late seventeenth century, with armies, treasure and swathes of territory at his command. But rivals, including local families of a provenance superior to his own, painted him merely as an over-strong rebel—a warlord with a frightful number of swords at best—so that in addition to actual power, what the Maratha hero urgently needed was legitimacy. The answer to Shivaji's woes came in 1674, when he decided to promote himself from warlord to king, with classical ritual in extravagant display. A genealogy was 'discovered' connecting him to an ancient royal line, and

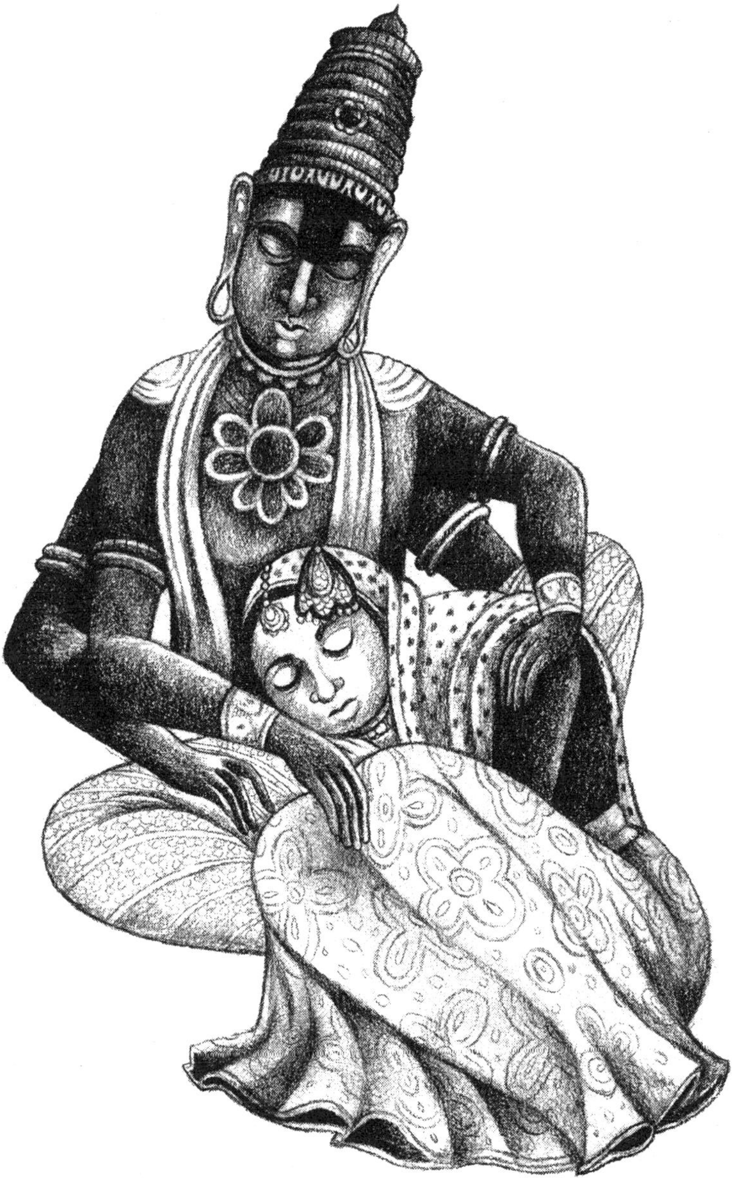

ostentatious rites permitted him to claim 'pure' kshatriya status, when hitherto local brahmins deemed him, like other Marathas, much lower in caste. It was a masterstroke: Shivaji now formally soared above all other Maratha clans (which remained in their previous, relatively inferior position), while simultaneously alerting his Mughal foes that they could no longer dismiss him as a 'mountain rat'. He was a lawful, anointed monarch after that day, and his investment in ritual paid the expected dividend soon enough: when he met the Qutb Shah of Golconda shortly afterwards, he was received with an embrace reserved only for a royal equal.

As a society, India has often negotiated disruptive change through such inventions of tradition. When Muslim might arrived in northern India alongside invaders, a new chapter was inaugurated in the story of the subcontinent. The old order collapsed in many places and a fresh structure was fashioned, with Islamicate ideals in the ascendant. One way in which elites on both sides tried to rationalise these painful changes was, to borrow historian Aziz Ahmad's terminology, through epics of conquest and resistance. Thus, for instance, we have Muslim accounts that exaggerate the 'destruction of infidels' in India, when, in reality, even the terrifying Muhammad of Ghor's early coins prominently featured the 'infidel' goddess Lakshmi without irony—the former legitimised him in the wider Islamic world through literary bombast and bravado, while the latter was a practical concession as he sought to rule a country full of non-Muslims. This was countered, as the scholar Richard H. Davis notes, by Hindu elites with their own exaggerations of suffering and valour, the case of the Rajput queen Padmavati preferring fire to a Muslim's harem being merely one prominent example. On all sides of power, rhetoric was amplified, legends and tales competing

The Courtesan, the Mahatma & the Italian Brahmin

for narrative dominance even as realpolitik was guided on the ground by battles and great armies. Both went hand in hand, adding yet another layer of detail in an already complex land.

One such remarkable story from the fourteenth century features a Muslim woman revered to this day as Tulukka Nachiyar (literally, 'Tughlaq Princess' or 'Turkish Princess'), who is said to have fallen in love with a Hindu god. Even a mere outline of the legend is fascinating: When Muslim troops from Delhi plundered temples in southern India, on their list was the great Vaishnava shrine at Srirangam in Tamil Nadu. The temple chronicle, the *Koil Ozhugu*, tells of the attack of the invading armies, and the fall of a heroic warrior in defence of the temple. The sultan's men then seize the idols, and the image of the deity is transported to Delhi. Unknown to the soldiers, a good woman devoted to the lord travels with them to the north in disguise, even gaining access to the sultan's residence and confirming that her beloved deity is now parked in a palace storeroom. This lady, recalled hereafter as Pin Thodarnda Valli ('she who followed'), now returns to Srirangam where she at once informs the temple authorities of the whereabouts of their lost deity. Liberated from their anguish and sorrow, the Vaishnava bhaktas rejoice, and led by their informant, sixty of them make their way to the court of the sultan to reclaim their god. Coming into the imperial presence there, they entertain the king with music and dance, and ask for the deity of Srirangam to be returned to his rightful place in the south. Pleased with their performance, the Tughlaq sultan happily grants them this wish, commanding his men to go to the storeroom and retrieve Srirangam's deity. Everyone is rather pleased with the turn of events, and there is hope in the air of a happy conclusion.

This is where the twist occurs. It so happens that the sultan's daughter had long before gone into the storeroom and collected the idol, taking it to her apartments and there playing with it as if it were a doll. The implication, however, is that by dressing him, feeding him and garlanding him, as is done to deities in Hindu temple rituals, the princess was essentially worshipping the image, winning divine affection—while during the day he kept her company in the form of an idol, at night, the *Koil Ozhugu* mischievously suggests, he played with the princess in a completely human avatar. As soon as the appeal from the Srirangam party is heard, however, the deity puts his Muslim beloved to sleep and agrees to return with his original devotees. With the consent of the sultan, who is somewhat startled by the animate image, they set out immediately, only for the Tughlaq princess to wake up distraught. She hastens to catch up with the brahmins, who meanwhile have split so that one group can conceal the idol in Tirupati, lest it be kidnapped again. For the princess, this separation is unbearable—arriving in Srirangam but finding her beloved absent, she perishes in the pangs of *viraha*. Her sacrifice is not for nothing, though, for when eventually the deity comes home—which is a separate adventure altogether—he commands the priests to recognise his Muslim consort. She is commemorated in Srirangam in a painting on the wall, where during his processional round, to this day, the deity appears before her in a colourful lungi (the costume associated with the peninsular Muslim) and accepts north Indian food which features such items as chapatti.

The story is a memorable one, with an exact parallel in the Melkote Thirunarayanapuram temple in Karnataka—in this tale, however, the princess is enshrined as a veiled idol in a shrine of her own and not in a wall painting. What is fascinating in either case is not the legend itself but what it seeks to convey. Though it seems unlikely that a Tughlaq princess actually came to the south, head over heels in love with an idol that nightly took human form, could it have been that a Muslim woman was instrumental in having Hindu idols released from Delhi? Or is it, as Davis suggests, a 'counter-epic' where the roles are reversed: Instead of a Muslim king chasing after Hindu princesses, we have a Muslim princess besotted with the Hindu divine? By accepting the concept of a Tulukka Nachiyar within the temple, were the leaders of the time creating a space to locate newcomer Muslims within the world of the orthodox Hindu? Were they seeking to prevail over Islamicate principles by celebrating the Hinduised daughter of a sultan? The truth probably lies in a combination of these, but we can be sure that what we have here is a colourful, revealing narrative with a splendid cast and an exchange between actors who are usually held to be firmly separate and even bursting with unconcealed hatred for one another. It tells us once again that while there were moments of tension between India's principal faiths, legend and myth allowed them to see eye to eye and engage on fresh ground, even while competing in the realm of ideas—a lesson we would be wise to remember in our own contentious times, when revenge is sought from people long dead and gone, and violence justified in the name of so many gods.

THE TALE OF TWO SHAKUNTALAS

In 1791, when Goethe first encountered the legend of Shakuntala, he was moved to the extent of declaring that if heaven and earth were to combine in a name, that name would be hers. Indeed, the German thinker's passion for Kalidas's epic heroine lasted a lifetime, and even on the eve of his death, he was referring to Shakuntala as 'a star that makes the night more agreeable than the day'. Goethe was hardly alone in his fascination for the *Abhijñānaśākuntalam*, which captured Europe's imagination after Sir William 'Orientalist' Jones produced his famous translation, *Sacontala, or The Fatal Ring* in 1789. Since then, this Indian heroine has emerged as one of our most widely recognised mythological characters, featuring in Raja Ravi Varma's canvases as well as on the movie screen, not to speak of endless literary works, at home and abroad. As time passed, as the historian Romila Thapar notes, Shakuntala was swiftly enthroned as the ideal of Indian womanhood, her integrity and blamelessness going down as virtues to be emulated by every good daughter and every self-sacrificing wife.

The Shakuntala Kalidas conceived, however, is markedly different from the original template that appears in the Mahabharata. In this older avatar, Shakuntala is a remarkably direct and confident figure. When Dushyanta, who has killed 'thousands of deer' in the course of his royal hunt, arrives unexpectedly at her adoptive father's hermitage, he calls out, 'Who is here?' Shakuntala appears without a hint of coyness or reserve, even as the royal visitor studies her 'beautiful hips', 'lustrous appearance' and 'charming smile'. Having welcomed him, our protagonist asks how she may be of service, and in the course of their conversation also explains her half-celestial origins. It is only a matter of time before the king is moved to declare: 'Be my wife, buxom woman!,' suggesting to this 'girl of the lovely thighs' that they ought to marry right away, in the gandharva style, where passion compensates for lack of ceremony (or patience). Shakuntala initially asks him to wait but is eventually persuaded that this is indeed a legitimate form of marriage. But even then, she seeks first a promise: Her son from this union must be the king's heir. 'If it is to be thus, Duhsanta, you may lie with me,' she declares. The lady in the Mahabharata is sensible, in other words, and able to command from the king a significant pledge.

The Shakuntala Kalidas's exquisite poetry breathed into life and who went on to inspire Goethe and his generation, was not, as the scholar Kanchana Mahadevan writes, 'the assertive woman of the epic'. Unlike in the Mahabharata, she barely even talks to Dushyanta directly—she is too innocent and sweet to do anything of the sort. In fact, as a companion explains, she is 'as delicate as a jasmine', which also means she knows nothing of the ways of the world. She falls in love with the king, in any case, and he is tempted by this 'flower that no one has smelled'. Their mutual attraction results soon enough in a consummation, and in a twist that might have been inspired by a Buddhist tale, the king departs after handing over to Shakuntala his ring. While she is lost in romantic dreams and yearnings, one day soon afterwards, a sage with a frightful temper appears at the ashram. And not finding her up to the mark in his service, he issues that devastating curse—the lover who so dominated her mind and thoughts when even in the sage's hallowed presence will forget her altogether. Following entreaties by others, he subsequently allows a caveat that when the king beholds the ring he left behind, he will remember Shakuntala,

paving the way for a reconciliation. And so, in this version, matters are taken beyond human control to the realm of fate that serves, in essence, to absolve our male lead of his subsequent betrayal.

The Courtesan, the Mahatma & the Italian Brahmin

The ring and the curse are interesting additions by Kalidas. In the Mahabharata, our heroine, after a pregnancy that lasts thirty-six months, appears at Dushyanta's court with their son to remind the king of his word. 'Remember,' she commands, 'the promise you made long ago when we lay together, man of fortune, in Kanva's hermitage!' Dushyanta, however, quite deliberately chooses not to recognise her. 'I do not know that this is my son … Women are liars—who will trust your word?' he sneers. A powerful exchange follows, and while Shakuntala is angry, she remains full of furious self-assurance. 'Even without you, Duhsanta, my son shall reign over the four-cornered earth,' she declares. 'My birth is higher than yours, Duhsanta! You walk on earth, great king, but I fly the skies.' Eventually, a magical voice confirms that the boy is the king's son, upon which Dushyanta announces that he had known Shakuntala was telling the truth all along. As Wendy Doniger translates: 'I knew … that he was my own son. But if I had accepted him … just from her words, there would have been doubt among the people.' The king, for reasons of public approval, then, had been loudly stating an untruth. And without irony, he then proceeds to forgive Shakuntala for *her* harsh words! (Clearly, patriarchy is as old as any Indian tradition.)

In Kalidas, this very episode is completely transformed, in a reflection of the changing mores of the poet's own time. In his version, Shakuntala is pregnant, and accompanied by others who speak for her in court—as mentioned earlier, cultured women like her do not presume to have a voice. The king does not recognise her and suggests that she is trying to pass off another man's seed as his own. 'Don't cuckoos let other birds nurture their eggs and teach the chicks to fly?' he asks in an unkind taunt. But through the device of the curse—which means the king has *genuinely* forgotten Shakuntala—Kalidas exonerates him, whereas, in the Mahabharata, Dushyanta is guilty and telling a calculated lie. The fact that Shakuntala has lost the all-important ring complicates matters. But unlike, to quote Thapar again, 'the spirited woman who argues her right' in the epic, Shakuntala in Kalidas's retelling sheds pious tears till her mother, the celestial nymph Menaka, comes to her rescue and takes her away. Eventually, after the ring reaches the king through the means of a dead fish, he remembers everything and sets out to reunite with his wife and child. Nobody is to blame here—Shakuntala is pure, the king's crudeness was the result of a curse, and what really determined matters was a tragic twist of fate, not human choice and action.

Kalidas's was a tremendously popular retelling of the story given that the hero and heroine are both romantic victims. But the play also encapsulates a moment when the powerful woman of the epic makes way for a new ideal—an ideal that was embraced by Western audiences in Goethe's day, and which Indians too accepted (in a nineteenth-century Urdu translation, Shakuntala is so chaste she even wears a veil). This Shakuntala, who travelled seamlessly from Kalidas's Sanskrit verses to the Victorian imagination, still eclipses the more remarkable woman who first appears in the great Indian epic: one who does not conform to notions of patriarchal correctness and stands proud, instead, as a challenge to the world of men.

A DALIT AT THE TEMPLE DOOR

In 1784, administrative officers of the Peshwa in Pune, the formal headquarters of the Maratha Confederacy, issued orders to the authorities in Pandharpur concerning the prominent shrine of Vithoba in that pilgrim town. There was, they pointed out, a stone image commemorating a low-caste Bhakti saint outside the principal temple, and untouchable men and women often gathered there to worship. However, 'the place is so narrow and crowded', the order observed, 'that the visitors [to the temple in general] are touched to one another and the brahmins are opposed to this. Therefore the untouchables should perform worship from near the stone-lamp', which stood close by, 'or from a nearby untouchable hamlet', steering clear of the path used by brahmins and their other high-born neighbours. 'Those who [continue worshipping in the old way],' the despatch warned in conclusion, 'shall be punished.'

About four hundred years before the Peshwa's orders arrived from Pune, Pandharpur was home to a man called Chokhamela—the very Bhakti saint whose image is referred to in the 1784 order. From early in his life, Chokhamela was devoted to the deity, and it was only his untouchable Mahar caste status that kept him from beholding Vithoba within the temple premises. He was resigned to his fate for the most part, though now and then his frustration took the form of appeals to the brahmin gatekeepers of the temple. 'The cane is crooked, but its juice isn't crooked,' he cried. 'Chokha is ugly, but his feelings aren't ugly. Why be fooled by outward appearance?' It was a question he asked in the fourteenth century, but even towards the dawn of the nineteenth century, those of his kind received in response only continued rejection, and no real answer.

Among Maharashtra's (male) Bhakti thinkers, Chokhamela is the first untouchable to appear, though he spent most of his life doing the peculiarly menial work that was the mandate of the Mahars. His fellow saints in the Bhakti pantheon, in comparison, came from relative privilege, though few could be reckoned as part of the elite—Tukaram was a failed shopkeeper, Namdev a god-fearing tailor. Yet, the fact that while they were low (sudra), they were not among the lowest (atisudra) meant certain liberties were permitted to them. Their verses, therefore, often took the risk of packing a punch. Jnandev, son of an ostracised brahmin, is said to have mocked the old guard by causing a random buffalo to produce sounds that resembled Vedic verses, while Tukaram was relieved that he was 'no wretched pandit splitting Vedantic hairs'. They could all, to some degree, get away with a certain radicalism even within a deeply hierarchical social order, while for Chokhamela the untouchable, this was never a feasible option.

The Courtesan, the Mahatma & the Italian Brahmin

Instead, he couched his devotion in terms of his social conditioning as a Mahar. Addressing the deity as he might an upper-caste superior, he sang: 'I am the Mahar of your Mahars, I am so hungry; I have come for your leavings, I am full of hope.' In another verse, he brings a 'bowl for your leftover food'—with no access to the shrine and its blessed occupant, perhaps he could satisfy his devotion by serving the deity as a low-born serves his overlord, eating his scraps and offering complete submission? 'O god, my caste is low; how can I serve you? Everyone tells me to go away; how can I see you? When I touch anyone, they take offense ... Chokha wants your mercy.'

Interestingly, though there is anguish, the Mahar poet rarely points a finger at those who designed his shackles and branded him at birth as undeserving. Indeed, he goes as far as to flagellate himself, blaming karma for his terrible plight. In a previous birth, he explains in an example of the fatalism caste engenders, he must have disrespected god; 'this [present] impurity is the fruit of our past'.

While there were moments when Chokhamela seemed on the verge of standing up to those in power ('The earth and the Ganga are common to all, irrespective of caste and religion'), it was his son who was more blunt in his criticism of the way things were. Karmamela, as the boy came to be known, spoke thus to the deity: 'Are we happy when we're with you? ... The low place is our lot; the low place is our lot; the low place is our lot, King of gods! ... It's a shameful life here for us. It's a festival of bliss for you and misery written on our faces.' It isn't surprising, as the historian Eleanor Zelliot found, that Karmamela, with his sharper critique, finds fewer devotees singing his verses during the annual pilgrimage to Pandharpur today. In contrast, Chokhamela has been elevated

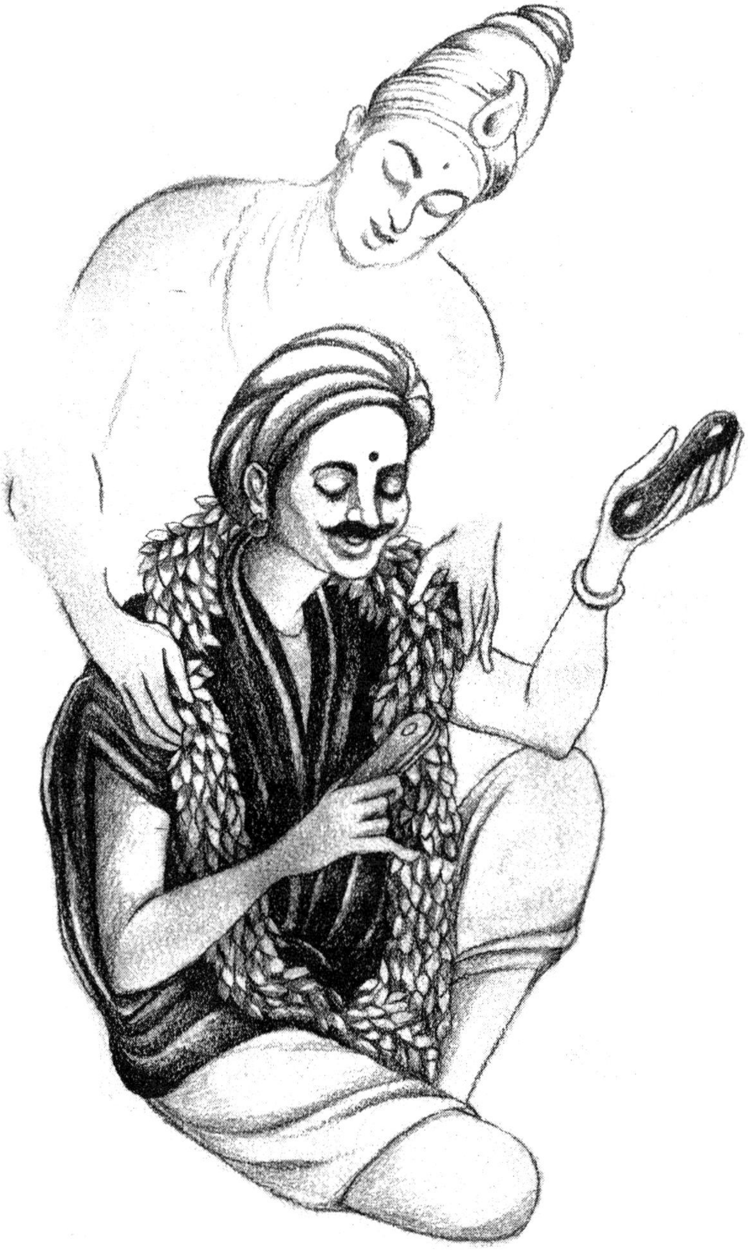

as the product of a divine birth: God met his mother once and bit into a mango she offered him. When he left and she looked at the half-eaten fruit, there lay in its place the baby Chokhamela.

Part of this posthumous promotion may have been due to his own efforts—borrowing the later sociological expression—to Sanskritise. He spoke out against animal sacrifice not only because 'you will be inflicting cruelty on another life and destroying it', but also because, one suspects, this was more in consonance with ritual 'purity'. He railed against alcohol, which in many parts of India was associated with certain 'low' forms of worship; this too seems to have helped his subsequent upgrade in the high-caste imagination. God, it is said, appeared to him in several forms: One version has Chokhamela struggling to drag away a dead cow, another duty that fell upon the Mahar, and the deity, manifesting as a young man, lends him a hand. But most memorably, after he is rejected at the temple's gates on yet another occasion, the lord comes to *him* instead, offering him commiseration as much as he does company, the two of them sitting quietly by the riverside like old friends.

At the end of the day, Chokhamela was devoted to Vithoba but did not transgress any concrete lines drawn by society and its privileged elders—nor did Vithoba, in any of his manifestations, insist that Chokhamela breach custom and step in through the temple gates.

Chokhamela died in an accident when labouring on a construction site, and legend has it that even his bones were chanting the name of god. These bones were carried to the temple and buried at a spot that still receives visitors. Such remains, however, are deemed impure, and so his memorial stands at the foot of the temple's steps—that very spot where, four hundred years later, the Peshwa's officers did not want untouchables to gather and cast their shadows and sweat on anybody else. All that Chokhamela had ever wanted was a chance to glimpse the deity within. But in the end, he had to settle forever by the door—precisely where they said he belonged even when he lived.

THE WORLD OF SHIVAJI MAHARAJ

In 1630, when the Maratha noblewoman Jijabai brought forth the second of her two sons, little did she imagine that the boy would grow up to shatter forever the might of the Mughal empire.

The Deccan into which Shivaji arrived, though, was already a fascinating place. Until four years before his birth, the hero of the plateau was a Muslim warrior called Malik Ambar, whose career began in slavery in Africa and culminated at the height of power and glory in India. The local sultan was the Nizam Shah of Ahmednagar, whose ancestors were brahmins but whose line welcomed brides of both African and Persian extraction. Shivaji's grandfather, Maloji, was closely affiliated with both Malik Ambar and the Nizam Shahi dynasty, while his maternal family lent its men and resources to the imperial Mughals of Agra. The horizon was one of unending military drama, and when Shivaji was still a child, the last of the Nizam Shahs was incarcerated in a

Mughal fortress, his ancestral dominions swallowed in bits and pieces by Emperor Shahjahan and his forces.

The Deccan was once home to celebrated Hindu dynasties which fell before Alauddin Khilji in the fourteenth century, making way for what became the Bahmani sultanate. These early military encounters provoked massive cultural disruptions, though soon enough, the new kings settled down and reached an accommodation with subjects of the old. The Bahmanis and their heirs in Maharashtra, the Nizam Shahs included, connected the Deccan to Islamic networks of international commerce, establishing also in the region a Persianised court culture. All the same, the newcomers

The Courtesan, the Mahatma & the Italian Brahmin

married Maratha women, patronised the Marathi language, and were nourished by local traditions—there could be no other way, for the urban Muslim aristocracy was handicapped without the cooperation of those who dominated the vast and impenetrable countryside. And so, wisely, they joined hands with older leaders of the land, and together birthed something new, enduring for centuries in splendour till the ambitions of a new northern emperor called Aurangzeb reduced them to another tragic chapter.

The Marathas, too, developed their identity in this age of Muslim power, embracing the best of Indo-Islamic tradition. Shivaji's father and uncle—Shahaji and Sharifji—were both named after a Muslim saint called Shah Sharif. If one travels to Ellora, the ancestral seat of the Bhonsle clan, the samadhis of Shivaji's grandfather and other relations so closely resemble Islamic mausoleums that they have been mistaken for 'tombs' like those of the Nizam Shahs and the legendary Malik Ambar. The African general, in fact, when he established the city that became Aurangabad, named its various quarters after Maratha commanders, paying homage to their loyalty. In costume, cuisine and vocabulary too, the sultans left their imprint, and many are the Maratha families that trace their glory to the service of these Muslim lords. Together they made history—when at the famous Battle of Talikota in 1565 the Deccan's sultans defeated Vijayanagar, fighting for the Muslim princes were Maratha warriors in the thousands. In matters of faith also, there was debate and discussion. Contemporaneous with the Bhakti saint Tukaram was Muntoji, a scion of the Bahmani dynasty who equated the bismillah with the invocation of Rama, while Eknath featured in his bharuds not only brahmins and mahars, but also Muslims and Africans.

Shivaji, however, was a man who envisioned power and its projection differently. Where his father was happy to be acclaimed by a sultan as 'the abode of intrepidity and grandeur', 'the pillar of the mighty state', and even 'my son', Shivaji saw in the decline of regional Muslim power an opportunity to consecrate a whole new order. Many were the Marathas who saw the choice as one between preserving regional Muslim potentates and accepting the Mughal embrace. Shivaji desired something different, a new order in which Persian and Islamicate influences were consciously discarded to celebrate a 'Maharashtra dharma'. When a Maratha grandee declined Shivaji's invitation to join forces, emphasising his loyalty to a Muslim superior, Shivaji reminded him that his own course was not one of disloyalty—instead, it was of a higher loyalty to their local deity, in whose name they ought to create a 'Hindavi' kingdom. No longer was he interested in accepting the supremacy of Persianised padshahs—not when he could become a Maratha padshah and establish a kingdom of his own. Of course, there were many who chose not to invest their energy and support in his project—he saw them as 'misguided', or at worst, 'snakes' who would eventually be persuaded by his charm (or might).

To be clear, no part of what Shivaji proposed could be described as communalism with large numbers of people waking up overnight to the realisation that they constituted 'the Hindus' and seizing arms to destroy a blanket category called 'the Muslims'. What Shivaji represented, however, was a crystallisation of a new ideology among the political elite of the land. Even as he employed Muslims and empowered qazis to dispense justice, Shivaji actively pursued a new form of political expression rooted in Sanskritic tradition. Genealogical claims linked him with the Rajputs in the north, and by the

The Courtesan, the Mahatma & the Italian Brahmin

end of his life, he was writing letters not in Persian—the language of diplomacy at the time—but in Sanskrit. As the *Rajyavyavaharakosa*, a dictionary he commissioned, declares, 'overvalued Yavana [foreign] words' were now to be replaced with 'educated speech'. He had nothing against individual Muslims, but he jettisoned older systems built on Islamic ideals and sought one inspired by Indian high tradition. While he allied with sultans like the Qutb Shah of Golconda (whose ministers were brahmins), when he challenged fellow Hindu Marathas (whose loyalties lay with assorted sultans), and even as he himself came close, on one occasion, to being absorbed into the Mughal court, Shivaji was creating a fresh self-image which the Sabhasad *bakhar* describes as '*navi paddhati*' or the new course. It was by no stretch nationalism defined in communal terms—it was very much a feudal order, derived, however, from Hindu roots.

Of course, the project was fraught with contradictions only natural in this age of diverse identities and fragmented political authority—self-image did not always reflect lived reality on the ground, and even the Mughals often spoke in a religiously charged idiom that concealed cooperation when it came to actual business. For instance, the man they sent to reduce the 'infidel' Shivaji was himself an infidel called Jai Singh, the famous Rajput.

The *Sivabharata*, a grand epic eulogising the deeds of Shivaji, was composed in the Maratha king's own lifetime, giving on the one hand a vision of his political philosophy, while also acknowledging long-standing links between Islamic and Hindu interests in actual transactions. Shivaji was, according to his court poet, an incarnation of Vishnu, who 'crushes unruly Muslims'. He protected brahmins and cows, and 'descended the earth to strike' enemy sultans. Islamic rule was a wicked force, manifest on earth 'disguised as barbarians' to conquer and command (though not as evil a force as the Europeans on the coast, who were even lower in divine estimation). 'Foreign religions (mlechcha dharma)' were growing, complained the *Sivabharata*, and there was 'great fear' among the righteous and the just. 'All these clans of Muslims are incarnations of demons,' we read at one point, 'risen up to flood the earth with their own religion.' Shivaji, then, is presented as the restorer of a classical idea of balance, the deliverer of a Sanskritic notion of justice.

But the heady picture here is a formal aspiration. In reality, even the *Sivabharata* recognises a more complex cultural universe. Like the Hindu god Kartikeya, who was protected by the gods as he battled an *asura*, the poem presents Malik Ambar, shielded by Shivaji's father and other lords in his war against the Mughals—Ambar, an African Muslim 'as brave as the sun', is likened to a Hindu god, while the mighty enemy to the north is cast as a demon. When Shahaji leaves the Nizam Shah's ranks, he is 'nostalgic' about their shared, intertwined past; as he accepts service with the Adil Shah of Bijapur, another of the Deccan's sultans, that kingdom is likened to the land of 'Lord Rama himself'. The Nizam Shah, whose associate Shivaji's grandfather was, is described as a *dharmatma*, to whom barbs against 'Turks' do not apply. And when Afzal Khan is famously dispatched to smash Shivaji, with him march Marathas—Jadhav, Bhonsle, Naik, Ghorpade and more—while Shivaji, we know, held the loyalty of men like Siddi Ibrahim. The Muslim side could be divided into 'good' and 'evil', never painted with the brush of presumed uniformity—Ibrahim Adil Shah II of Bijapur, a Sunni who venerated Hindu gods, was 'dignified', while a successor was seen as wicked. The Mughals, meanwhile, saw only themselves as legitimate Muslims; the Muslims of the Deccan were enemies of Islam as much as the Marathas were agents of evil.

In theory, then, the *Sivabharata* visualised a 'Hindavi' kingdom built on a rejection of Islamic kingship, but even Shivaji's poet could not ignore the reality of Muslim–Maratha entwinement in this turbulent period. There was ideology that was different from the court culture of Shivaji's political predecessors, and then there was a mixed reality—each fed off the other, and neither was absolute in its influence. The *Sivabharata* also had another significant role to play, one in which an emphasis on Sanskritic tradition was integral. Completed in time for the coronation ceremony that saw Shivaji transformed from warlord to consecrated king, a poem like this was essential for cementing his legitimacy as a sovereign. It was not, in itself, original—the emperors of Vijayanagar had applied the word 'Hindu' to define their self-image, even as, without irony, they battled other Hindu kings and employed Muslims by the thousands. A Telugu text, which we shall encounter later in this book, similarly, articulated even before Shivaji was born a 'Hindu' ideology of statehood, comparing some Muslim kings with the devil while speaking of the Mughals as blessed by the gods. Islamic texts too exaggerated themes such as 'the destruction of infidels', as noted in a previous essay, when the reality was often somewhat different.

Black and white were not the colours through which these voices perceived their world—there was an elite visualisation of 'Turks' and there was another of Hindus, but boundaries between the two were not rigid. Indeed, in one canto in the *Sivabharata*, among the lands Shivaji proposes to conquer are not only those of 'evil Turks' but also those of the rulers of Madras and Kandahar; Kashmir and Kerala—and many

Hindu principalities which, like Muslim states, did not meet the standards of his Hindavi vision. Shivaji, then, was a challenge to the establishment of his day, an establishment defined in terms that were Persianised and Islamic, but he was the 'lion' that challenged Hindu as well as Muslim 'elephants' that stood against him. His was certainly a challenge asserted in a consciously Sanskritic fashion. But was he launching a nationalist 'Hindu state' as his Hindavi kingdom is today sometimes defined, or was his world far more syncretic, a melting pot of cultural influences? The answer lies somewhere in the middle—where culture and the lives of the people were an ocean of shared experience, the politics of the elite sought to define itself in language that sought to establish competing narratives. Energised by both, the eclectic traditions of his land and the righteous force of ideology, Shivaji established his Maratha swaraj.

The Deccan where he was born had seen Hindu princes absorb Muslim influence and Muslim kings celebrate Hindu divines; it had seen brahmins become sultans and a Muslim seek brahminhood. Now, however, it opened a new chapter in the history of India, one in which this land was destined to go down also as the graveyard of the Mughals and their formidable empire. And the man who stood at the cusp of this great transformation was Shivaji the Maratha, Vishnu-reborn in Sanskrit poetry, pragmatic warrior-king in reality.

BASAVA, WOMEN AND THE LINGAYAT TRADITION

India has a long tradition of bright minds poking holes in some distinctly un-bright ideas. And one such mind lived over eight centuries ago in the south, tearing a hole so large through that disastrous institution called caste that a flood of people—about 6.5 million today—escaped the old order, arriving at an identity of their own. Of course, this identity, when formalised, invited its own peculiarities and contradictions, but over the years, as a section of the Lingayat community sought recognition outside all-subsuming Hinduism, custodians of the majoritarian cause were gripped by understandable anxiety. And this despite the feelings that Basava, the twelfth-century intellectual preceptor of the Lingayats, himself expressed about such self-appointed custodians in his own day. 'Loaded with the burden of the Vedas,' he pithily remarked, 'the brahmin is a veritable donkey.'

Basava could get away with saying outrageous things because he himself was a brahmin (which was precisely the kind of privilege Chokhamela, as we saw earlier, did not possess). But he was a brahmin repulsed by brahminism, and the intellectual and material debilitations wreaked on society by caste. 'False, utterly false,' he declared, 'are the stories of divine birth. The higher type of man is the man who knows himself.' His was a kind of humanism that rejected man-made inequalities justified in the name of the divine, wedded though it was to the worship of Shiva. 'On the same earth stands,' one of his vachanas goes, 'the outcaste's hovel, and the deity's temple. Whether for ritual or rinsing, is not the water same?' Just like the outcaste chandala, the brahmin, too, was born from a human womb. Or 'is there anybody in the world,' scoffed Basava, 'delivered through the ear?' If he expected anybody to answer, they stewed instead, in anger.

Basava, son of Madiraja and Madalambike, was born in 1105 in Bagewadi. Poets subsequently embellished the tale with typical apocryphal excess—that his arrival was a boon from Shiva, or that the baby only opened his eyes when an image of the deity was dangled before him. But myth-making aside, the boy was sharp—at sixteen, he is said to have discarded the brahminical thread, and by twenty-eight he was clear in his vision of a society without caste. In the fashion of his day, the vocabulary of his reform was also religious. And so Basava sought to break the monopoly temples and priests enjoyed over god by popularising the portable Ishtalinga, a symbol of Shiva worn around the neck. From his centre in Kudalasangama, the idea of the temple was diluted, as was the popularity of polytheism. 'Gods here, gods there, with no space for our feet!' Basava exclaimed. Shiva alone was, he argued, a truly divine force in an ocean of pointless

The Courtesan, the Mahatma & the Italian Brahmin

divinities, and Shiva came to mean for Basava what Krishna would to Meera.

Many were those of dazzling intellect who joined him. Tired of social shackles and determined to chart an alternative course, they found in Basava's anti-caste, egalitarian crusade a resonance that has survived the ages. Perhaps the most revealing test of the sincerity of any drive for reform lies in how welcoming it is of the voices of women—and here Basava proved himself sincere. Of the 210 saints associated with him, as many as thirty-five were female, fourteen of them unmarried. These were women of uncommon brilliance who, in addition to their battles against caste and inequality, also challenged patriarchy's grip over their bodies and thought. As with most in the Bhakti tradition, their ideas were expressed in the language of devotion, evoking, as the scholar Vijaya Ramaswamy says, 'very strong sexual imagery' that was 'erotic in style and metaphor'. Thus, for instance, we have the saint Remmavve of the weaver caste, who sang ecstatically of her union with the patron deity of the Lingayats, Shiva himself:

> All husbands have seeds
> My husband has no seeds
> All husbands are above
> My husband below, I am above him!

Like elsewhere, women in medieval Karnataka found their lives cemented in patriarchal norms: father, husband, son and family were the frontiers of their universe. Those seeking freedom from this prescribed existence received sanctuary in Basava's movement, also insulating themselves from social opprobrium through a pronounced commitment to god. The celebrated Akka Mahadevi left her royal husband's palace behind, wandering naked and singing praises of Shiva. 'You shall be doomed if you touch the woman married to [the lord],' she warned, but even then the road was not safe. In a version of the *Shunyasampadane* that holds the Lingayat vachanas, there is a figure who attempts to violate Mahadevi. 'She is not,' we are informed, 'desecrated.' But the fact was that even with their voices couched in spirituality, women thinkers were not always safe and had more battles to fight than their male counterparts could truly know or imagine.

Basava, cognisant of this, went out of his way to promote equality between the sexes as much as he fought for equality among the castes. Menstruation, for instance, ordinarily entailed ritual pollution for women, but Basava rejected this—women could continue to worship Shiva regardless of whether or not it was their time of the month. When Mahadevi's nudity became a source of controversy within his circle, he came to her defence and asked: 'Does the one who has loved the sky-clad one have need of a girdle cloth?' He also raised questions of institutions built around gender. 'Look here, dear fellow,' goes one of his vachanas. 'I wear these men's clothes only for you. Sometimes I am man, sometimes I am woman.' The singular Mahadevi, meanwhile, argued the opposite. 'A woman though in name, I am, if you consider well, the male principle.' Clothed in Shiva's 'light', she was not bound by shame. 'Where is the need for cover and jewel' when she was under the gaze of the divine? It was all about devotion—but within it lay also an assertion of who Mahadevi was.

If these were more personal expressions of individuality in a time when community reigned supreme, Basava and the Lingayats had questions for society too. Their age was one of brahmin supremacy, and the orthodox did not welcome Basava's call for a society unrestricted by caste, open to introspection and embracing of women who seemed, to

The Courtesan, the Mahatma & the Italian Brahmin

them, unpredictable freaks. The Lingayats were dismissed as contrarian for the sake of it, their female saints simply branded strange. Strange, in fact, even the men must have appeared in any case—a fellowship of rebels from the most unaristocratic backgrounds. Basava was certainly a brahmin, but Allama Prabhu was a drummer; Siddharama a cowherd; Maccayya a washerman; and Kakkaya a skinner of dead cows. What was positively infuriating, however, was their pointed criticism of conservative brahminical hypocrisy. As Basava put it sarcastically:

They say: Pour, pour the milk
When they see a snake image in stone.
But they cry: Kill, kill!
When they meet a snake for real.

But then Basava, who was simultaneously a bureaucrat since 1132, having advanced from royal accountant to chief minister at the tumultuous, fractious court of the local ruler in Kalyan, went one step too far. Already his Hall of Experience (Anubhava Mantapa) was attracting men and women from all castes to gather freely and express radical new thought with ever growing liberty. He proceeded to eat meals with untouchables, flouting age-old law. What could have been written off as a new, somewhat eccentric Shiva cult now began to shake the very pillars on which powerful social hierarchies were perched. 'Today he dines with [the low-born]. Tomorrow he will encourage mixed marriages,' cried the orthodox, fearing 'caste mix-up' and the 'utter ruination' of the status quo. Their alarm was, as it happens, valid, for Basava did proceed to intermarriage. The king was prevailed upon to warn his minister to behave—and the king was politely disobeyed.

The event was cataclysmic—and not merely because it was happening in 1167 in a country where inter-caste unions still provoke violence and murder. The daughter of a brahmin, Madhuvarasa, was wedded to the untouchable son of Haralayya in the full gaze of the public. The monarch and the establishment were apoplectic—the respective fathers, it is said, had their eyes gouged out, after which they were thrown under elephants to painfully meet their maker, casteless in death. Basava himself survived the calamity, but the kingdom descended into political chaos (chaos which was simmering also on account of other factors—after all, Basava was a political figure too, and politically motivated charges of corruption had been used to topple his reform movement earlier). The last thing the king wanted on his hands at a time of turmoil was social disorder. Basava's career ended, and he left for Kudalasangama, for the riverside where he had first declared his love for Shiva.

He did not live for long afterwards, however, and for over two centuries after his death in 1168, his *sharanas* (followers) kept the movement alive but unprovocative. It was only in the fifteenth century that Lingayat identity evidently reasserted itself after one of their own became minister to the emperor of Vijayanagar. By now Basava's vachanas had been compiled, and the movement invested with a structure of its own. In order to survive, a certain accommodation with the brahminical order was arrived at, essentially turning the Lingayats into one of the very many other castes that exist in Indian society. To Basava himself, such a compromise might have seemed unfortunate, but he had long departed and those left behind had to be pragmatic in the face of hostility. Today, however, Lingayats question this classification. Are they who celebrate Basava's heterodox teachings, who uphold the vachanas of many remarkable women, who bury their dead and go to no temples, really Hindus? Those on the extreme right insist they are—where majoritarianism is the goal, one can hardly allow the dilution of the majority. And so, as many Lingayats contemplate a second divorce from the Hindu fold, it is the Hindus who seek to retain Basava's children within their order—not so much due to a similarity of vision as to the naked expediencies of cultural politics.

'JODHABAI'
MORE THAN AKBAR'S WIFE

In 1575, authorities in the port of Surat prevented a woman called Gulbadan Begum from embarking on her pilgrimage to Mecca for an entire year. Negotiations dragged on, and eventually, she had to bribe them with the entire city of Valsad in order to board the boat. It was no surprise that the begum paid in town, not coin—Gulbadan was the daughter of Emperor Babur and aunt to the mighty Akbar, then sovereign of all of upper India. It was, however, revealing that even a senior representative of the imperial harem found herself applying for leave to sail: The truth was that the Mughal emperor's power met its limit at the beach. It was the writ of the king of Portugal that prevailed in the Arabian Sea, and without Portuguese consent, no princess, of whatever consequence, could depart India's shores. Even as Akbar dismissed the Portuguese as 'chickens', Mughal ships quietly paid to carry on their business—the Europeans might have been overpowered on land, but on international waters their

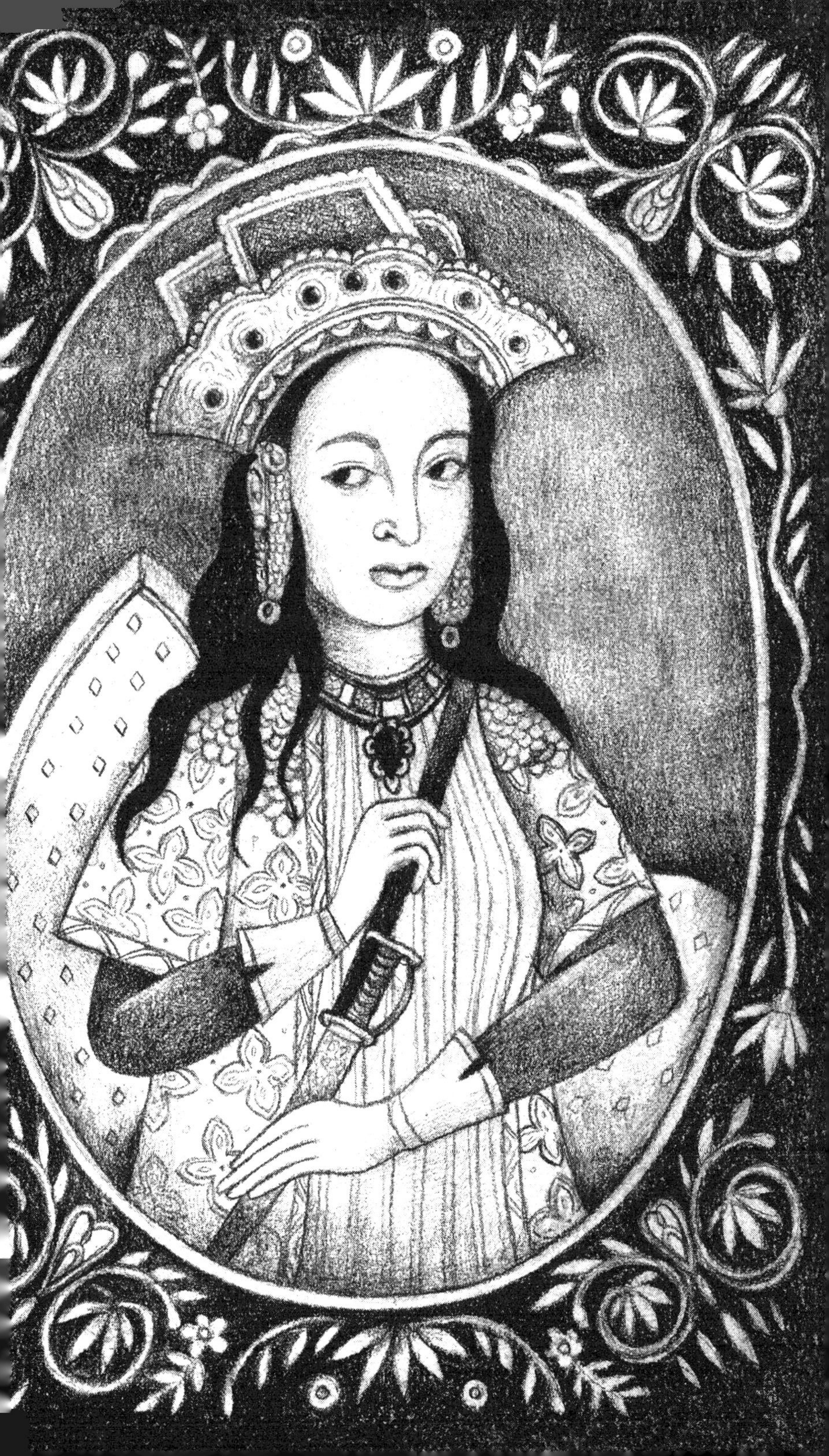

mastery of navigation ensured that even the imperial family gnashed its teeth but, ultimately, fell in line.

In 1613, during Jahangir's reign, however, the Portuguese, already imperilled by the arrival of the Dutch and the English, went a step too far, hastening their decline in India. The emperor, to be sure, was a friendly, curious man—as we shall see in a subsequent essay—and may have allowed things to carry on as before given his lack of personal interest in matters such as warfare. But in September of that year, Portuguese provocation was so brazen that only firm action could restore Mughal prestige. The underlying issues were many. Politically, the ignominy of seeking licences was a demonstration of the limits of Mughal power, always somewhat embarrassing when the emperor was officially 'Conqueror of the World'. Then there were religious concerns: The Portuguese were such fervent Christians that each *cartaz* (licence) carried images of Jesus and Mary—a troubling detail for orthodox Muslims compelled to buy these documents in order to do the haj. Also in 1613, a Hindu lady got embroiled in these Mughal–Portuguese dynamics, her wrath bringing down the full force of the empire, ringing the death knell of the latter's long-standing power at sea.

The lady in question was Mariam uz-Zamani, though she is often erroneously called Jodhabai, the Rajput princess who was Akbar's wife and Jahangir's mother. While conventional depictions are fairly predictable—she was beautiful and regal in a predictable, overblown sense, as seen in a 2008 Bollywood portrayal—in actual fact, the dowager was a formidable woman. Described by a contemporary as 'a great adventurer', she headed phenomenal business enterprises even while sequestered in the Mughal harem. At court, as scholar Ellison B. Findly notes, she was one of the four seniormost figures and the only woman to hold a military rank of 12,000 cavalry, entitling her to the right to issue *firmans* of her own. She was also the proprietor of the *Rahimi*, believed to be the largest Indian vessel trading in the Red Sea, displacing 1,500 tonnes, its mast some forty-four yards high—it was, one account tells us, 'verye richlye laden, beeinge worth a hundred thowsande pounde'. In addition to such goods worth millions of rupees, the dowager empress regularly conveyed Muslim pilgrims to Mecca on her ship. Add to this the fact that she funded the construction of numerous mosques, even while she remained a devout Hindu, and her prestige is patent.

In 1613, the Portuguese decided it was a clever idea to seize and subsequently burn the *Rahimi*. The action was unprecedented, and, given who the owner of the vessel was, the insult landed straight on the otherwise cheerful, opium-loving Jahangir. The whole affair was meant to gain leverage at a time when the Portuguese were threatened by competition from other European companies. But the move backfired. As one observer noted, Jahangir immediately had Daman besieged, blocked all Portuguese trade in Surat, and 'hath likewise taken order for the seizing of all Portingals [sic] and their goods within his kingdoms'. Furthermore, the emperor 'sealed up their church doors and hath given order that they shall no more use the exercise of their religion in these parts'. Rattled, the Portuguese made amends by offering three lakh rupees as compensation, but on the condition that the Mughals expel the English from Agra. Jahangir refused to blink and welcomed soon afterwards, in 1615, Sir Thomas Roe, the famous English ambassador. 'The Portuguese folly in the capture of the *Rahimi*, then,' writes Findly, 'tipped the scales in favour of the English.'

But it was not as if the newcomers were granted a red-carpet reception; on the contrary, the playing field was merely levelled somewhat. Mariam uz-Zamani herself wasn't sympathetic to the English: In 1611, after an Englishman outbid her representative at the indigo market in Bayana, she exerted enough pressure on her son to ensure that Roe's unofficial predecessor, William Hawkins—the 'English Khan' who till then was friendly with Jahangir—had to pack his bags and leave the empire for good. It was clear enough that the emperor's mother was a force to reckon with, the affair around the *Rahimi* merely cementing such thinking. And in 1623, when Mariam uz-Zamani died—still immensely rich and powerful—due honour was given her by burying her in a mausoleum close to that equally redoubtable man to whom she was once married: Emperor Akbar.

A WEAVER AND HIS MESSAGE

When Kabir, the poet-saint, died five centuries ago, he could not have predicted that he would be reimagined over and over again, to allay the anxieties of every succeeding generation. To most, of course, this icon of Bhakti is a champion of Hindu–Muslim unity, his Arabic name sitting cheerfully alongside the chant of Rama, which he repeated so often in his quest to realise god. Indeed, only a few years after his death, Abul Fazl, Emperor Akbar's chronicler, described him as 'the asserter of the unity of god', one who 'discarded the effete doctrines' of his time and came to be 'revered by both Hindu and Muhammadan for his catholicity of doctrine and the illumination of his mind'. Sikhs too looked upon him with admiration, dedicating to his work whole passages in their Adi Granth. And in the nineteenth century, European missionaries laid claim to the weaver-saint of Benares, delighting in his barbs against caste, finding in his sayings a reflection of such thought as could only, they were convinced, be Christian in origin.

'Kabir appears to modern India,' Charlotte Vaudeville pointed out, 'to be the true symbol of nonconformity.' And yet, everything about him is immersed in myth and awe. He was the poor son of Muslim weavers, though the lexicon of his devotion led early on to Hindu claims upon his memory. Some invented for him a miraculous birth—he was the conception of a brahmin widow, delivered through her palm. Abandoned, he was raised by Muslims. Others said he descended enveloped in lotus leaves and light from the heavens, floating upon a lake where he was discovered by his *julaha* father. He certainly did celebrate Hindu imagery over Muslim theology, evidently also enjoying the tutelage of the guru Ramananda. But by most accounts he was definitely a Muslim, with a wife and two children, coming to mean so much to Hindus that stories about non-Muslim roots were invented to drag him, as Wendy Doniger notes, 'over the line from Muslim to Hindu'.

While he lived, there was enough in Kabir's message to upset Hindu and Muslim elites alike. To brahmins he asked (much like Basava some centuries before in the south) whether they were born with a caste mark on the forehead, or whether their mothers delivered them through a special canal. 'And if you say you're Turk,' added Kabir, 'why weren't you circumcised before birth?' So too, he sneered, it was 'dumb' if people sought salvation in ritual. 'If going naked brought liberation, the deer of the forest would attain it first. If a shaven head was a sign of piety, ewes would be pious too.' That low castes and *kafirs* were doomed to their fate by the accident of birth was nonsense, he declared. Only those 'who don't have Rama on their lips' were ignorant; they alone were the low-born of the earth. 'Those who read the Vedas call themselves Pandits, those who read the Koran call themselves

The Courtesan, the Mahatma & the Italian Brahmin

Maulana; they give themselves different names, these pots made of the same clay. They are all,' announced Kabir, 'in their own delusions, not one of them knows the Lord.'

Like those before and after him in the Bhakti tradition, Kabir too knew persecution. Many are the tales that place him at the receiving end of the ire of Sikander Lodi, Sultan of Delhi. Punishment was ordered, and suffering was inflicted, but here again Kabir laughed at the irony. Giggling, it is said, in the presence of the emperor himself, the palm-born weaver declared, 'All my life I have tried to impress upon the Hindus and Muslims that god is one.' He had tried to build a bridge between different paths, only to be ridiculed: 'How could a brahmin demean himself by joining hands with a low-caste weaver? How could a *maulvi* degrade himself by allying with a kafir?' They did not listen to words of wisdom, but hate achieved what Kabir himself had failed to bring about: 'They could never bear to stand together in the court of [god] the King of Kings, but today it amuses me to see them standing united in the court of a [mortal] king.' And this because custodians of the faiths universally disliked Kabir and his dissident message.

It was his large following—those like him, illiterate, weak, and devoid of books—that made him an asset to wardens of the great traditions *after* he went to the grave. Indeed, they fought over his remains when he died, till, legend claims, only flowers remained under the funeral sheet: some were buried, the rest cremated, and both sides got to claim a share of Kabir's great legacy. He would have chuckled at the feud over rites and ownership had he witnessed what transpired. 'His death in Benares', he once declared, 'won't save the assassin from certain hell', just as 'a dip in the Ganges won't send frogs—or you—to paradise'. Matters of ritual were all futile:

mere instruments to enthrall the susceptible, shrouding true wisdom from the masses. But no sooner had he died than Kabir, too, became an instrument. 'I say the world is mad,' he had laughed earlier. 'If I tell the truth they rush to beat me; if I lie they trust me.' Now that he was in the grave, the need to own him trounced the upholding of his message—and for this, the very ideas, practices and institutional norms he eschewed became suddenly imperative.

Of course, Kabir was no perfect man. His message resonated with the masses, and with quiet confidence he stood up to the power of those who held the keys to heaven. But he too had prejudices, he too was far from ideal. 'Woman', he declared once, 'is the refuse of the world' so that 'noble men will put her aside, only the vile will enjoy her'. Elsewhere he compared the female to a twenty-hooded serpent, and 'if she stings one', he warned, 'there is no chance to survive'. But we can try and console ourselves that perhaps this streak of misogyny (offset though it was with contradictory verses where he is less suspicious of women) was a reflection of his age, and that he never himself claimed to be a perfect man, or the one true soul in whose words lay answers for all. He was merely Kabir the weaver—a product of his times, a mortal made of flesh and weakness—and he cared for Rama alone, not for the world and its numerous other quarrels.

A CITY FOR A COURTESAN?

In 1543, when the first Qutb Shahi ruler of Golconda was stabbed to death, one of his sons fled to neighbouring Vijayanagar to save himself from his parricide brother. For seven years, he lived in exile at this Hindu court, before coming home after the death of his murderous sibling. What followed was a phenomenal reign: the new Qutb Shah Teluguised his name from Ibrahim to Abhirama, patronised poetry on the Mahabharata, produced thirty children of his own (two of whom he put to death for plotting against him, fearing his father's fate), and inaugurated an era of prosperity and splendour (despite, that is, the general violence of his age). Golconda's ports attracted merchants from the world over, while its mines threw up diamonds in heaps, and by the time Ibrahim went to the grave in 1580, he was lord of one of the richest realms in India.

But the Qutb Shah—who once, curiously, also compared the moustaches of his enemies to the pubic hair of 'public women'—was never fully pleased with life in his old fort. He

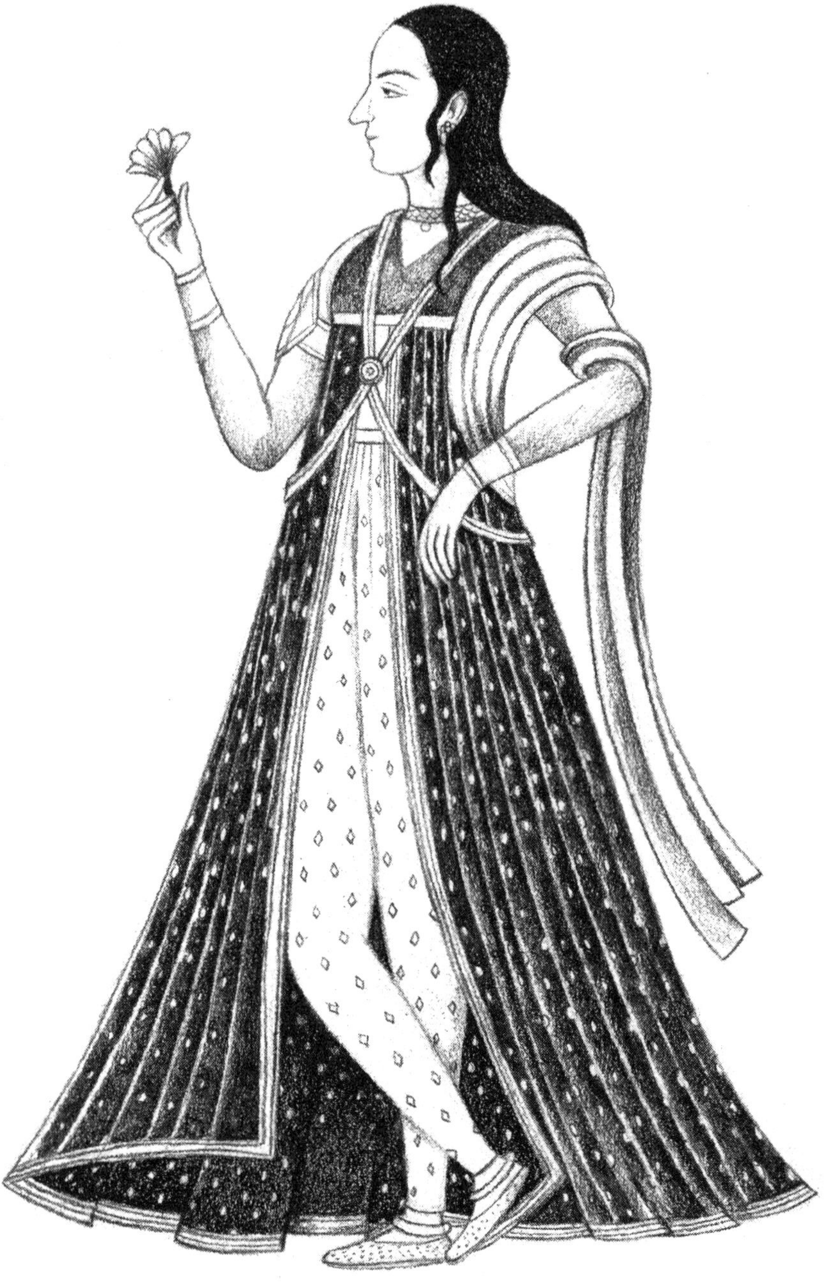

tried first to build an unwalled city towards the west. But when want of water aborted the enterprise, he constructed a bridge over the Musi river and looked instead to the east. His death meant that it was his heir, Muhammad Quli, who realised Ibrahim's dream, founding what is today the city of Hyderabad—another place that has in our own time attracted the zeal of that special variety of politician anxious to rename great cities of the past, instead of confronting challenges in the present. Hyderabad, either way, was only one of many feathers in Muhammad Quli's cap. As a patron of the arts, too, he was substantial, authoring a celebrated collection of works called *Kulliyat* that covers everything from *kabaddi* to the festival of Basant Panchami.

Hyderabad, however, was an ambitious project and from early on seems to have attracted the envy of the Qutb Shah's rivals. Fourteen thousand shops and public buildings were envisioned in the new city, with the magnificent Char Minar built over its central crossroads. The palace was a sensation, said to exceed any contemporary Mughal building—seven or eight floors high, with interiors studded with gems and gold. 'A citie that for sweetnesse of ayre, conveniencie of water, and fertility of soyle, is accounted the best situated in India,' is how the English merchant William Methwold described it, while the French traveller Jean-Baptiste Tavernier thought the bridge 'scarcely less beautiful than Pont Neuf at Paris'. Indeed, what the Qutb Shah envisioned in Hyderabad was not only a city unparalleled by rival capitals, but a 'replica of paradise' itself.

The founding romance of Hyderabad is a story repeated by every self-appointed tour guide in the vicinity. One day, we are told, when Muhammad Quli was out riding, he encountered a woman of exceptional beauty. Her name was Bhagmati, and having married her, he decided to name his new urban project Bhagnagar. Later, when she was styled Hyder Mahal, the city became Hyderabad. The story is certainly old—we have the contemporary Mughal poet Faizi writing to Akbar that the place commemorates 'a hardened whore'—but it is unlikely that it reflects fact. Hyderabad celebrates Ali (also called Hyder, the Prophet Muhammad's cousin), who was venerated by the Shia Qutb Shahs (whose Shiism was also lambasted by Faizi), and while coins record both Hyderabad and Golconda, no mention occurs of Bhagnagar. Indeed, Muhammad Quli, who catalogued the names of his seventeen beloved ladies, himself makes no mention of Bhagmati, and in the *Kulliyat*, the city he founded is always referred to as Hyderabad.

What is more likely, as the historian H.K. Sherwani noted, is that Mughal antagonism towards the smaller but powerful and prosperous Deccan sultanates—which they would annex after generations of strife—meant everything impressive about them had to be disparaged. Just as the Qutb Shahs were never acknowledged as independent padshahs by the Mughal emperor, it is likely that this grand new city had to be dismissed as nothing but a vanity project that flattered 'an old mistress'. Such a tale, in fact, may well have found an audience even in the other Deccan sultanates, which oscillated between friendship and war with the Qutb Shahs on account of their own ever-changing dynamics. So, in the end, as Sherwani concludes, a 'sneering sentence' from a Mughal officer grew 'into a paragraph, the paragraph into a section, and the section into chapters', repeated often enough to imitate the truth.

The weight of historical evidence does seem to lie with Sherwani, but Bhagnagar continues to live in the popular imagination. European travellers in the seventeenth century used the name, for instance. Indeed, proponents of the Bhagmati story argue that if the lady does not exist in local records, it is because she was proactively wiped out—the idea that the new capital was named after a courtesan appalled enough people for it to be expunged. Such an erasure is possible—Ferishta, who wrote in the Deccan in the lifetime of Muhammad Quli, notes that Bhagnagar was named after a 'prostitute' called Bhagmati, but that the Qutb Shah felt 'ashamed of his amour' and renamed the city. But the fact that Muhammad Quli named over a dozen of his mistresses, including his five favourites, in a candid work spanning 1,800 pages, and did not mention Bhagmati at all renders the matter open to debate.

In any case, for the garden variety bigot seeking to rename Hyderabad Bhagyanagar—a Sanskritised version of Bhagnagar—it may come as news that the last laugh will still be had by the ghost of the Qutb Shah. If he was forced to erase Bhagmati's name, this might be justice done for a Hindu woman who loved a Muslim king; if she never existed at all, the Qutb Shah's memory still triumphs. After all, he built a city that still endures, while the men seeking to wipe out his contributions in the service of religious bigotry have only a pretended glory—one that begins and ends with waging war on the past.

WHAT IF VIJAYANAGAR HAD SURVIVED?

When Vijayanagar was defeated in the Battle of Talikota in January 1565, what fell with it was the last formidable empire to tower over the Indian peninsula. To be clear, the old kingdom continued to exist for many more decades in a truncated form, but Talikota marked the end of all glories for a power that once boasted of such monarchs as Krishnadeva Raya. Weakened and emasculated, its rulers watched as their authority dissolved and regional dynasts emerged, inaugurating the so-called Nayaka period in the south. In the northern Deccan, meanwhile, Vijayanagar's traditional enemies—the sultans who emerged victorious at Talikota—ruled for a century more till the Mughals swallowed their independence during the reigns of Shahjahan and his son. With the fall of Golconda in 1687, even their tale was concluded, and the next chapter pivoted around the feud between Shivaji the Maratha and Aurangzeb, the last Great Mughal.

The Courtesan, the Mahatma & the Italian Brahmin

What, however, might have been the course of history had Vijayanagar survived? What if, instead of having his severed head impaled on a spear, Rama Raya, the de facto emperor, had triumphed at Talikota? He did reign, after all, over one of the wealthiest empires of his day, lacking neither in men nor money; it was better artillery and fortifications that typically helped his rivals to the north. Had he defeated them, would he have annexed their lands or merely demanded tribute? The Qutb Shah of Golconda, in fact, was an old friend, whose years of exile as a youth were spent in Rama Raya's court. The Adil Shah of Bijapur, another of Talikota's triumphant sultans, was Rama Raya's adopted son. It is likely that Vijayanagar would have allowed these Islamic states to continue as vassals, just as the sultans did not comprehensively attach Vijayanagar's lands after victory in 1565. But their independence would have been limited, their riches transferred from their vanquished capitals to be heaped before the Raya.

What would this have meant for the Mughals? The picture is a fascinating one: to think of Akbar presiding over an ambitious, swelling empire from Agra, while the south remained the sphere of influence of Vijayanagar's Rayas. The Deccan's sultans might have formed buffer states between these two great empires—one moment seeking friendship in Vijayanagar, the next trying to persuade the Mughals to help unshackle themselves from the southern yoke. They were close, too, to the Shah in Persia: would he have played politics through his Deccani allies to balance Vijayanagar and the Mughals? Or would he have allied firmly with the Hindu dynasty that dominated the peninsula—one which was more actively part of international networks of trade—than the Mughals, who were his rivals in the wider world of Islam? And where would the Portuguese have fit into this? After all, trade in the Arabian Sea had been dragooned into their hands, and overtures had been made from Vijayanagar for special understandings and friendship. Would the Portuguese have had to choose between the Mughal and the Raya?

To think of India divided between two dominant powers allows for a grand (even if entirely imaginary) picture: the Mughals with their influence stretched across the Gangetic belt, and from Afghanistan to Bengal, while all that lay south of the Narmada became the dominion of the heirs of Krishnadeva Raya. At some point the two would certainly have clashed—Mughal ambitions and the ballooning of their empire could only lead them towards the frontier of the southern emperor, just as the latter's ancestral conflict with Orissa's monarchs would have mobilised Vijayanagar's armies towards the north. So, instead of the sensational confrontation that the seventeenth century saw between the Marathas and the Mughals, would Aurangzeb have found himself battling the might of an imperial equal? Whose arms would have triumphed? The Mughals, after all, drew talent from across the Islamic world—warriors, administrators, artillerymen, and others—while Vijayanagar, even in its rivalry with regional sultans, was often unable to source the latest technology, or even the best horses. Would, perhaps, the Portuguese have filled the gap and become Vijayanagar's agents and arms dealers?

The Courtesan, the Mahatma & the Italian Brahmin

Then there is the matter of culture. Persian sartorial tastes and much else from the Islamicate world touched life in Vijayanagar—its temple sculptures, its architecture, and even the famous bronze of Krishnadeva Raya and his wives in Tirupati stand testament to this. A Vijayanagar princess was once given in marriage to a sultan, while another emperor is believed to have toyed with the idea of seeking a bride from Catholic Portugal. Could an alliance with Akbar have led to a matrimonial bond between the two empires, perhaps after a military confrontation? Or would Akbar have had to concede victory to the Raya, ceding territory and becoming the lesser of India's two great emperors? It would most likely have been difficult for either to completely overpower the other—but the constant balancing of power between north and south might have birthed interesting dynamics, even as these two major courts patronised a fascinating universe of ideas and culture, poets and scholars, artists and artisans.

If Vijayanagar had survived, India might have entered the modern age looking a great deal different. Its experience with the European trading companies that sought to colonise this land could have taken a different shape—a powerful emperor in the peninsula might have been able to contain Portuguese, Dutch and English influence. Many later heroes—from Shivaji down to Tipu Sultan—might not have emerged at all, had Vijayanagar's imperial order held. But fantasy is perhaps best tempered with the evidence left by reality: great empires often fell because of internal contradictions, not external enemies; due to the misguided policies of their rulers rather than the arms of any invader. So for all we know, if Vijayanagar had survived after Talikota, it may yet have collapsed a few generations later, inadequate minds and incapable men bringing about what the Deccan sultans' armies achieved by force of arms in 1565.

SULTANS AND RAJAHS
TEXTS AND TRADITIONS

At the dawn of the seventeenth century, decades after Vijayanagar fell before the might of the sultans of the Deccan, a fascinating new work of poetry took form in the Tamil temple-town of Madurai. The *Rayavacakamu* (Tidings of the King) is ostensibly about Krishnadeva Raya (r. 1509–29), but the composition stands out primarily for its polemics against Muslim kings.

'What are the Turks,' it declares, 'but drunkards and opium eaters!' while brahmins, with 'their diet of rice with salt and sambar', are cast as a vastly better sort who 'don't suffer from pride and malice'. Elsewhere, Hindu agents of the Deccan's sultans lament how 'Our lords are drunkards who have no faith in gods and brahmins. They are,' these characters cry, 'barbarians and cow-killers.' When spies from Vijayanagar travel to the sultanates, they witness the most unspeakable horrors. 'People were being sliced into

The Courtesan, the Mahatma & the Italian Brahmin

two at the waist or slowly cut apart with saws,' reports one informant, and even officials who fail to deliver gold to their greedy monarchs, are 'tortured to death' in 'the middle of the street'. The lands held by these sultans—the Nizam Shah of Ahmednagar, the Adil Shah of Bijapur and the Qutb Shah of Golconda—are likened to the realms of Yama, god of death, all three rulers painted as vulgar, unrefined upstarts who know neither honour nor true kingly dignity. Dharma as construed in classical texts is elevated, while the adharma of Muslim rulers is violently castigated, boundaries drawn between 'us' and 'them' in colours that are unprecedented.

The *Rayavacakamu* is a remarkable text in retrospectively ascribing a hatred of Muslim princes to Krishnadeva's time. The history of the Deccan shows that in actual fact, while rivalries existed, the world was not perceived in terms of communal acrimony as we understand it today. Many, for instance, popularly perceive the 1565 battle that destroyed Vijayanagar as a plot by Muslim monarchs to demolish a Hindu kingdom. The matter is complicated, however, when you recall that the (de facto) ruler of Vijayanagar at the time had spent his early career as a nobleman in the court of a Muslim sultan. In that battle was also the Qutb Shah who, in turn, as alluded to in the previous essay, had lived seven years in Vijayanagar. Similarly, further challenging this notion of a blunt Hindu–Muslim conflict is the little detail that while thousands of Marathas fought in the tragic 1565 battle, their swords were raised not in support of the Hindu rulers fated to fall, but of Muslim kings this side of the Tungabhadra. Generals and aristocrats too easily shifted between the sultanates and the Hindu empire in the south: One of them, known as Ain al-Mulk Gilani, began his career with the sultans, but by the 1550s was a prominent courtier in Vijayanagar, in which realm he made gifts of land to as many as eighty brahmins. Indeed, even a century before, there were high-born Muslims resident at court: Fath Khan, for instance, was a descendant of Firoz Shah Tughlaq, who chose exile not with fellow Muslims in the Deccan but in Hindu Vijayanagar, where he did his (unsuccessful) best to persuade the Raya to march with him and seize the throne of Delhi.

The *Rayavacakamu* does, however, signify a crystallisation among Hindu elites (as opposed to the masses) of a sense of common identity in competition with the 'Turks'. While its tone has been assessed by scholars to be a result of the fall of Vijayanagar—a 'culturally disruptive act' which left large numbers of poets and others without patronage—this mood did not yet lead to what can be construed as a Hindu–Muslim communal divide. For instance, the very same work, while degrading the Deccan's sultans as low-born and mean, elevates the Mughals in Delhi to levels of Sanskritic divinity. This might be partly on account of Mughal inroads into the sultans' lands—they were enemies of an enemy and therefore friends. But what is striking is that the Mughals are painted as blessed by Hindu gods. India, in the conception of the *Rayavacakamu*, had three 'Lion-Thrones': Vijayanagar's was blessed by Vishnu in Tirupati, Orissa had the blessings of Jagannatha in Puri, and the suzerains of Delhi shone in the glory of Visvanatha in Varanasi. These three rulers are likened to the devas or gods of Hindu mythology, while the sultans of the Deccan are seen as asuras, or demons, inevitably destined for defeat. In other words, while certain Muslim kings are disparaged as barbaric, others are seen as refined; and where the Adil Shah, Qutb Shah and Nizam Shah are demons, the Mughal emperor sits confidently among the gods.

The Courtesan, the Mahatma & the Italian Brahmin

What, then, does one make of the *Rayavacakamu*? There was certainly a notion in the corridors of power of 'us' and 'them', derived from diverging ideologies of power and statecraft. To repeat an important point, while one group designed court culture with Islamic ideals in mind, the other elevated Sanskritic tradition and classical Indian notions to great heights. That one was native to the land and the other of outside origins was also clear to the poets of the age—Venkatadhvarin's contemporaneous *Visva Gundarasana Campu*, for instance, describes Muslims (called 'Yavanas', a term originally applied to Greeks) as 'terrifying' clans that were a threat to 'temples of Siva and of Vishnu on his serpent couch'. The same text, interestingly, also disparages other 'evil people' who 'treat brahmins with contempt, as if they were no better than blades of grass'—in this case, the 'evil people' are Europeans settled in Madras. As early as the mid-fourteenth century, even the founders of Vijayanagar saw the 'Turks' as people different from them. From the 1350s, among the titles flaunted by the Rayas of Vijayanagar was an especially revealing one: they called themselves 'Hinduraya Suratrana', or 'Sultans among Hindu Kings'. The term 'Hindu' was one applied by the 'Turks' to the native peoples of India. It was internalised in Vijayanagar, where the rulers saw themselves consciously as Hindus, even as they also borrowed the new title, 'sultan', introduced to India by the same Turks. Calling themselves 'Sultans among Hindu Kings' was to equate themselves to powerful Muslims while at once establishing a cultural difference by asserting their identity as Hindus. 'Sultan' was an acknowledgement of a new order in India; the term 'Hindu' was their self-image in a time when a whole new host of identities had entered the land.

To the brahmin on the street, however, the 'Turk' was not more alien than the untouchable. Identities on the ground were diverse and fragmented, and indeed, cultural exchanges were exceedingly syncretic. Muslims adopted Hindu habits, and Hindus became disciples of Sufi masters. The annual *urs* of one particularly famous sultan was presided over by Shiva-worshipping Lingayats, while among the Bhakti saints in the time of Tukaram and Ramdas was a Muslim student of Advaita philosophy. Against a background of cultural exchange, texts like the *Rayavacakamu* were not so much a reflection of reality as an articulation of elite political preoccupations, with one or two other agendas. Soon after Vijayanagar was founded, for example, it ejected Muslim rulers from Madurai. The epic *Madhuravijayam*, on the face of it, is full of laments about the destruction of the dharmic balance by foreigners, with a prince of Vijayanagar restoring order. What is often forgotten is that before Madurai, the Vijayanagar forces destroyed another enemy—the Sambuvarayas, who were Hindus. Besides, in painting themselves as restorers of classical high tradition, the Telugu–Kannada rulers of a new empire were also legitimising themselves in the eyes of their Tamil subjects around Madurai. In showing the Turks as foreign barbarians, they were making their own relative newness to the scene seem less foreign. Rhetoric was a space in which all kinds of grand designs could be articulated—reality was generally a more practical negotiation.

Muslims, in other words, once they established themselves, were given a place in the conception of Indian rulers. It was not a flattering place, but it was an acceptance of their claim to rule in the subcontinent. That is why literary sources incorporated sultans into age-old Sanskrit metaphors. The king of Orissa was the Gajapati (Lord of Elephants); the Raya of Vijayanagar was the Narapati (Lord of Men); and the sultans of the Deccan (or, alternatively, the Mughals) were Ashvapatis (Lords of Horses), linking them to their military expertise in cavalry warfare. Bukka, one of the founders of Vijayanagar, was celebrated in overblown verse as Krishna reincarnated 'to deliver the world when it was overpowered by Mlechchas' (Muslims). A simple reading of this would suggest that the king saw Muslims as enemies. In reality, while he certainly had political ambitions in the Deccan, from which he wished to oust local sultans, to do so he sought the aid of another 'mlechcha', the sultan of Delhi. Turks, furthermore, were to Bukka just one of many enemy clans to be destroyed. So in one instance, we have him eulogised as follows: 'When his sword began to dance on the battlefield, the faces of the [Muslim] Turushkas shrivelled up ... the Andhras ran into caves, the Gurjaras lost the use of their limbs ... the Kambojas' courage was broken, the Kalingas suffered defeat.' Muslims are listed along with other Hindu dynasties and not marked out for any pronounced hostility here. At certain moments, then, literary and political texts incorporated them as legitimate members of society, while at other times they challenged the legitimacy of 'Turks' in the Sanskritic order of things. But the presence of the Turks in and by itself was not unusual.

This perhaps explains an action of Krishnadeva Raya in the sixteenth century which is somewhat at odds with the claims and ambitions of the *Rayavacakamu* a hundred years later. In 1523, the Raya marched into the Deccan, defeated the Muslim powers that existed there, and put their armies to flight. Did he, thereafter, take over their lands or seek to swallow their realms whole? He did not. Instead, he resurrected an older Muslim dynasty, the house of the Bahmani sultans, and by his own royal command had them crowned monarchs of the northern half of the plateau. He did not replace Muslim power in the Deccan with Hindu might in the name of a grand dharmic cause—instead, he restored the legitimacy of a much older Muslim line and placed them in a position of official authority. Then, to commemorate this action, Krishnadeva added to his list of styles and titles a fascinating new one in 1523, one that encapsulates the world of the early modern Deccan: the Raya of Vijayanagar, it was announced to all, was now the 'Yavana Rajya Sthapana Acharya'—the Hindu king who re-established the kingdom of Turks.

DARA SHUKOH
POET AMONG WARRIORS

By the end of August 1659, everyone in the imperial court in Agra knew that Dara Shukoh would soon find himself minus his head. Emperor Shahjahan's eldest and favourite son, beloved of mystics and poets, had lost the war of succession, outsmarted by the shrewder Aurangzeb. Plundered by his own soldiers, abandoned by old retainers, his wife dead (possibly by suicide), and betrayed by a man he thought loyal, Dara seemed conscious of his impending doom. He wrote to his royal captor from his place of confinement, promising to spend the rest of his days praying for the new emperor's welfare. But his pleas were rejected—the victorious Aurangzeb's hatred for Dara had accumulated over decades, and in the sham trial that followed, the elder brother was accused of every kind of crime, from perverting imperial judgement to scandalous heresy, till the younger confirmed, self-righteously, the sentence of death.

The life Dara had led before was full of splendour and privilege. He sat on a golden chair in his father's court, and was styled, in happier days, Prince of Lofty Fortune. Before both chair and fortune were abruptly toppled, he had enjoyed two crore silver rupees a year in income. He was his father's closest adviser, provoking envy from more than one of his several siblings. Dara's personality was fascinating, and while he wrote sentimental verses on renunciation, he was no stranger to the notion of self-interest. When Aurangzeb cornered the Shia sultanates of the Deccan, it was to Dara that their rulers sent their appeals. The senior prince, the sultans knew, had the ear of the emperor—and since Dara had no desire to see ambitious Aurangzeb swell in power, he prevailed on their father and had his brother's designs thwarted. Indeed, if Dara had won the war of succession, there is no reason to expect that he would have been kinder than Aurangzeb in dispatching his rivals.

He did have natural defects of character. 'He entertained,' wrote François Bernier, who was Dara's personal physician for a brief period, 'too exalted an opinion of himself [and] believed he could accomplish everything by the powers of his own mind ... He spoke disdainfully of those who ventured to advise him, and thus deterred his sincerest friends from disclosing the secret machinations of his brothers.' Added to this fatal overconfidence, born of soaring intellectual talents, was disdain for proud men with narrow minds. 'Paradise,' he proclaimed, 'is where no *mullah* exists'—naturally, even sympathetic mullahs turned away from Dara. And so, for all the love and regard his father fed him, the man assembled enemies with resentments as sharp as Aurangzeb's. His chief military campaign, moreover, was a flop, and he lacked with ordinary troops that bond which brought success to his brothers—while they picked the sword, Dara collected Sufi saints.

The Courtesan, the Mahatma & the Italian Brahmin

But the Mughal prince's weaknesses were only of the kind that one might find in any human being. His mind far surpassed that of his contemporaries. At twenty-five he authored his first book, and two years before his execution, he was still composing lines of pure delight. 'He was constantly in the society of brahmins, yogis and sanyasis,' complained a poet employed by Aurangzeb, till he regarded 'these worthless teachers of delusions as learned and true masters of wisdom'. He composed the *Majma-al-Bahrain* (The Mingling of Two Oceans), seeking, like his ancestor Akbar, to unite faiths to fashion a new vision for society. It was Dara who translated the Upanishads from Sanskrit to Persian, which a century later allowed Voltaire in France to immerse himself in Indian wisdom. These were, Shahjahan's ill-destined son wrote, 'without doubt of suspicion, the first of all heavenly books'—a line that would one day be used against him as representing a direct challenge to the Quran to which he was pledged.

But the times were violent and while Dara scaled the heights of intellectual attainment, he failed to claim the power of arms that sustained kingship in that complex age. When Shahjahan fell ill, his son made tactical mistakes. He yet had chances of success, with the royal forces and treasure vaults at his disposal, but on the battlefield Aurangzeb was the real warrior, Dara a poet in armour. He was defeated and fled Agra, wandering from province to province, while his father wept, till Aurangzeb's men defeated him once again. He should have fled to Persia when he had a chance—perhaps he might have returned like Akbar's father to fight another day. But bad judgement and betrayal by someone he had once helped delivered Dara his warrant of death. His wife, for instance, urged him to carry on but the man thought too soon that

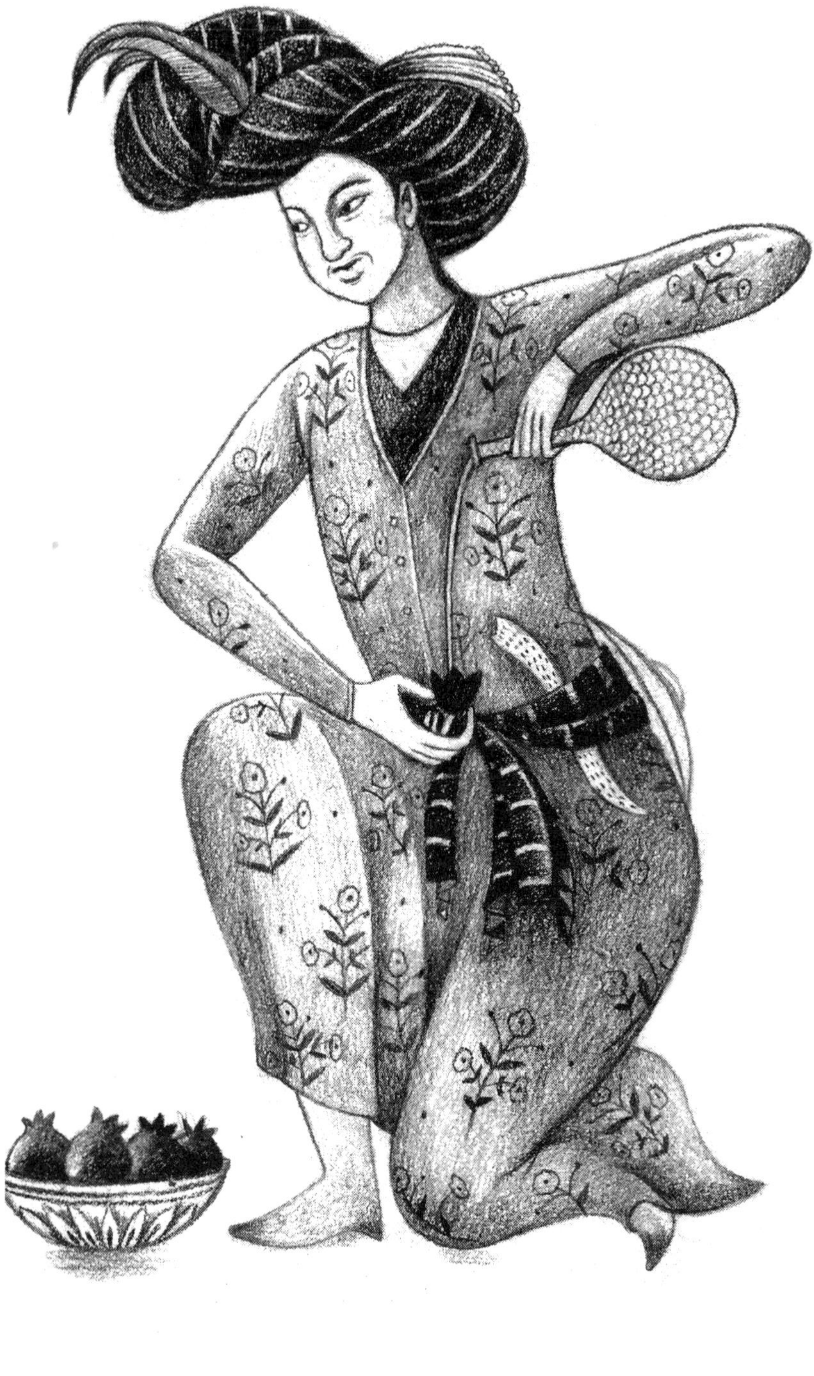

they were out of danger; his helpers were suspicious of a regional grandee whose hospitality Dara accepted, and he was proved wrong and these sceptics correct.

When Dara came shackled to Delhi, the people shed tears of sincere regret. 'From every quarter,' noted Bernier, 'I have heard piercing and distressing shrieks ... men, women, and children wailing as if some mighty calamity had happened to themselves.' Aurangzeb had, then, to eliminate this popular rival, and men were sent to do the deed on the last day of August. His younger son died with him, while the older was captured and slowly poisoned to death. For these brutal political events, of course, a religious vindication was expertly prepared. As Aurangzeb's chronicler wrote, with his obsession with the Vedas and his attention devoted to 'the contents of these wretched books', Dara was an apostate. 'It became manifest that if Dara Shukoh obtained the throne ... the foundations of faith would be in danger and the precepts of Islam would be changed for the rant of infidelity and Judaism.' The murder of brother by brother, then, was both imperial justice and god's fury in direct play.

It is tempting, even if futile, to imagine how Mughal history might have been shaped had Dara reigned and not Aurangzeb. Would he have saved the empire by becoming the Akbar of his age, using the sword where necessary but not fearing to also offer a diplomatic embrace? Might he have won over the Marathas as Akbar succeeded with the Rajputs? Or would he have remained too long in the company of his poets and saints, allowing statecraft and power to fall by the wayside? It is impossible to say, though as a historian once wrote, Dara Shukoh was perhaps destined to fail either way. He had many flaws and he had his strengths, but what really marked him out as a man of tragedy and dismay was one peculiar detail: he was far too civilised for his age.

THE LOST BEGUM OF AHMEDNAGAR

In 1565, after what is popularly called the Battle of Talikota, Husain Nizam Shah returned victorious from Vijayanagar to his court in Ahmednagar. There had been horrific bloodshed—ending with the enemy's head on a spear—and much gold and silver had been gained. But Husain seemed not destined to savour his victory: That very year, he would die, and while some held alcoholic excess to be the cause of his end, at least one Portuguese chronicler decided it was poison, not drink, that took the Nizam Shah to his grave. Deccan politics was dangerous to begin with, and in this instance, it was the ruler's own wife who was blamed for his death. She was a devadasi-turned-begum, wrote the European historian, and to plant her own son on the throne, instead of a rival's, she decided to take the life of the man who made her his queen.

Khunza Humayun was a remarkable woman, and while she was never a devadasi, she was in every sense extraordinary. Aftabi's *Tarif-i Husain Shah Padshah-i Dakan*, a eulogy

The Courtesan, the Mahatma & the Italian Brahmin

commissioned around the time of the king's death, is full of praise for his queen. Indeed, alongside beautiful paintings (including one where she appears in her husband's lap), this unusual text describes vividly Khunza's loveliness and physical voluptuousness, comparing her breasts at one point to ripe pomegranates. Other sources present her ancestry—she was descended from a ruler of Baghdad, though a fall from power meant scions like her father joined hordes of other Persians seeking employment and a future in India. Here he joined the court of the Nizam Shah—the Muslim dynast with brahmin forebears—and before long, Khunza was married to Husain.

Few women appear in retellings of the history of the Deccan, and if there is a queen who shines, it is usually Khunza's daughter, Chand Bibi. At the end of the sixteenth century, she bravely resisted the Mughals, and her tragic assassination enshrined her as a romantic heroine. Khunza, however, did not die at the end of a sword: her power was thwarted and restrained, and death in prison years later did not quite attract glamorous poems. And so she was forgotten, even her form and face crudely painted over in many of the miniature paintings. If Chand Bibi was celebrated even by the Mughals for her valour, Khunza came to be resented by her own son. There was no place for an inconvenient woman like her, and what survives is in bits and pieces, her fall from influence obscuring her fame forever.

Even in her husband's day, Khunza appears to have had some say in politics. One poem, in fact, ascribes an insult to her as the provocation for Husain's war against Vijayanagar. Of course, the battle in 1565 followed generations of tension and rivalry and had various causes, but it is telling that the *Fath Nama-i Nizam Shah* cites, in the words of scholar Sanjay Subrahmanyam, 'a potentially sexually loaded' reference to the queen as rousing the fury of her husband. The sultans of the Deccan often traded insults with Vijayanagar, but in this instance a line was crossed: in an inflammatory letter demanding tribute from Husain, the ruler of Vijayanagar listed, besides diamonds and rubies, the anklets of the begum. Disgusted and furious, Husain the 'lion' was roused against the 'pig' to whom he delivered death.

Leaving literary bombast aside, the death of Husain in 1565 enthroned Khunza's son in Ahmednagar. The boy was fated for instability and eventual murder, but for the next six years power was in the hands of his mother. She governed with the aid of trusted men—there was a eunuch and there were her brothers. She sat in court and gave orders, proving strong enough to ensure her commands were obeyed. She even went into battle—including against Chand Bibi's husband, who ruled a principality next door—and showed herself unafraid. It wasn't like the men around her saw this as admirable: a coup was thwarted in 1567. Her own son was involved, but chickening out in the last minute, he told his mother about the plot. For the time being, Khunza prevailed.

Powerful women like her, however, always had to tread with care. In the thirteenth century, the empress of Delhi, Razia Sultan, was murdered by men of her own court, and Khunza's daughter too was betrayed by those she thought she could trust—though war with the Mughals raged, Chand Bibi's assassin was not an invader but an insider. Khunza was always on her guard, but after half a decade at the helm, when the nobility decided to terminate her 'petticoat government', her downfall was confirmed. Khunza's foreign policy had proved a disaster—alliances were destabilised by impetuous demands, and those inclined to support her left her side in disapproval. Then there was the internal politics

The Courtesan, the Mahatma & the Italian Brahmin

of the realm: there was an African faction, a Persian faction and a local faction, all of them perpetually at loggerheads.

By 1571, the Nizam Shah was ostensibly liberated from the hold of his mother so that he could start making mistakes of his own (which included trying to kill his son in due course) and earn the epithet *deewana*, or madman. Khunza, abandoned by the men she had raised to power and wealth, was imprisoned and spent the rest of her days in oblivion. A similar unhappy fate her relations elsewhere too endured—the Mughal emperor Akbar's regent, Bairam Khan, was an extended family member, though assassination meant that he too was remembered with some poetic regret. Khunza wasted away with time, written out of history, disfigured in works of art her husband had lovingly had made. Only fragments remain of her tale, and like so many women, she went to the grave uncelebrated and unmourned, as history continued to be written by unforgiving men.

THE STORY OF THE *KAMASUTRA*

In 1883, when the *Kamasutra* first made its appearance in English, European readers of Vatsyayana's treatise hadn't the faintest idea that its publisher—the wordily nomenclatured Hindoo Kama Shastra Society—was, in fact, an entirely non-existent body. Ostensibly headquartered in Varanasi, with links to London and New York, the 'Society' was actually a work of fiction, born from the imagination of a couple of British officials and their associates in faraway India. That the translation, despite its numerous infirmities, was indeed of Vatsyayana's 1,600-year-old disquisition was not doubted. But even as the *Kamasutra* made its way into the great libraries of the West, the true identity of its translator remained shrouded for years behind this fictitious organisation.

There were several reasons why Sir Richard Francis Burton was paranoid about advertising his identity as translator on the book that went on to become a global bestseller—British laws on obscenity were so draconian that printing anything

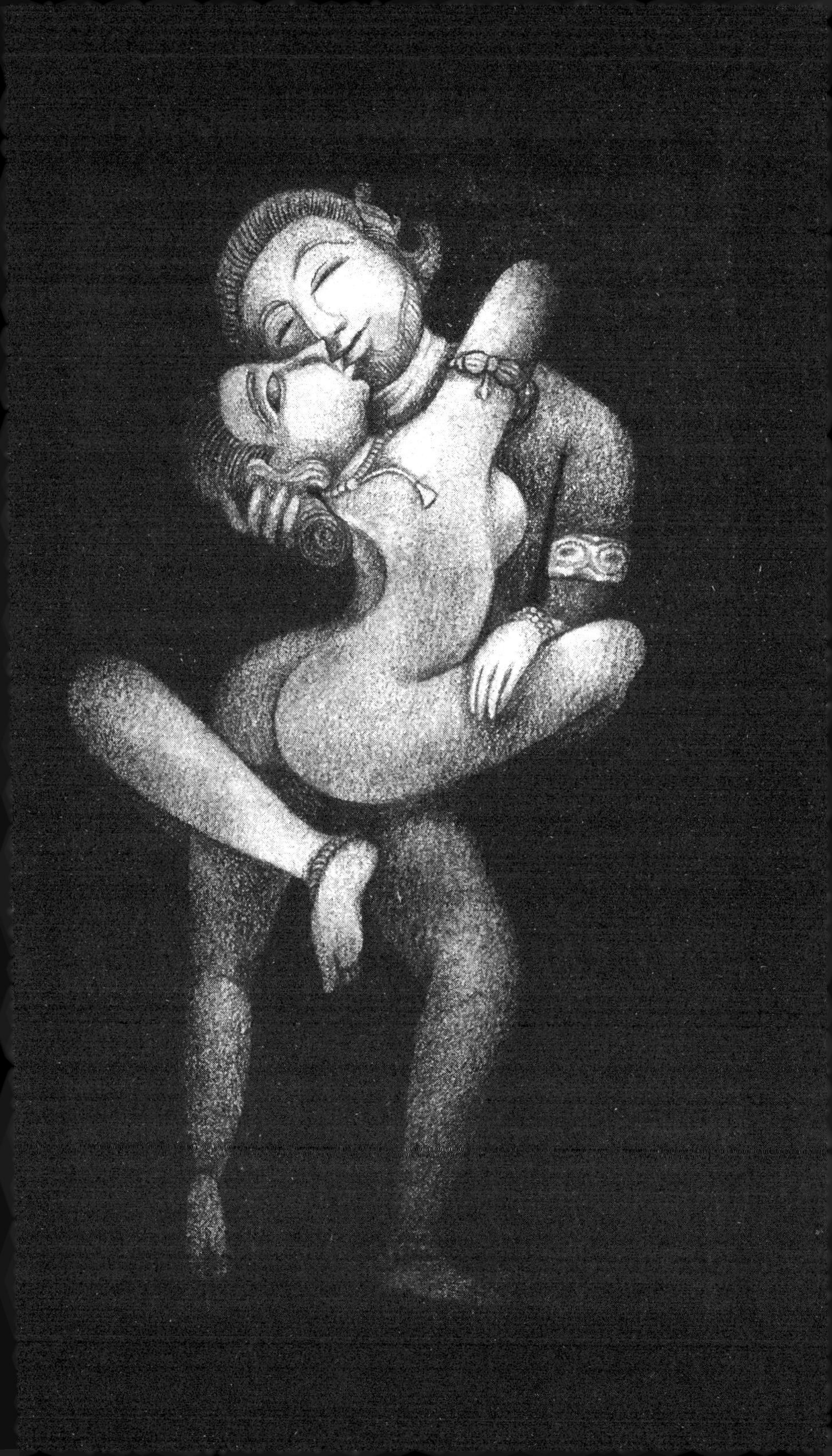

even vaguely sexual could show writers the door to prison. For the *Kamasutra* to be published then, it took some creative thinking to evade Victorian prudery. The Sanskrit word *yoni*, for instance, was used in the English text for the vagina, even when Vatsyayana himself never used that word in the Sanskrit original. But the gamble paid off—in time, the bogus Kama Shastra Society's translation would become, as one scholar notes, 'one of the most pirated books in the English language', registered across the world as the oldest and foremost classical text on all matters pertaining to love and human sexuality. This, even when it wasn't exactly sincere to Vatsyayana's moral outlook from centuries before.

The loosely held opinion that the *Kamasutra* is a catalogue for boudoir gymnastics also owes much to this context: The pronounced disapproval with which topics around sexuality were viewed meant that its most colourful components acquired, ironically, a heady momentum of their own, feelings of taboo fuelling a mischievous appetite for the text. In actual fact, the *Kamasutra* is more than a manual for lovemaking—of the seven books that constitute its body, only the second is strictly concerned with methods of human congress. Sir Richard, bent as he was on 'the sexual liberation of Victorian society', seems to have highlighted these while watering down the other elements. But despite such interventions and exaggerations, even in that first 1883 translation, of 175-odd pages, he could devote only forty to this theme. The remainder of the *Kamasutra*, in fact, offers a much wider series of discussions for the benefit of its wealthy and primarily male audience, covering not only sex but also matters of aesthetics and more.

Book Five, for example, concerns itself with extramarital affairs and how one ought to go about sliding into bed with another's spouse, while another section in the same book investigates, tantalisingly but ultimately disappointingly, 'Why Women Get Turned Off'. In Book One, we learn that if men of culture want to remain men of culture, they must allocate time every five or ten days to the removal of all their body hair: an idea that has some resonance today. Married women are generally not to be seduced, we are taught, but if it helps gain influence over a powerful husband or even perhaps to erase him from the world and acquire his wealth, it is acceptable to bed the wife as a weapon for one's personal ambitions and avarice. In these sections, then, the *Kamasutra* might well have been inspired by cold, calculating Chanakya and his utterly pragmatic *Arthashastra*.

The writer Hanif Kureishi noted that the *Kamasutra* is less like Lord Byron's heady romances and closer to P.G. Wodehouse's wit in its tone. 'One can wager on kisses,' argues Vatsyayana, for 'whichever of the partners first gets to the other's lower lip wins.' In order to seduce a woman, a man must be prepared to go flower-picking with her, to play in her doll house, and, perhaps most essentially, cultivate her closest friend (who, in an ideal society, would be her wet nurse's daughter). Where courtesans are concerned, Vatsyayana advises them to avoid by all means patrons with worms in their stool—or whose breath 'smells of crows'. They must also, he warns, never surrender reason, feeling free to manipulate men for money and goods. And if a patron were no longer capable of providing the aforementioned money and goods, he was to be discarded at once. One suggested route was to alienate him with markedly unpleasant behaviour: 'Curling the lip in a sneer' and 'stamping on the ground' promised success; 'ignoring him' was also an option.

There are, however, parts of the *Kamasutra* that make for uncomfortable reading, especially in our time of reluctant, troubled introspection; sections that, as scholar Wendy Doniger notes, seem to justify the seduction-by-sexual-assault school of thinking in which alarmingly large numbers of men are even today specialists. So while one can laugh at the *Kamasutra*'s assertion that the male 'instrument', pierced, and smeared with honey, powdered thorn apple and black pepper, provides divine ecstasies to the female, one cannot quite digest that a man can confidently proceed with intercourse with a woman when 'her mouth says no, but her eyes say yes'. Where at one point he is clear that 'a girl who is asleep, weeping or absent' (!) cannot be a bride, Vatsyayana still allows a wedding technique that involves getting the lady drunk and taking her 'maidenhead' while she is unconscious. Of course, given its age and context, it is not surprising that the *Kamasutra* speaks primarily in a male voice with erroneous male preconceptions. But compared to contemporaneous texts like the *Manusmriti*, the *Kamasutra* is replete with commentaries by women—and it recognises the right to pleasure for the female too.

Vatsyayana's approach to the third gender, and to homosexuality and bisexuality, also makes for gripping reading (and interpretation), so that in the overall analysis of the work one feels partly surprised, partly amused, but always interested. For all its sometimes outlandish views on life, marriage and intimacy, the *Kamasutra* remains a thoroughly fascinating work of art and cultural heritage, one we must read for more than a list of positions and bedroom acrobatics. That, in the end, is the secret of its enduring appeal, and in that also lies Vatsyayana's genius.

SULTANS AND PADSHAHS
FOREIGNNESS IN INDIANNESS

In 1352, Bukka Raya, one of the five brothers who founded what would become the empire of Vijayanagar, flaunted a most extraordinary title in a royal inscription. Along with such typically flamboyant styles as 'punisher of enemy kings', 'vanquisher of kings who break their word', and 'auspicious hero', this son of Sangama introduced something unusual, used only once before in India—by his own brother, a few years earlier: He assumed for himself the title of 'Hinduraya Suratrana', sultan among Hindu kings. It was, as has been alluded to in a previous essay, a remarkable claim to make, adopting all at once the nomenclature of 'Hindu'—hitherto applied by foreigners to describe Indians in general—while also transcribing into the Sanskritic vocabulary and imagination the concept of 'sultan', a potent new form of kingship which resounded across the land as Islamic dynasties entrenched themselves in the north, and took fire and steel into the south.

As part of imperial bombast, 'Hinduraya Suratrana' was essentially employed in Vijayanagar, though a stray reference appears also in a 1439 inscription in Sadri, Rajasthan. But the Sanskrit translation of 'sultan' as 'suratrana' itself was not Bukka's innovation. In 1323, Ghiyasuddin Tughlaq appears as Suratrana Gayasadina, and three years before Bukka, we find the term in Nepal—after his invasion in 1349, Shamsuddin of Bengal was remembered there as Suratrana Samasdina. Even in the seventeenth century, the term was in vogue, used to describe the Mughals. And yet some deny any connection between this Sanskrit term and its Arabic root. Suratrana, to them, comes from *sura* (god) and *trana* (protector), which would mean that Bukka saw himself as a protector of Hindu deities, and was not borrowing an Islamic title. The etymology could be entertained, but the fact is that, in practice, the words were certainly used synonymously: where the Delhi sultanate's coins used the Arabic 'sultan' on one side, the reverse was inscribed in Sanskrit with 'suritana'. So too, when literary works referred to the Suratrana of Yoginipura (Delhi), it is unlikely they were flattering Muslim kings as guardians of Hindu gods.

In the larger picture of the interaction Islam had with India's diversity of traditions and cultures, this indigenisation of a foreign title is hardly surprising. The dominance Muslim rulers enjoyed for centuries saw the import of Persian culture into the subcontinent, and much from Farsi and Arabic blended with Indian tongues. The place of Persian as the language of diplomacy meant that as late as the 1810s, communication between a Malayali queen (whose minister was her *dewan*) and the English East India Company was conducted in that language. In some Indian languages, in fact, Persian and Arabic left imprints that are indelible, marking their nature as much as their cultural and literary identities.

The Courtesan, the Mahatma & the Italian Brahmin

Marathi, for instance, borrowed a great many words from these foreign *bhashas* so that, as the scholar V.K. Rajwade noted, 'old Marathi documents are as unintelligible to a non Persian-knowing Maratha, as to a foreigner'. The nineteenth-century Maharashtrian thinker Vishnushastri Chiplunkar had no qualms admitting that the 'roots of our language' lay as much in Persian and Arabic as in Sanskrit. And just as the emperors of Vijayanagar projected themselves as Hindu sultans, the Deccani hero Shivaji was described in the Sabhasad bakhar (i.e. chronicle, derived evidently from the Persian *akhbar*) as a Maratha padshah.

While suratrana and padshah were titles related to dynasts and kings, foreign influences made their presence felt even at lower levels, travelling down to our own time. Scribes who worked for Muslim kings and wrote their letters in Farsi were called Parsnavis, from which emerged today's surname of Parasnis, just as the Maharashtrian name Daftardar is descended from an official bureaucratic title. Fard-Navis, or secretary/note-taker, is what birthed Fadnavis. The *bharud* drama-poems of Eknath, the celebrated Bhakti saint, are replete with words of Persian origin, while even personal names used by Marathas sometimes had a foreign provenance: names like Sahebrao, Serfoji, Rustamrao, and so on. Shivaji's own father and uncle, as we saw earlier, were named Shahaji and Sharifji to celebrate a Muslim pir called Shah Sharif, whom his grandparents admired.

Shivaji, it is true, made a pointed effort to erase Persian influences and concepts from Marathi, even commissioning a dictionary to help discard *yavana* (foreign) words and replace them with Sanskrit alternatives. But as the power of the Marathas spread across large swathes of the country, the status of Persian as a link language made its resurrection inevitable. The Peshwas, a dynasty of hereditary ministers to the Maratha king, were orthodox, but even their title was Persian. In a 1775 letter that the prominent Maratha figure Nana Fadnavis sent on behalf of the Peshwa to the British monarch, the scholar Sumit Guha highlights words that are of Perso-Arabic origin (*daulat*, *biradar*, *bahut*, *mahzabat*, and so on), noting that though not as extensively as before, these were back in circulation. Such Islamicate influence was not limited to language, administrative jargon and titles alone: The Marathas also, as we saw earlier, adopted Persian sartorial fashions and styles of architecture, so much so that the *samadhi* of Shivaji's grandfather has been mistaken for a Muslim tomb on account of its striking resemblance to Islamic mausoleums.

Considering the plurality of influences that makes up Indian culture—a civilisation with no single origin—none of this ought to surprise anyone. By the nineteenth century, however, efforts were already under way to 'purify' languages and give them a classical pretence by overcompensating with Sanskrit words and trying to divert everything Persian and Arabic along religious lines to a specific class of people. In many respects, the project is still ongoing, and there is among certain sections of people even today a quest to find the 'true' essence or the purest version of the past. The irony is that such a past does not exist, and what exists is not 'pure' but rich and layered and marvelously complex—a past where there are Hindu sultans and Maratha padshahs, where the forebears of a Hindu king could seek the blessings of a Muslim pir.

MEENAKSHI
FIRST A WARRIOR

To visit the great temple in Madurai today is to navigate a dozen streets and discover an army of beggars besieging the 700-year-old structure. Some of these beggars are old, but many are young and quick. There are beggars with bowls, and beggars with babies. But they all have a peculiar confidence when seeking donations. The temple, after all, welcomes about 15,000 visitors on a routine day, and collections from even a fraction of this host are more than adequate to sustain their thriving economy on the streets. The solicitation of money is made with an almost defiant sweetness—if *you* don't drop coins, there are others who most certainly will.

For all its known history, Madurai has been dominated by this temple, with its 33,000 sculptures and magnificent towers of monumental height. The Greeks traded here, and as early as 21 BCE, a Tamil embassy was welcomed in Rome. The eunuch general from Delhi, Malik Kafur, came uninvited to relieve the city of its burdensome riches in the early fourteenth century, and for many decades thereafter, the place was under the rule of a fearsome sultanate (a princess of which became wife to the traveller Ibn Battuta). Some generations later, Roberto de Nobili showed up seeking flocks of Christians. The Italian, as we have seen, did his best to convince local priests that he was also a brahmin, flaunting a sacred thread, and by 1610 teaching the gospel in fluent Tamil and Telugu.

The story of the Meenakshi temple, though, is the tale of a woman—a fearsome warrior-queen transformed into a lovable goddess; a formidable mortal tranquillised into divine immortality. *Tiruvilaiyadal Puranam* (The Story of the Sacred Games), a thirteenth-century poem in 64 rich chapters, begins with a melancholy Pandyan king. 'I was without a son,' he says, 'and I performed great sacrifices for a long time. [And when that failed] I performed the sacrifice that was supposed to produce a son.' Soon he extended his arms and received a child, but the three-year-old that emerged from the flames was a girl. 'But god!' cried the king, 'even though this girl has come with a face that shines like the moon, she has three breasts!'

So it was that Meenakshi—she with fish eyes, a political superlative since the fish was the totem of the Pandyas—made her appearance on earth. Her father worried that her three nipples 'will make even enemies laugh', and languished in 'depression and unhappiness'. He had sought a child—a son, valiant and unparalleled in might—but what he got was a freak. A voice from the heavens, however, reassured him and the three-nippled girl was raised a boy, dissolving boundaries of gender and sex. When (s)he came of age, her parents said it was time to marry. (S)he, however, decided it was time to conquer the world.

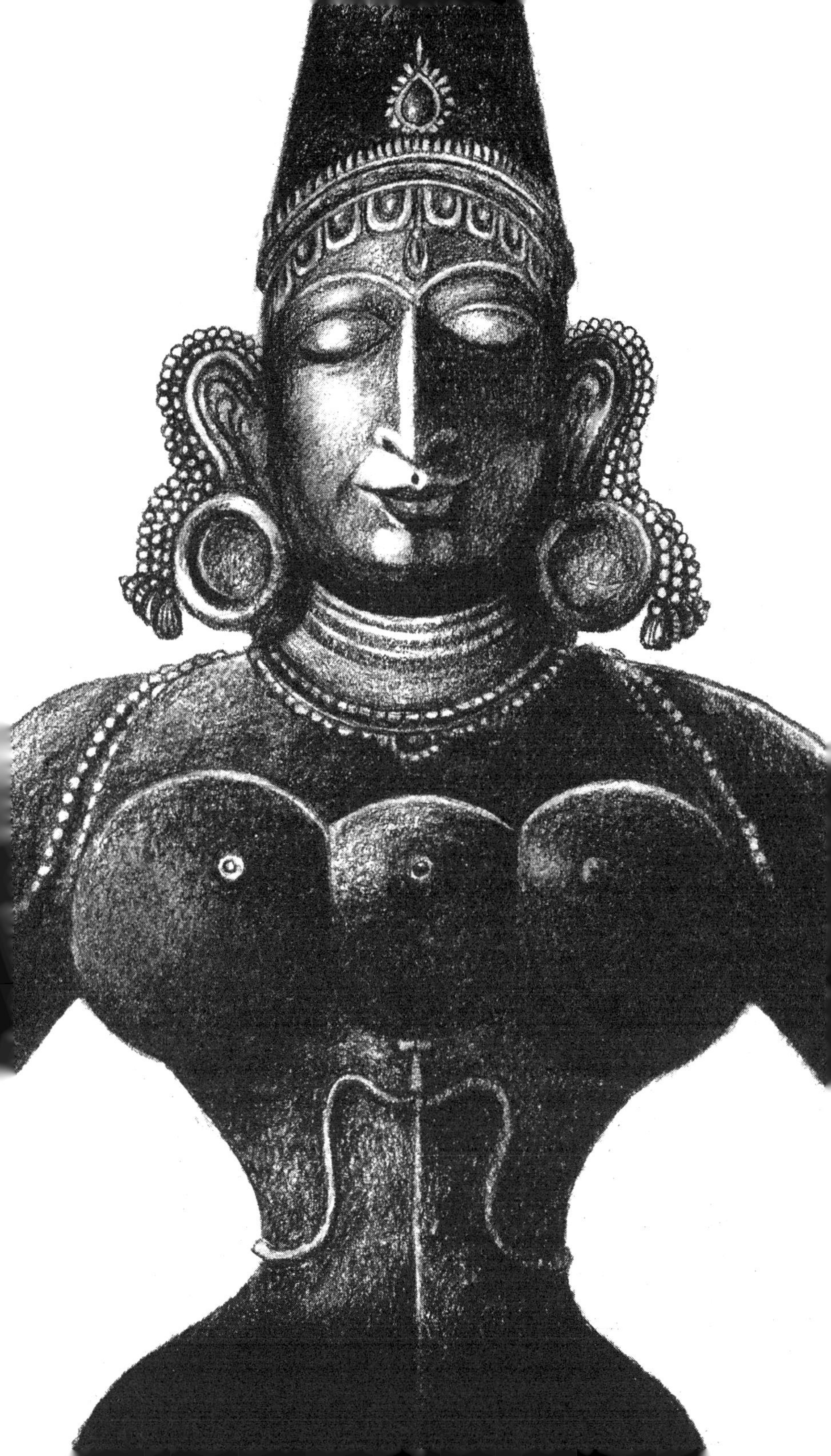

With a powerful, formidable army, Meenakshi set out from Madurai. Indra, Lord of the Heavens, fled at the very sight of his foe—and nobody laughed any more at the third nipple. Soon the conqueror climbed the Himalayas to battle Shiva. But when the fish-eyed one gazed upon him, the third breast disappeared and she became a regular woman. Or, as the poem tells it, she 'became bashful, passive, and fearful. She leaned unsteadily, like the flowering branch of a tree under the weight of its blossoms. Her heavy dark hair fell on her neck. She looked downward, toward her feet … And there she stood, shining like lightning, scratching in the earth with her toes.'

Soon they were married, and the rest of the poem shows Shiva as its hero, pulling the strings where once his wife had led. It is interesting how *Tiruvilaiyadal Puranam* seeks to establish his power, almost as if to compensate for the reality that was the superiority of his wife—to this day, it is Meenakshi who is worshipped first, not Shiva, even when in theory he is held superior. They share eight festivals, but she has four dedicated only to her while her husband has none. Shiva, too, in practice, was Pandyanised. His animal skins were discarded for silk, the serpents he wore replaced by bejewelled ornaments. He is Shiva in name but a different kind of Shiva, rarely to be found elsewhere.

Inside the temple, there are sculptures still of others who, like Meenakshi, were born different. There is a representation of her in stone, all three breasts intact, before her union with god made her more 'normal'. There is Arjuna, not only as the feared warrior of the Mahabharata but also as Arjuni, in female form, and as Brihannala, in the third gender—he has the face of a man, with a drooping moustache and a long beard, but the body of a woman, with full breasts. Besides transgenders, there is also room in the tube-lit temple premises for autosexuals—the halls feature self-fellating lions, under some of whom sit pilgrims, children and ticket vendors, next to pious women chanting slokas and prayers.

Was there really once an androgynous queen with three nipples whose exploits inspired the *Tiruvilaiyadal Puranam*? Megasthenes, the Greek envoy to India, refers to the legend of a princess wedded to a god, and perhaps there is some historical truth to what we have received in song. What matters more is the devotion Meenakshi inspired then and still inspires today. Some view her marriage with Shiva as the absorption, at last, of a resilient local goddess into the wider Hindu pantheon, where her independent power was surrendered in favour of a greater cause and more correct femininity. But the pilgrims who come to Madurai to pay obeisance to Meenakshi—not her husband—keep alive the flame of the original triple-breasted warrior. And like the politely defiant beggars outside, every pillar and stone defies the story woven in the *Tiruvilaiyadal Puranam* in celebration of a memory from long, long before, when the abnormal resisted the normal, and when a princess reigned before she was turned into a goddess.

THE WOMAN WHO HAD NO REASON FOR SHAME

In the kingdom of Thanjavur there once lived a courtesan called Muddupalani. To her came fame and riches, while modesty, she declared, was a shroud for the timid and colourless. 'Which other woman of my kind,' asked this eighteenth-century poet, 'has felicitated scholars with gifts and money?' 'To which other woman of my kind,' she added, 'have epics been devoted?' The queries were rhetorical, of course, for in the Thanjavur of her day, Muddupalani was a woman unequalled. Her face, she triumphantly proclaimed, shone 'like the full moon', and to gaze upon her was to behold beauty and brilliance in harmony unparalleled.

Muddupalani (c. 1730–90) was a jewel in the court of Pratapasimha (c. 1739–63), a patron of the arts and Maratha heir to swathes of Tamil country. But a century after their time, the world was inherited by men who cloaked fragile sensitivities in thundering hypocrisy. Some took to calling

The Courtesan, the Mahatma & the Italian Brahmin

Muddupalani 'Muddu Pillai', as though she were a man—for this devadasi and her 'kind' were no longer respectable, and her Telugu epic, the *Radhika Santwanamu*, offered not edification through art, but ignominy and scandal. Where once the great temple in Thanjavur celebrated devadasis by the hundreds, where once they were feted for their beauty and artistic prowess, they were now savaged and violently deplored as old kings fell and foreigners emerged to rule. If Muddupalani found admirers in this new generation, they had to hide her behind a fictitious name, inventing an imaginary man.

In the course of the nineteenth century, Indian society absorbed from the British an overblown sense of Victorian piety: this much is well known. And in this age of duplicity, Muddupalani—that woman with a singular voice—was cast as the author of raging vulgarity. Krishna came to her in a dream, she said, inspiring her poem of love. But now her words were used against her, as the confabulations of a 'shameless prostitute'. There was, the critic Kandukuri Veeresalingam grudgingly admitted, charm and scholarship in her writing; 'this woman's poetry' was both 'soft and melodious'. But she was too obsessed with ecstasies of the flesh for her palm-leaf verses to be elevated to the dignity of modern print and paper. What appeared in an 1887 translation of Muddupalani's composition was vandalism, her soul excised and discarded. But with the woman made invisible, the elders could remain unthreatened and sanctimonious.

Every line in the epic's 584 poems threatened disorder, but some passages were especially calamitous. Not only did Muddupalani show Radha grooming Krishna's bride, Ila, for their wedding night, she also highlighted Radha's furious envy thereafter. At first it is concern for Ila that Radha expresses, like a 'good' older woman ('How will the lips of this young girl suffer his bites ... How will her breasts bear his clawing?'). Then it is advice for the girl ('He is the best lover, a real connoisseur, extremely delicate. Love him skilfully and make him love you'). But after she has delivered his bride to Krishna's chamber—and given *him* counsel on how to make love to this young thing 'new to the art'—Radha collapses into an ocean of jealousies, 'her mind a jumble of misery and joy'.

Once, laments Radha, it was she who made love to Krishna. Now she was supplanted by another whose body was as 'soft as bananas'. Lying restless in bed, she pictures them together, tortured by the images arrayed in her cruel mind. 'Inside her,' tells Muddupalani, 'she was burning. As for Krishna, he was busy with the [other] girl.' But the story does not end in torment or tragedy: Krishna returns to Radha and appeases his first love. She is comforted, and soon it is the hero who expresses exhausted discomfort. 'If I ask her not to get too close,' protests Krishna, 'she swears at me loudly. If I tell her of my vow not to have a woman in my bed,' he complains, 'she hops on and begins the game of love.'

In other words, when Radha had Krishna in her embrace again, she commanded unforgiving allegiance. Muddupalani's Radha was not timid like the newly-wed Ila. Indeed, she was not like any other Radha. She turned convention on its head and claimed her right to bodily pleasure. For the first time in compositions of its type appeared a woman determined to quench her desire. She yearns for her lord, not coyly but insisting on physical affection. At first, she fears betrayal, but when her lover returns, she collects her dues and demands physical satisfaction.

Muddupalani—named after the deity in Palani—was a woman who composed a whole epic bursting with eroticism.

The Courtesan, the Mahatma & the Italian Brahmin

As her biographer Sandhya Mulchandani records, 'Writing with unabashed frankness and unbridled enthusiasm, [she] feels no anxiety or remorse in so truthfully expressing her desires.' Some believe her work is autobiographical: Pratapasimha was initially patron to Muddupalani's grandmother, herself an acclaimed courtesan called Tanjanayaki. Was Radha's envy a reflection of what the poet's own forebear felt when her partner transferred his affections to one so much younger? Was the appeasement of Radha at its core the tale of a Maratha prince who returned, at last, to placate a neglected Telugu lover?

Devotional poetry by women in language charged with erotic feeling was not Muddupalani's innovation. She was, in fact, heir to a tradition as long as it was illustrious. Raghunatha Nayaka, lord of Thanjavur in a previous age, had a wife, Ramabhadramba. In streams of Sanskrit verse, she paints him as the embodiment of kingly ideals, bursting with masculine strength and physical vigour. When Raghunatha seeks women's embraces, his consort 'compares him admiringly', writes Vasudha Narayanan, 'to Lord Krishna'. She 'extols his sexual prowess as he goes through a typical night' making love to 'an astounding series of women'. There is heroism and there is ardour. But here, as in works before, it is the man who commands love and attention—it is his pleasure that is central.

With Muddupalani, however, the gaze is reversed—it is the deity who must satisfy the erotic yearnings of his female devotee. Shudder as some might at these verses, their eroticism was not what upset the elders. It was the fact that their author was a woman—one with wealth, learning, beauty and culture—that horrified her two-faced readers. From men, they lauded *padams* full of *sringara*. Ksētrayya, in the voice of a lovelorn woman, sings to his beloved god in lines that are famous:

I can see all the signs
Of what you've been doing
Till midnight, you playboy.
Still you come rushing through the streets
Sly as a thief to untie my blouse.

Elsewhere, he is still more playful:

When we are on the bed of gold
Playing at love talk
He calls me Kamalakshi
The other woman's name.
I am so mad
I hit him as hard as I can
With my braid.

But Ksētrayya was a man, his verses, therefore, naturally sublime. Muddupalani was female: 'an adulteress' who had not the 'modesty natural to women'. Where was virtue, demanded her critics. Where was shame? 'Several references in the book are disgraceful and inappropriate for women to hear, let alone be uttered from a woman's mouth,' they screamed.

Then, in the early twentieth century, Nagaratnamma, a devadasi from Bangalore, resurrected Muddupalani from darkness. She turned to these men and asked sharply in turn: 'Does the question of propriety and embarrassment apply only in the case of women, not men?' Was desire only a feeling permitted to men and forbidden forever for women? But the world was not ready; the elders still reigned. And Muddupalani went underground again, far from the self-righteous eyes.

As for Nagaratnamma, the self-righteous sneered at her. A 'prostitute had composed the book,' announced a magazine, 'and another prostitute has edited it.' Surely no 'literate gentleman can realise god by reading that he enjoyed sex in forty different ways'. But Nagaratnamma remained devoted. 'However often I read this book ... I feel like reading it all over again ... this poem, brimming with rasa ... written by a woman.' While her contemporary Ancukam, a devadasi in Colombo, invited her 'kind' to follow the path of virtue, wearing not jewels but rudraksha, not make-up but sacred ash, Nagaratnamma hungered for Muddupalani, who had no reason for shame, no desire for 'reform'.

Then, at long last, after many decades had passed and India became free, the ban was withdrawn and justice done. Scholars like Susie Tharu and K. Lalita set out to retrieve Muddupalani, encountering on the way men yet opposed to such unholy plans. One alone offered words of wisdom ringing with an inconvenient truth. Said Yandamuri Satyanarayanarao: 'These epic poems are well-formed works, complete with all the nine *rasas*. If we look at them with our present view of women, they might appear low and unrefined.' But that is 'the inadequacy of our culture, and not that of the epic or the poet' herself.

It's a simple point, but it needed to be reiterated. If today we are afraid of Muddupalani's song, it is not she who is to blame. If her poem is a moral threat, it is not she who must hide in shame. Muddupalani ruled over a different age, and there she remains eternally enshrined. It is those who came after who proved themselves history's unworthy heirs.

ALAUDDIN KHILJI
RULING BY THE SWORD

Alauddin Khilji, the fourteenth-century Muslim king of Delhi, had a fearsome mother-in-law. The conqueror—captured in a 2018 film as the very picture of unwashed ferocity, complete with sinister, surma-lined eyes, an insatiable appetite for gore and gold, and much lust for virtuous Hindu princesses—does not seem to have enjoyed any domestic tranquillity during his very eventful life. His first wife and her mother, described variously as 'fool of fools' and 'silliest of the silly', were supremely dominating, so much so that some of his early campaigns were also partly an excuse to place as much distance as possible between himself and them. Things got a little more complicated after he seized the wife of a Gujarati king—the lady missed her young daughter, so another round of battles had to be fought to seize the object of her motherly affections. Then he had in his harem a slave girl who was sent out to do battle and died in the process. Finally, he also fell in love with Malik Kafur, the eunuch general, who cheerfully exploited this sentiment till he found his way abruptly to a forgotten grave.

Alauddin was nephew and son-in-law to the first of the Khilji sultans, a man who killed his predecessor and then belatedly found himself consumed by guilt. This uncle wouldn't sit on the throne, for instance, because he was convinced he was unworthy. While older nobles at court were sufficiently moved, those of a more aggressive temperament thought this sentimental nonsense. They began to plot to replace the mild-mannered monarch with a more manly substitute. When news of one of these intrigues reached the ruler, he summoned its participants to his august presence. And there, instead of relieving them of their seditious heads, he proceeded to lecture them on alcohol and the importance of not getting carried away into making murderous plans while under its influence. The young men nodded, wept and begged forgiveness, but among those who realised that the sultan was more heart than head and ambition was Alauddin. In 1296, after he raided Devagiri without imperial permission and returned with phenomenal quantities of plunder, he sought his royal uncle's pardon and invited him to come in person to collect the treasure. Trusting and naïve, the old sultan went where he was told—and very quickly found himself in more than one piece.

'While the head of the murdered sovereign was yet dripping with blood,' writes the chronicler Ziauddin Barani, 'the ferocious conspirators brought the royal canopy and elevated it over the head of Alauddin. Casting aside all shame, the perfidious and graceless wretches caused him to be proclaimed king by men who rode about on elephants.' The new king was touched. After he put his uncle's sons to

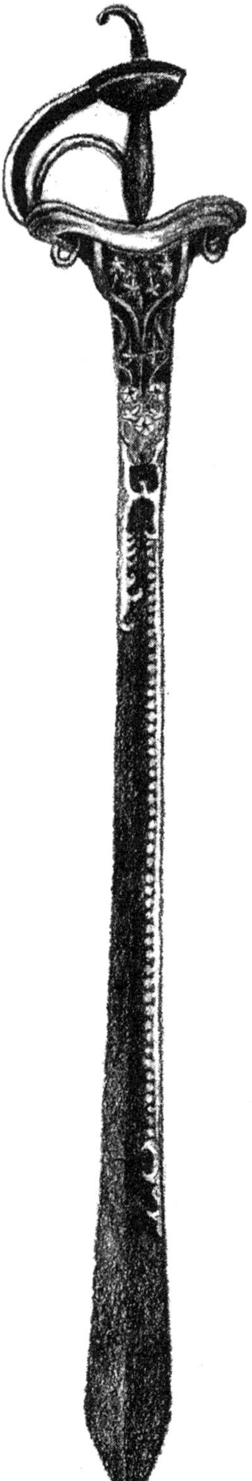

flight and eventually imprisoned his infuriating mother-in-law, the men who helped raise him to the throne were also rewarded with death—that is, leaving aside two who had been already destroyed by leprosy or madness. The loot from Devagiri (later called Daulatabad) was put to good use. After all, gold could erase all traces of a less-than-conventional succession to the throne, purchasing loyalties that could not be immediately inspired. In subsequent policy, Alauddin was firm. 'I issue such orders as I conceive to be for the good of the State, and the benefit of the people,' he declared. 'Men are heedless, disrespectful, and disobey my commands: I am then compelled to be severe to bring them into obedience.' An elaborate network of spies was formed, so that if anything unwise was said against the sultan, His Majesty was perhaps also among the first to hear it.

Alauddin's career was not easy, though, despite all its violence and fury. Having murdered his uncle, he could hardly point fingers at his own nephews for seeking to follow in his august, blood stained footsteps. One tried to shower him with arrows, and for this his head appeared on a spear. Two sons of a sister decided the time was right for rebellion, so they were both blinded. In due course, however, it was clear that the sultan meant business, and the court fell in line. The times were such that to claim and retain power, one also needed to indulge in periodic violent demonstrations of its use. Alauddin became an empire builder. Kingdom after kingdom in northern India fell to him, while his trusted commander Malik Kafur acquired mountains of gold in the south. When hordes of Mongols invaded India soon after the sultan's ascent to power, they were defeated. In 1303, however, when Alauddin was away, the Mongols destroyed Delhi. The king returned and locked himself up in a fort, unable to do much on this occasion, though he put to good use the lessons he learnt from the experience. For the rest of his reign, he never once allowed the Mongols a victory.

Interestingly, the sacking of Delhi in 1303 occurred because Alauddin was at the time in Chittor, doing battle. *Padmavat*, an Awadhi poem that has since been embraced as historical fact, offers a most imaginative motive for the sultan's presence there. A parrot had told the already married ruler of Chittor about a dark-skinned Ceylonese beauty. After many adventures, this beauty became queen in the desert, from where a wicked sorcerer was expelled by her Rajput husband. This character told Alauddin all about her, and so it was that the Muslim king marched his men and demanded the princess's enlistment in his harem. To cut a long story short, battles were fought, masses of people died, and the lady jumped into a fire. Alauddin himself never knew this story, for it first appeared two centuries after his death. It would hardly have mattered though, for his end was not very happy. Illness depleted him, and he spent his time fearing his own sons, lapsing more and more into the hands of Malik Kafur, who may even have had something to do with his death. Either way, Alauddin died in 1316, and a fresh cycle of intrigues and violence began, ending with the fall of his dynasty and the inevitable advent of a new one.

THE COURTESAN WHO BECAME A PRINCESS

In the summer of 1795, soldiers attached to a Mughal jagir in present-day Uttar Pradesh rose up in mutiny and chained their commander-in-chief to a gun carriage. It was the nadir of their ultimately foiled enterprise, but the whole episode was packed with extraordinary drama. To begin with, the commander-in-chief—who languished for a whole week in excruciating heat—was a woman. She had launched her career as a dancing girl, not only rising to become the begum of Sardhana, but also to win the affection of the Mughal emperor, who styled her Zeb-un-Nissa (Jewel among Women), Farzand-i-Azizi (Beloved Daughter), and even Umdat-al-Arakin (Pillar of the State). She had spent her youth by the side of a much older German lover, inheriting his fortune and lands, and later joined a Frenchman in a doomed marriage. Now, as she lay shackled and humiliated in public, riding heroically to her rescue was a former Irish paramour, one who would title himself the 'Raja from Tipperary', becoming famous in due course for his own colourful military exploits.

Begum Samru, as our protagonist is best known, was born in the 1750s to the junior wife (or mistress) of a petty Mughal nobleman. The early death of her father saw both mother and child turned out on to the streets, and by her teens the part-Kashmiri girl, who would one day take the name Joanna Nobilis, was a courtesan in Delhi. It was at this time that she encountered Walter Reinhardt. A serial deserter turned mercenary, this man of obscure origins had upset practically all of his employers, including the French and the British. He had originally served the French, assuming the name Somers when he transferred his loyalties to the English—this was later amended to 'Sombre' when he flipped again to the French side, which identity was finally Indianised into the 'Samru' of legend after he abandoned both European companies and took service with the Nawab of Bengal. In 1763, at the nawab's orders, Reinhardt presided over a massacre of dozens of Englishmen in Patna: the prisoners were invited to dinner and after 'his guests were in full security, protected as they imagined by the laws of hospitality', he ordered his men 'to fall upon them and cut their throats'. Only a doctor was spared, and the horror of the atrocity clouded Reinhardt's reputation for the rest of his life.

Even as the furious English authorities placed a bounty on his head, our German mercenary with many identities now entered the service of the Nawab of Awadh, essentially putting as much of a physical gap as he could between himself and East India Company justice. It was no wonder, then, that when even his latest master lost to the English, Reinhardt moved on yet again, travelling with much treasure and a large body of men to the court of the Jat ruler of

The Courtesan, the Mahatma & the Italian Brahmin

Bharatpur. Here, in his newest capacity, he joined the 1765 Jat attack on Delhi. And now, at last, he encountered the courtesan who would take his name and bring to it a sheen of unusual glamour and magnetism. At the time, incidentally, Reinhardt already had an Indian wife and a son, but very quickly his romantic associate from Delhi became his principal partner. Indeed, Begum Samru would live with him for over a decade, sharing in his numerous adventures. At first, this unlikely couple—the 'butcher of Patna' and the dancing girl from Delhi—stayed in Bharatpur. But in 1773, when the Jats were defeated by troops fighting for Emperor Shah Alam, Reinhardt switched sides again. It was the final gamble of his life, but a remunerative one. He received from the Mughals the jagir of Sardhana, which at last lent him a semblance of prestige, becoming also the stage where his begum would leave her own indelible mark.

The years she spent with Reinhardt transformed Begum Samru. Accompanying her 'husband' on his numerous military campaigns, she became his right hand in managing Sardhana, investing in its growth and watching its revenues multiply. After Reinhardt's death in 1778—something that infuriated the English, since it denied them the chance of ever avenging his barbarity—she played her cards with uncommon shrewdness, having the emperor recognise her, and not her husband's hopeless son, as heir to his estate and all its appurtenances. Even while her dead spouse's reputation continued to plague her, Begum Samru won admirers across the board, all of whom noted her determination, charm and store of wisdom—after all, she had come begrimed from crisis and want, and here she was now, wealthy, strong, and a force in her own right. Indeed, successive commentators recorded her 'masculine' gifts, which, in this patriarchal age, as Julia Keay wrote, was their highest compliment. The begum, too, encouraged such an image: she sported a turban and appeared unveiled in paintings, with a hookah pipe in her hand. She was essentially making, as art historian Alka Hingorani argues, 'subtle alterations of traditionally masculine prerogatives', carving out a space for herself in contemporary India. And that made her, at the time, completely extraordinary.

In 1781, Begum Samru, now confirmed master of Sardhana and commander-in-chief of all of Reinhardt's troops, took the unusual step of converting to Catholicism. It was an act as much of religious conviction as of political imagination. Though she shared no tongue with the priest who baptised her, and despite disapproval over her retention of an Islamic appearance even after her conversion, the begum spent lakhs of rupees on Christian institutions, constructing also what is still one of north India's largest churches. Becoming a Christian seemed also a suitable strategy for a woman unhappy with Islamic restraints on her sex: Catholicism gave her the freedom she required to rule Sardhana while creating a legitimate (and distinct) space in Hindustani politics. Her very story and rise were unusual; now, even in power, she retained distinction by securing a place unlike any other for herself. Some, in fact, claim that Begum Samru foresaw British dominion and wished to curry favour with India's future masters by accepting the Christian faith—a claim not borne out by evidence, even if it lends itself to speculation, not least because she corresponded enthusiastically with the pope.

As a military commander, Begum Samru showed all the qualities that marked leadership in her tumultuous age. When necessary, she could be ruthless: while she never ordered large and indiscriminate massacres, when two murderous maidservants set fire to her buildings, she had no hesitation in having them buried alive. In the 1780s, when the Mughal emperor was imperilled and surrounded by enemies, it was she who rode more than once, for not only the defence of his imperial person but also of his capital. It was this service that earned her those aforementioned titles, and it was her genuine affection for his well-being that saw the former dancing girl become one of Shah Alam's most beloved confidantes. (Unfortunately for the emperor, on the one occasion he needed her most, Begum Samru was unable to come to his aid: falling into the hands of a particularly sadistic enemy called Ghulam Qadir, he saw his daughters violated and was himself blinded before he could be rescued.)

The begum also had to balance factions within her own armed forces. A motley crew of European adventurers and assorted Indian sepoys, whose moral compass was barely more evolved than Reinhardt's, they had their own politics and rivalries. That is how, for instance, when she went ahead and married an unpopular French gun-founder in 1795, she provoked the mutiny which saw her tied up and left to die in the scorching heat. She survived the debacle and was restored to power, but never again permitted her heart to reign over her head. Her husband, of course, could learn no lessons—he was shot dead by the begum's men.

By the early nineteenth century, the middle-aged begum ('a bejeweled vision of delight'), who had hitherto loyally served the tottering Mughal crown, knew that English power was in the ascendant, and soon she was their ally—a potential adjustment to altered political realities after the emperor and his dynasty went into terminal decline and British supremacy became India's new normal. Instead of military engagements, it was her soirées that now attracted Europeans for whom she was also an object of curiosity. As late as 1834, when she was 'bent in two' and 'shriveled like dried raisins', her energy never ceased to dazzle. In fact, writes the scholar Brijraj Singh, she actively 'preferred European people and things to their Indian counterparts'. It was another matter that despite admiring her, Company officials never saw her as an equal. But that didn't depress her either, in the big picture: she had begun life in poverty and worked in a public house. By the eve of her demise, she not only enjoyed military salutes, but was also one of India's richest women. As her memorial in Sardhana records, when 'Her Highness Joanna Zeb-ul-Nissa' died on 27 January 1836, she was 'revered and lamented by thousands of her devoted subjects'—not a predictable ending for someone who was once a courtesan, and whose successes so bewildered the world that rumour insisted she was actually a witch.

MEERABAI
A DIFFERENT KIND OF VALOUR

Perhaps if Meerabai of Mewar had jumped into a fire, she too might have had armies of twenty-first-century men prepared to smash glass and destroy public property in the name of protecting her honour. After all, nothing rouses patriarchal masculine pride more than illusions of stoic sacrifice by unreal beauties, who, between managing their heavy jewels and rich skirts, spout tedious lines about valour and fortitude. So while (the possibly fictional) Padmavati, by dying the way she is supposed to have, went down as the right kind of tragic heroine, the definitely real Meerabai presents a minor problem by refusing to bow out in the correct fashion. On the contrary, far from yearning to kill herself after her husband succumbed on the battlefield, Meerabai declared firmly, 'I will not be a sati.' She chose instead, to live for decades more, singing praises of her favourite deity, Krishna, while rejecting pressures from the muscular guardians of Rajput society. Patriarchy accommodated her as an icon of feminine, god-loving devotion, but in her own verses, we find a lady with a mind of her own; one who stood up to all established norms of honour, and to the authority of every mortal man around her.

Meerabai was born at the dawn of the sixteenth century in Merta in Rajasthan. According to hagiographies composed by her earliest admirers, this motherless child was raised in her grandfather's household, and from a tender age showed great affection for Krishna. Around 1516, when in her late teens, she married Bhojraj, son of the legendary Rana Sangha of Mewar. Their complicated union did not last, however. In the next decade, Meerabai lost her husband and her footing in his royal household. Her refusal to commit sati may have added to the erosion of status that came automatically with widowhood, but she did not care about being perceived as a troublesome woman. As one of her verses, addressed to her husband's heir, declares: 'Rana, to me this slander is sweet ... Mira's lord is [Krishna]: let the wicked burn in a furnace.' There is no doubt that Meerabai was passionate in her love for god—some of her greatest works are those expressing deep sorrow at her 'separation' from her divine beloved. But there is also no doubt that hers was a voice that challenged the world, refusing the control her husband's relations sought to exercise in the name of their own prestige and her patent lack of aristocratic reserve.

Some of this resistance is encapsulated in Nabhadas's *Bhaktamal*, composed soon after Meerabai's time. 'Modesty in public, the chains of family life/Mira shed both for the Lifter of Mountains,' the saint writes. She had 'no inhibitions' and was 'totally fearless'. 'She cringed before none, she beat love's drum.' In other words, far from leading an unobtrusive life in widow's garb or fitting into the role of a *pativrata* (devoted wife), as Padmavati is supposed to have done, Meerabai engaged freely with other devotees and moved in spaces not ordinarily permitted to women. Her interlocutors, furthermore, included a diverse cast of men, from backgrounds that did not make them ideal companions for a Rajput widow. Where custom demanded social invisibility of her, Meerabai chose the opposite, further enraging her family. Still, she did not care—'I don't like your strange world, Rana,' she records. 'A world where there are no holy men, and all the people are trash.'

In the face of her resolve, there was even an attempt to poison her, but our poet was uncowed: 'Rana,' she announced, 'nobody can prevent me from going to the saints. I don't care what the people say.' Eventually, Meerabai was cast out and became even more determined in her ways. 'Fools sit on thrones,' she sang, while 'wise men beg for a little bread.' Elsewhere she proclaims: 'If Rana is angry, he can keep his kingdom/But if god is offended ... I will wither,' making clear where her loyalties resided. 'She danced,' writes Dhruvadas, 'with anklebells on her feet and with castanets in her hands. In the purity of her heart, she met the devotees of god, and realised the pettiness of the world.' Much had to be given up, but she did so readily in the pursuit of her calling. 'What I paid,' writes Meerabai, 'was my social body, my town body, my family body, and all my inherited jewels.' With Krishna as her focus, she was able to survive every loss and become one with the people. She would sing his songs and, through him, be also her own person.

In due course, Meerabai became a travelling saint, an outcast where she was once a princess. Her *satsangs* were attended by many, but the path was riddled with privations

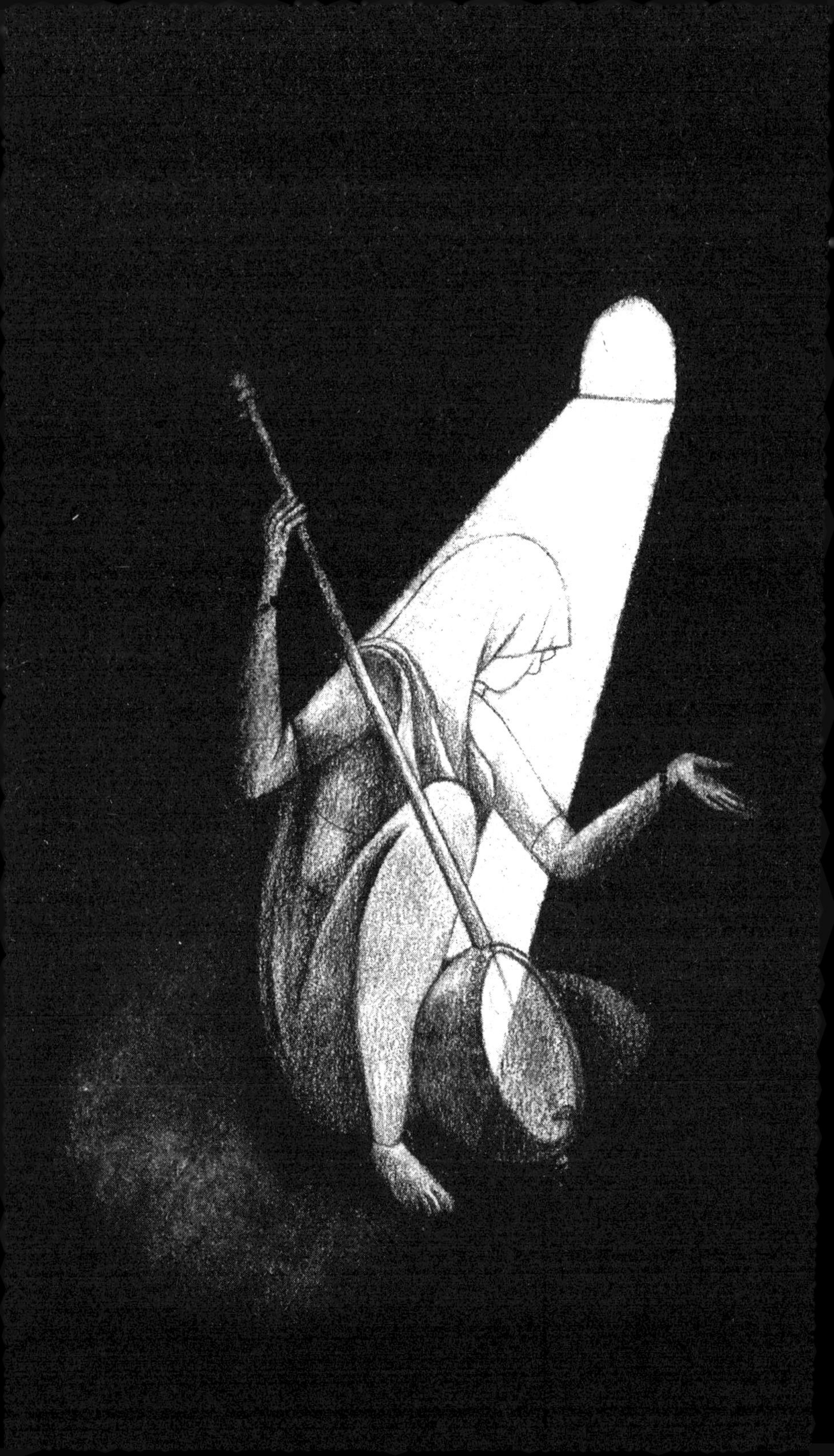

and tests—there were those within the Bhakti tradition who challenged her or sought to take advantage of this woman on her own. But she survived, dying on her own terms, in Dwarka by the middle of the century (and not in a blazing flame). Her story has since found several takers—Mahatma Gandhi saw an exemplar of non-violent resistance, while Carnatic singer M.S. Subbulakshmi highlighted Meerabai's religiosity at the cinema. But just as importantly, Meerabai also 'disowned, defied and subverted the ... values associated with powerful and entrenched institutions—family, marriage, caste, clan, royalty and even the realm of Bhakti.' She threw off the weight of expectations from every quarter, and painstakingly embraced only that which brought her closer to god. Passion, flaws, rejection and greatness were all woven into this mortal one, remembered to this day by that fascinating, immortal name, Meerabai of Mewar. And so she went down as the woman she truly was, refusing to become another Padmavati, that imagined paragon of monochrome glory.

THE AKBAR OF THE DECCAN

In the twenty-fourth year of Jalal-ud-din Akbar's reign, a ten-year-old boy was installed on the throne of the Adil Shahs of Bijapur. Ibrahim II was the Mughal emperor's junior by several years, but if the two had met, they would have delighted in each other's company. For though separated by distance as well as a generation gap, there was a great deal the Mughal badshah and the Deccan sultan had in common. Both were patrons of the arts, and each was a man of ability as well as charisma. And in what is directly relevant to our own times, Akbar and Ibrahim both embraced the plural impulses of the societies over which they reigned, birthing a magnificent age and lighting a path that still shines, centuries after they went to the grave.

The horror with which Akbar's religious views were perceived is well chronicled. But in the shadow of the emperor, Ibrahim languishes forgotten. Ibrahim Adil Shah II of Bijapur was a man full of surprises, and not only because he coloured his nails red. As a boy, he once came across a

The Courtesan, the Mahatma & the Italian Brahmin

party of Shaivites and was so profoundly influenced by their exchange that it ignited a lifelong fascination in him for Hindu traditions. Indeed, though formally a Sunni Muslim, when he died, such were the suspicions around his true loyalties that his epitaph served primarily as a reassurance to all concerned: 'No, Ibrahim in truth was not a Jew, neither a Christian; but he was a Muslim, and one pure of faith; certainly he was never of the idolators.' The last line was, of course, insincere, for the Adil Shah's universe was bursting with Hindu influences, and his career had seen him endow temples, affirm the rights of pilgrims at popular shrines, and consciously exalt Hindu gods to the heights of kingly devotion.

This is not to ignore this gentleman prince's military avatar (like Akbar's) that allowed brothers to be killed and overpowering regents blinded. But when he was in his gentler, more constructive mood, Ibrahim could charm the world. Calling himself Adil Shah Sufi, a number of his *farmans* begin with an invocation of the Hindu goddess Saraswati. It was, in fact, such unconcealed devotion to this deity that eventually convinced a section of his court that the Adil Shah, if he was not already secretly a practising Hindu, was flirting dangerously with apostasy—at one point, he renamed Bijapur (originally Vijaypur, the City of Victory) as Vidyapur (City of Learning). In a poem Ibrahim composed, he expressed ideas that to the conservative appeared dangerously heterodox, and antithetical to their brand of puritanical Islam. Thus, for instance, we have the prince declare:

> There are different languages;
> But there is one emotional appeal.
> Be he a brahmin or a Turk,
> He is only fortunate on whom
> The Goddess of Learning [Saraswati] smiles.

Indeed, when Ibrahim produced his celebrated *Kitab-i-Nauras*, what he offered the world besides 'an engaging text that is ... highly visual in its imagery and metaphor' was a glimpse of the splendid syncretism of his age. The *Kitab* refers to the world of politics as much as it does to his royal household, featuring characters such as the warrior queen Chand Bibi, not to speak of his pet elephant, Atash Khan. There are Hindu gods like Shiva and Parvati, alongside influences from the great Sanskrit epics. In what is equally noteworthy, among the several paintings he commissioned is one of Saraswati where she appears on a golden throne, with all her traditional instruments and symbols—the peacock, the conch, a veena, a lotus, and so on. But unlike her familiar representations today or even in sculptures of yore, Ibrahim's Saraswati is dressed in white robes, appearing more 'in the form of a royal [Muslim] princess' than in any immediately recognisable 'Hindu' style. Equally striking are the words that appear within the painting, embodying the depth of the Adil Shah's love for the goddess: Ibrahim is described as he 'whose father is guru Ganapati, and mother the pure Saraswati'. No wonder some at court were apoplectic.

While the Adil Shah—often painted with rudraksha beads and proclaimed, in Sanskrit, as 'protector of the weak' on his coins—thus embraced Hindu traditions in all their richness, his policy had practical repercussions too. Following the fall of Vijayanagar in 1565, large numbers of Hindu artists were set adrift; Ibrahim opened his heart and his treasury to support them in Bijapur. Marathi brahmins were already powerful in the bureaucracy; Ibrahim now introduced Telugu and Kannadiga professionals into the fields of art, music and architecture. The Adil Shah himself, a Mughal envoy was surprised to discover, preferred speaking Marathi in court, and one of his harem favourites was a Maharashtrian dancer called Rambha. It was also well known that Ibrahim had an excellent grasp of Sanskrit, far superior than his grip over Persian, the language of his Iranian ancestors and of the emperor's durbar in the north. To the more orthodox, the Adil Shah's 'native' preoccupations seemed almost like a betrayal, given that only some generations before, his forebears were an exact contrast in conduct, exalting Persian, banishing local influences with vehemence and even having soldiers imitate Iranian patterns in their uniform and drills.

It was not surprising, then, that a reaction from the orthodoxy awaited only round the bend in Bijapur, just as Badauni held Akbar 'in defiance and contempt of the true faith' in the north. In the Adil Shah's case, interestingly, the backlash originated not from conservative clerics as much as from the Sufis. When one saint arrived in the city and learnt that the ruler was 'enamoured' of 'Hindu singing and playing', he insisted that Ibrahim proactively cease to surround himself with such ungodly influences. The latter said, like young people do to evade tiresome old men, that he would try—and then, eventually, had the old Sufi shipped off to Mecca with a pension. Another saint's hagiography has large numbers of people seeking his aid to 'rescue' the Adil Shah from the hands of a Hindu *yogi*—in the story, the Sufi succeeds, and not only does Ibrahim return to the right path, but the yogi also converts to Islam. Regardless of the veracity (which is dubious) of the account, the picture is clear: the ruler was surrounded by enough non-Muslim influences to give cause for worry to powerful parties in Bijapur—and to attract the attention of people in the capital of the Mughal emperor in Agra.

If Akbar and Ibrahim returned to gaze upon our world, they would see, like them, many with minds full of curiosity and spirit—but they would also see, as in their own time, others issuing diktats on what one should think, whom one should obey. Centuries and many ages separate us, but in the story of society, these kings might chuckle, some things clearly never change.

JAHANGIR
THE ENDEARING ECCENTRIC

If ever there was a Mughal ruler who lived the good life, that man was Emperor Jahangir, in whose veins flowed Persian, Turkic and Rajput blood—besides double-distilled spirits and a whole lot of wine. Jahangir, who died on 28 October 1627 aged 58, was the least militarily inclined of the great Mughals (that is, at a personal level), and though he once led a half-baked rebellion against his illustrious father, he preferred having other men fight the battles that mattered. In an age of violence this was something of a character defect, but Jahangir's indulgence was a mark of stability in the empire he inherited—after all, if he could afford to live the way he did, it was because he was parked at the apex of an order well settled by his father Akbar. Far from the heat and fury of conflict, deep in the embrace of art and aesthetics, he quickly came to represent both self-assured power and the height of Mughal imperial splendour.

Even today, reading the *Jahangirnama* is a fascinating exercise. For the figure that emerges is at once pampered

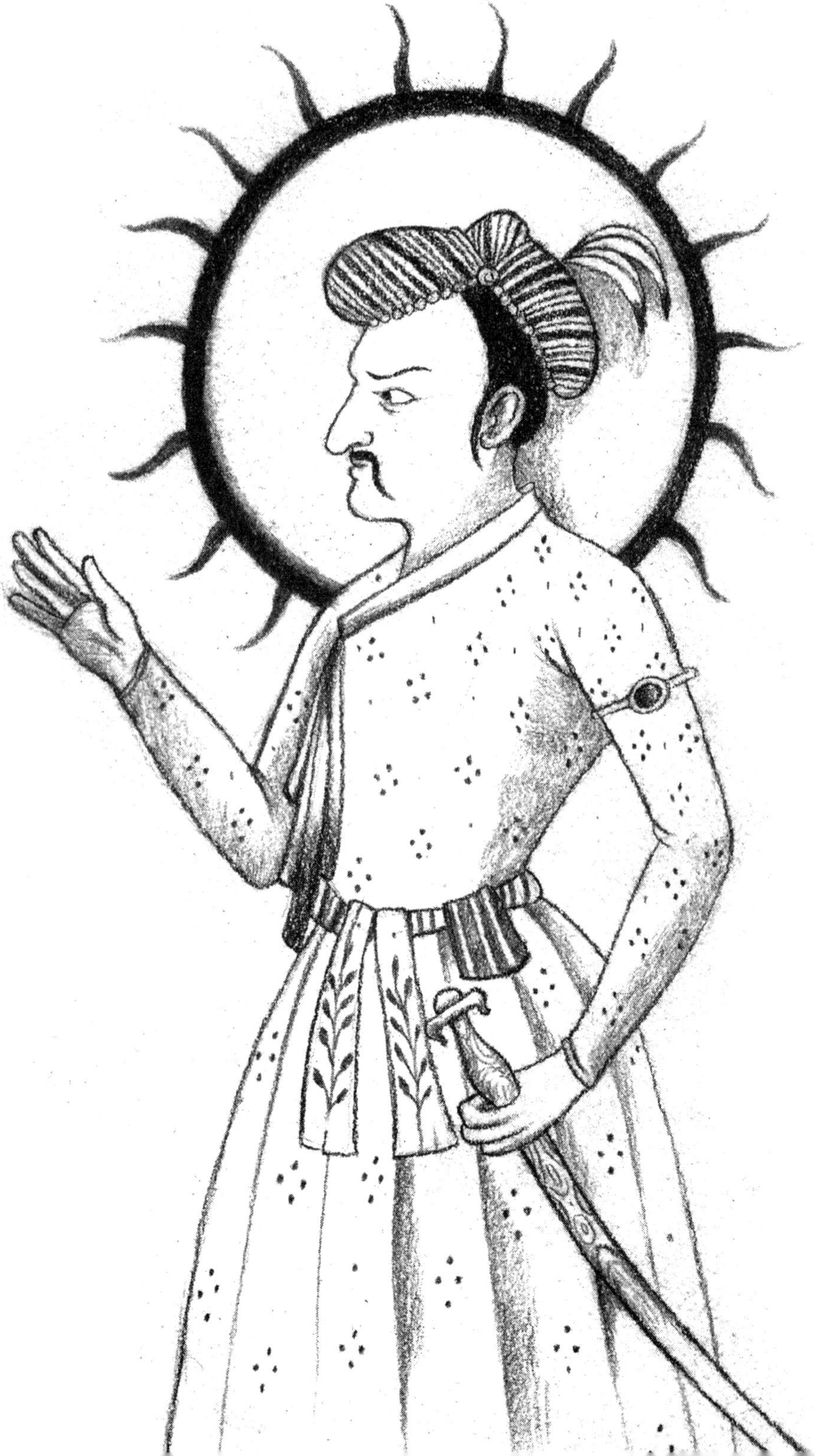

The Courtesan, the Mahatma & the Italian Brahmin

prince, curious dilettante, ruthless emperor, and sentimental man. The first-born of Akbar and the so-called Jodha Bai, Shaikhu Baba, as Jahangir was lovingly known, was one upon whom luck bestowed an early blessing. By eighteen, he was falling in love with his goblet; luckily for him, his brothers were worse. Not even royal commands could move him if he didn't wish it: once, when his father sought to appoint him leader of a campaign, the prince simply absented himself from court. One of those ill-fated brothers accepted the charge and won a few battles before losing himself forever to drink. Akbar, meanwhile, turned his hopes towards Jahangir's son, provoking a hundred intrigues and yet more tragedy.

Shaikhu Baba, however, was too shrewd to drown in wine and die. He understood quickly what was at stake and where to draw the line—no son of his could be emperor before he had had his time. So while he continued to drink—pretending after his accession that he only indulged 'to promote digestion'—he toned down the quantities. He even presented himself to the orthodox faction as a more pious Muslim than Akbar, to win them over before his favoured son. To be sure, having become emperor, he dabbled in more than one religion, till rumours floated that he was a Christian, and he commissioned art in which he appeared cross-legged and shirtless—more Hindu deity than a Muslim sovereign.

Even before his reign, Jahangir was a man of curiosity. All his life, as his biographer Parvati Sharma shows, he went about measuring things—the size of a peach, the weight of a melon, the dimensions of a cave opening—just as he recorded strange and peculiar sights. So while on the one hand his generals took fire and steel into enemy lands, Jahangir took delight in watching pet cranes mate. He thundered from afar at his enemies (the Marathas he dismissed as 'a people of unlimited stupidity') while investing in a menagerie at home. The way to please him was to bring him animals: the English gifted him mastiffs, for whom the emperor arranged palanquins. On another occasion he was introduced to a lion that lived with a goat, while his travels threw up everything from a snake swallowing a rabbit to a spider that strangled a snake.

Art flourished under Jahangir. Europeans were delighted with his affection for the Madonna, while Hindus noticed symbols from their own traditions. Then there were images prepared of the oddities that caught the emperor's eye. Sharma notes the story of an emaciated courtier, thin beyond belief, who asked for leave from court. Jahangir agreed to let him depart—but only after he had his likeness made. A dervish from Sri Lanka, similarly, brought him a slender loris—'really horrible looking'—and immediately, the emperor ordered that its likeness be painted. On yet another occasion, Jahangir was presented a zebra. A sceptic, he was suspicious at first that it was perhaps a painted horse, till much washing and cleaning refused to erase the creature's stripes. In fact, as far as Jahangir was concerned, few living beings were left alone: but if there was one thing that revolted the sovereign of Hindustan, it was worms crawling out of the corpses of animals he'd shot.

Jahangir's relationship with Nur Jahan is well recorded, but he was also close to other women. There was a sister to whom he was so attached that his father made him drink her breast milk so she 'may be like a mother to you'. When his wet nurse died, he carried on his own shoulder one end of her funeral bier. And in the *Jahangirnama* are multiple expressions of grief on the death of various imperial women, including, for instance, a Rajput wife, who chose suicide. There is vulnerability in this Jahangir, though another side

The Courtesan, the Mahatma & the Italian Brahmin

shows also cruelty, one where interrupting a hunt could cost a servant his life, and a gardener who cut down beloved trees found himself missing a few fingers. Even the elite faced the emperor's wrath: when a rebellious nobleman was presented, 'Were it not for what people would think,' Jahangir fumed, 'I would have throttled him with my own hands.'

Of all the Mughal emperors, Jahangir led the most comfortable life, free from many problems that afflicted those who ruled before and after him. He packed his twenty-two years on the throne with the most diverse interests, less focused than Akbar or Dara Shukoh, but rich in its sheer detail. He showed himself a remarkable man, one who could marvel at the gems sent him in tribute, just as he could stun an ambassador by gleefully driving a bullock cart. The future emperor Shahjahan's propaganda cast Jahangir as a henpecked debauchee. But, as new insights show, and the *Jahangirnama* attests, the man was a little bit more: an endearing eccentric, but every inch an emperor worth remembering.

VARARUCHI'S CHILDREN AND THE MAPPILAS OF MALABAR

There is in Kerala a fascinating legend featuring the Hindu sage Vararuchi and a pariah girl who bore him twelve children. The story is rich in metaphor, and to this day there are families along the coast that claim descent from one or another of their fabled offspring. The eldest, for instance, was raised a brahmin, while the youngest, who oddly had no mouth, is venerated as a temple deity. One son was a celebrated master carpenter, folklore connecting him to shrines across Kerala, while another was a madman whose chief delight lay in rolling a boulder uphill, only to watch it tumble down, over and over. Yet another brought to his esteemed Brahmin brother's feast beef to eat, while one more of Vararuchi's tribe settled as a trader. And in a tale that weaves together brahmins and Nairs, a deity as well as a dalit, it is this sibling, Uppukoottan, who introduces a final interesting identity. For Uppukoottan, son of Vararuchi, is believed to have been raised a Mappila, adhering not so much to his father's Hindu traditions as to the word of the Prophet Muhammad.

While to some the presence of a Muslim in a popular Hindu legend might seem outlandish, to Malayalis the story is by no means unusual. After all, across the length and breadth of Kerala, history and legend are united in featuring Muslims (and Christians) prominently in a shared cultural universe. Arabs had mastered the seas even before the Prophet was born, and soon after its dawn, Islam was delivered to Kerala through long-standing channels of commerce. The oldest mosque in the region, for instance, is said to have been established in the lifetime of the Prophet himself, in 629 CE, though archaeologists quibble about the exact age of the structure. By 849 CE, at any rate, Muslim traders were consequential enough to witness a royal grant (made, incidentally, to Christians), their signatures inscribed in archaic Arabic. When Ibn Battuta, the Moroccan diarist, came here in the course of his travels, he saw men from Persia in settlements along the coast, and one of the most beautiful mosques in Calicut, the turquoise blue Mishkal Palli, was founded soon afterwards by a commercially prolific merchant who began his life and career in faraway Yemen.

The influence of the Mappilas, born from the union of Arabs with local women as well as from subsequent conversions, quickly found reflection in Kerala's already diverse culture. Some of the principal officials of the Zamorin of Calicut were Muslims, and in the great Mamankam festival at Tirunavaya—the most important religious gathering in Kerala till the eighteenth century—Muslims participated in the colourful revelries just as they did in formal royal ceremonies. At Sabarimala, where hundreds of thousands converge to worship the Hindu god Ayyappa, homage is also paid to Vavar, the deity's Muslim friend whose name sounds (painfully to some) like Babur. The language of the Mappilas, meanwhile, developed into a unique blend of Malayalam sound and Arabic script, influenced over time by Persian as well as by Tamil and Kannada. Their architecture, too, absorbed Kerala's indigenous style—the oldest mosques feature no domes or minarets, bearing instead the gables and tiled roof that crown temples and even Christian churches from this era. The *nerchchas* of the Mappila community, celebrating saints and divines, resemble Hindu festivals—the tall brass lamp, the elephants, bright parasols and fireworks, all integral to the temple *pooram* as much as to these Muslim commemorations. There is even, in fact, a Mappila Ramayana, featuring Ravana as a sultan; Surpanakha's proposition to Rama in this version seeks sanction from the Sharia.

Even prominent Hindu lineages embraced Islam. Legend has a king, Cheraman Perumal, journeying to Mecca himself, while a Nair nobleman founded the Muslim dynasty of Arakkal. His line would come to rule over the Lakshadweep Islands, forging links with Tipu as well as the Ottoman sultan, but retaining through the centuries the matrilineal system of succession that allowed women to rule, unencumbered by purdah or seclusion. Such, in fact, was the mass of seafaring Muslims in the coastal towns and ports of Kerala that Ma Huan, the Chinese traveller, was convinced in the fifteenth century that most of the region's dwellers must be adherents of the Quran. One of the Hindu princes of Calicut certainly commanded every fisherman in his realm to bring up one son for Islam—this would enable them to sail the seas, man the royal navy and contribute to the prosperity of a land where commerce was everything.

It was when the terms of that trade began to suddenly change that the Mappila community encountered its first chapter of decline. The Portuguese, who arrived in 1498, quickly seized control of the seas, marrying commercial rivalry with religious bigotry. Arabs who had reigned supreme for a thousand years were expelled from their pedestals of power. As one authority recorded, the Europeans, with their guns and prejudice, 'forbade the Muslims to trade in pepper and ginger, and then later cinnamon, cloves and other commodities ... They prevented Muslims from making commercial voyages to Arabia, Malacca, Achin and Damao.' Mappila ships were set ablaze, pilgrimages obstructed, and mosques were destroyed by white men who brought unfair dynamics into the game. At first the Zamorins, in whose dominions resided the vast majority of Mappilas, fought back. But in due course, the cold logic of economics prevailed—the sea of foreign Muslims coming to Kerala was reduced to a trickle, as Hindu rulers came to terms with the Europeans. A few Mappila heroes emerged such as the Kunjali Marakkars, naval guerrillas who gave the Portuguese a real fight. But in the end they too were destroyed, and Muslim influence, it was patent to all, was on a cascading low.

Songs of the Mappilas to this day bear witness to this. The Mappila-*pattu* fall into several categories. There are festive songs, sung at weddings and ceremonies. Then there are *mala* or 'garland' songs, some praising great saints, and others celebrating warriors and heroes, including those who fell as recently as in the Mappila Rebellion of 1921. Among the oldest, however, is the Kotturpalli Mala, and in this Europeans are the villains. A brave Muslim youth, we hear, is informed of a girl being forced aboard a Portuguese ship. The courageous Mappila abandons his own wedding ceremony to rescue the abducted girl, but is killed. His body, cut into pieces, washes up on different parts of the coast, where great miracles follow—a story that bears unspoken links to the Hindu story of Sati, whose scattered limbs are worshipped in shrines across India. Either way, though the Portuguese prevailed, it was the Mappila who earned true honour, his adversaries merely agents of greed and merchants of ill repute.

The emphasis on honour, however, barely obscures the existential crisis of the Mappilas in the colonial age. By the middle of the eighteenth century, with few exceptions, the community was poor, with many Mappilas tenants of Hindu lords. When Hyder Ali and Tipu of Mysore conquered Malabar, these Hindus fled while the Mappilas saw value in collaborating with the invaders, fortified also by their shared religion. But when defeat came to Tipu, the tables were turned: the old guard returned, and with them arrived British rule. Religious animosity swelled on both sides during the nineteenth century. In 1851, a Nair landlord was killed after he forced a Mappila to replace the call to prayer with a 'summons to eat swine's flesh'. Violence was also driven partly by economics—a fifth of the land revenue in northern Kerala came from eighty-six landlords, only two of whom were not Hindus. Mappila tenants could be evicted at will by superiors who, even in the best of times, charged anywhere from fifty-nine to seventy-seven per cent of the produce as rent. All legal clauses privileged the owner—even when the landlord, such as the Zamorin, wasn't fully certain where his extensive lands began or ended. The colonial establishment, meanwhile, had no desire for reform. Even in 1917, the British were convinced that legislation to prevent arbitrary eviction would be a 'grave political mistake'.

It was no wonder, then, as one rebel expressed it in 1843, that 'it is impossible for people to live quietly while the ... [landlords] treat us in this way'. To such economic anxiety was also married an extremism born from a group of fanatics—in 1844, a British official noted that, encouraged by overzealous religious men, some Mappilas had started to believe that the 'murder of a heretic is a passport to heaven'. As recently as 1896, when a Mappila was captured after a temple attack, he confirmed his suicidal convictions: 'We came to the temple intending to fight ... and die.' And what would come after death? As testimony from an earlier survivor went, 'I had heard that there was a reward in heaven for those who got shot.' Indeed, in 1898, one Mappila even pointed out that his biggest fear was that he would get shot in the legs and live: only a fatal shot opened the gates of paradise.

Without economic resources, pushed to the corners and radicalised by an extremist minority, the men who sparked the outrages exemplified a combination of factors that birthed violence. To this was added the trigger of the Khilafat Movement in 1921, with protests against the post-First World War unseating of the Ottoman Caliph being fanned, in Kerala, into outright rebellion. As a telegram received by Lord Reading, the British Viceroy, read: 'The situation is now clearly actual war, and famine, widespread devastation and prolonged rebellion can only be avoided by prompt measures.' Unprecedented savagery was unleashed. Hindu and Christian homes were targeted by Mappilas and, as a declaration by the Zamorin claimed, cows were slaughtered in temples, with assailants 'putting their entrails on the holy image and hanging skulls on the walls and the roofs'. It was a horrifying display of fanaticism that came at the end of a long history of alienation: the stake Mappilas had in society had been watered down, till it was felt that the order itself must be toppled if they were to find purpose. In the end, 2,339 rebels were killed, 6,000 captured and 39,000 persuaded to surrender. Much blood flowed through northern Kerala. But from this disaster was also born introspective wisdom. For it was understood that if there was to be peace between different men, each one of them had to feel that important thing: a sense of common belonging.

The year 1921, then, became the year of the last major communal incident in Kerala. In the decades that followed, lessons were learnt and extremism was shunned. When in 1969 a Muslim-majority district was created in Malappuram, there were temporary fears that this would be a 'Moplastan' within India, a local manifestation of the two-nation theory. But that was not to be, and instead the Mappilas returned to a previous history from a more confident age, where a mosque could donate land for a temple, and a temple could host an *iftar* for local Muslims. There are today fears of radicalism imported from abroad, but then there is also the force of heritage and the wisdom of a beautiful past. New challenges will emerge, but there still remain in Kerala those wonderful old songs: where a Mappila could join hands with his Hindu brother, and even Vararuchi the sage could have a Muslim son.

THE WOMAN WITH NO BREASTS

Her name was Nangeli and she lived in Cherthala, a watery alcove on the Kerala coast. We do not know when she was born or who sired her. They say she died in the early nineteenth century, her spirit cast in a hundred moulds in the two hundred summers that followed. Today, Nangeli has champions on the Internet, her story told by men and women seeking inspiration and courage on this side of time. And they too have recast her sacrifice, celebrating a tale that would have been alien to its protagonist. Nangeli has been reduced from a woman who thrust a dagger into the heart of society to one who died to preserve those artful shackles that many of us know as 'honour'.

The contours of the tale are well known. Nangeli and her man, Chirukandan, were Ezhavas—primarily toddy tappers—who laboured in that awkward gap that society fashions for those who are low but not the lowest. They had a little hut where they lived, and they had no children.

Life for Nangeli and Chirukandan was as hard as it was for their neighbours. They survived hand to mouth, toeing lines drawn by caste and bowing before the pretensions of their superiors. Nothing about them was remarkable till Nangeli stood up. The elders proclaim that she stood up to preserve her dignity, but that is because they are afraid to admit that she stood up to them. Nangeli was a rebel, but like many rebels, in death her memory became the possession of those she opposed. She threw off one tyrant and found her legacy in the grasp of another.

The Kerala that Nangeli and Chirukandan knew was not the Kerala celebrated today for its healthy children, emancipated grandmothers and literate masses. It was a hard, difficult landscape, and Cherthala was a speck on the map of Travancore, a state with a ruler of its own, to whom was owed allegiance—and tax money. Land tax was low, but the rajahs made up for this ancestral blunder through other levies. If you were a landless fisherman, you had a tax on your fishing net. If you were a man sporting a moustache, your facial hair fell within the mandate of the revenue inspector. If you owned slaves, you most certainly had to pay tax on those bleeding units of muscle. Nangeli and her husband acquiesced like loyal subjects, but today's storytellers will tell you that she stood up to the one abhorrent tax that touched upon her honour; that when it came to her rights as a respectable woman, she declared: 'No more.'

They came one morning, the story goes, to tax her breasts, leering at their shape and dimensions, to calculate the figure owed. It was called *mulakkaram*—the breast tax—and women who were not high-born were surveyed as soon as they advanced from girlhood to adolescence. Nangeli had probably been taxed for years, but that year when the villains

The Courtesan, the Mahatma & the Italian Brahmin

of the tale came to her hovel, she was prepared for the act that would cleave for her a place in history and lore. She went inside calmly while they waited by the threshold, it is said, and returned with the tax offering on a plantain leaf. Since they had come for the breast tax, that is what they got: Nangeli's breasts, severed by her own hand and placed on the leaf in a bleeding lump. She collapsed in a heap and died in agony, her corpse cradled by Chirukandan, who returned to find his home turned into the scene of one of history's great tragedies. Some say he jumped into the pyre as Nangeli burned and perished in flames of grief—for him, too, there was the redemption of sacrifice.

The legend of Nangeli was birthed in blood and injustice. Women of low caste, they will tell you, couldn't cover their bodies if they didn't pay the breast tax. They silently wept and lamented their fate, shame building upon shame under the gaze of lewd old men who decreed that the right to dignity came with a price. But Nangeli was a woman of virtue—she would not barter money for honour. And so she chose death.

Embarrassed and horrified by the tyranny of their own ways, the rajahs abandoned the tax on breasts. Nangeli became a heroine. Womanhood prevailed.

This is the tale they will tell you of Nangeli. As it happens, it is all a travesty.

*

For a society as open as Kerala once was, breasts came to provoke a grave panic in the Victorian age. This was the land where Portuguese merchants in the sixteenth century beheld bare-breasted princesses negotiating treaties of trade and leading bare-chested troops in battle. It was here that a seventeenth-century Italian found himself in the court of a prince, packed with royal women covered only around the waist—two young nieces of the ruler wondered with amusement why on earth the visitor was so covered up in the tropical heat. This was also the land where women enjoyed physical and sexual autonomy, where widowhood was no calamity and one husband could always be replaced with another. The coast was rich with tales of great women—from Unniarcha of the northern ballad of Malabar, an accomplished warrior from Nangeli's caste, to Umayamma of Attingal, a princess who reigned over kings. These were brave women of towering personality. But in the nineteenth century, Kerala's moral conscience grappled not with their achievements as much as the conundrum that their unabashed bare-breastedness presented.

Virtue, as we recognise it today in its patriarchal definition, was not a concept that existed in Kerala. And till our colonial masters—and fellow Indians from patriarchal backgrounds—sat in judgement over the matrilineal streak heavily infused among the dominant groups here, women, their bare torsos and their sexual freedoms did not in the least attract attention or odium. Where elsewhere polygamy was a practice available to men, in Kerala there was polyandry on offer, because women were not unequal to their brothers (or, to be more exact, they were less unequal). They owned property and controlled resources, living fuller lives than the domesticated child-rearing destinies ordained to their sisters elsewhere. But this was, of course, the case of women of privilege. For women like Nangeli there was no question of living a life of heroic glamour with armies or ballads; she had to earn her way through every day of uncertainty. It was in death that the songs followed, and they focused not on Nangeli's message but a perversion of it that was more palatable to changing social mores.

The Courtesan, the Mahatma & the Italian Brahmin

The advent of the British meant more than just a new political order; they brought to Kerala a new sense of morality, reinforced by missionaries who had the ear of these foreign masters. Polyandrous marriage was deemed 'very revolting'—women were told that they ought to be virtuous, which meant deference to one husband, one master. They had to cultivate modesty, and toplessness was not a step in that direction. The sexual gaze of the patriarchal Victorian was turned towards the breast in Kerala, till then not a cause of concern. When men and women entered temples, they both took off their top cloth. Today only the men are obliged to do this. As late as the 1920s, when Namboothiri brahmin women for the first time acquired the blouse to cover themselves, purists excommunicated them for breaching custom—modesty and true moral superiority lay, they argued, in not covering up. As Aubrey Menen remarked of his grandmother's attitude to his Irish mother, it was thought that 'married women who wore blouses were Jezebels' and 'a wife who dressed herself could only be aiming at adultery'. To cover breasts because younger men demanded it was abhorrent to elders. But these elders were a minority in the face of young 'progressive' men bent on making their women 'virtuous'.

Across the coast, the torso—male and female—was not something that was covered. Higher castes sported shawls, not for reasons of modesty or because they had notions of virtue more consistent with those of a patriarchal society, but because the shawl was a mark of honour. When Christian converts from lower castes covered themselves in the 1850s, riots broke out after violent upper-caste attacks on them. The bone of contention was not that the converted women wanted to cover themselves; it was that they had covered themselves with the shawl permitted only to the high-born.

Peace was restored when the converts invented a blouse; the covering was not the issue in the first place.

The tale of Nangeli that they will tell you today has her fighting to preserve her honour, where honour is construed as her right to cover the breast. But in Nangeli's time, the honour of a woman was hardly linked to the area above the waist. As F. Fawcett remarked, dress was 'a conventional affair, and it will be a matter of regret should false ideas of shame supplant those of natural dignity such as one sees expressed in the carriage and bearing of the well-bred ... lady'.

But the import of Victorian patriarchy also imported shame, and women were told that a bare body was a mark of disgrace. Dignity lay in accepting male objectification; honour was located in docility. Men, studying in colleges in big cities, received jibes about their topless mothers who may have had more than one husband. Could they ever be sure about who their fathers were? These men dragged into Kerala the masculinity of their patriarchal interlocutors, and women too, exposed to the West and a new conception of femininity, succumbed. 'We will publish nothing related to politics,' declared one of the region's earliest women's magazines in 1892, adding that 'writings that energise the moral conscience'—tips on cooking, stories of 'ideal women'—and 'other such enlightening topics' alone would be covered. A lady's job was in the home as a mother, as a loyal wife and housekeeper, not outside as a topless harlot who exercised her customary right to divorce. 'As women,' another declaration went, 'our god-ordained duty is the care of the home and service towards our husbands.'

New icons needed to be found—women who fit the bill of the new order rather than those who were emblems of a now disgusting bare-bosomed past. And where such women

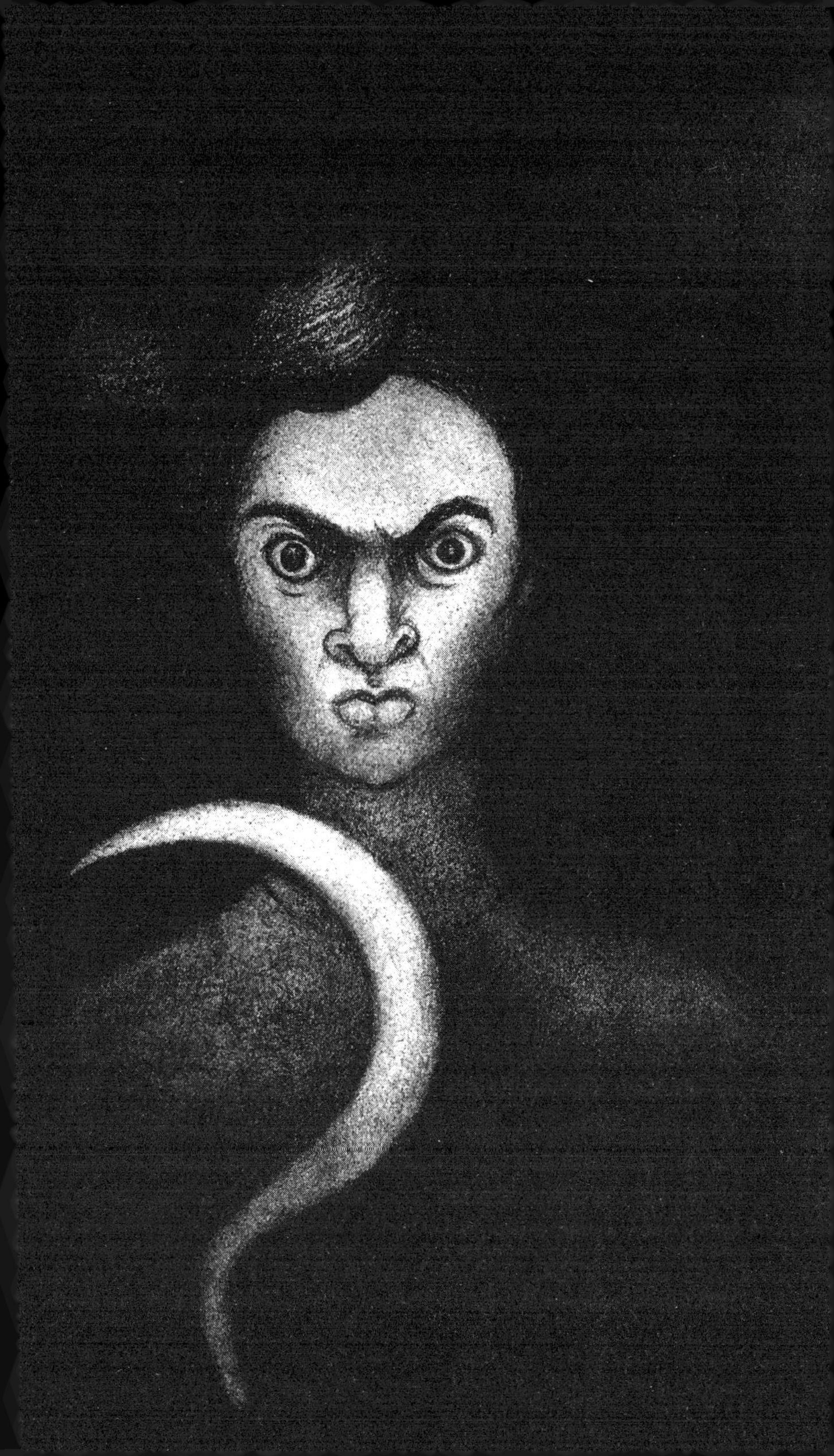

were in short supply, existing women were reincarnated, as J. Devika has shown. Umayamma of Attingal, the topless queen whom the Dutch noted for her 'noble and manly conduct', who was 'feared and respected by everyone', and who was a 'young Amazon', became in S. Parameswara Iyer's poetry a melodramatic damsel in distress, a helpless mother (when, in fact, she had no children) pleading for a male protector. Where once the English had (with perhaps some exaggeration) reported that the 'handsomest young men about the country' formed her seraglio and 'whom and as many [men] as she pleases to the honour of her bed' could be had by her, now she became a loyal, patriarchal icon of womanly virtue. The women of the past were turned into ciphers for the present, filled with doses of honour and draped in garbs tailored by men. The wheels of time had turned and this is what was needed for a changing society in Kerala.

*

Nangeli too was recast. When Nangeli offered her breasts on a plantain leaf to the rajah's men, she demanded not the right to cover her breasts, for she would not have cared about this 'right' that meant nothing in her day. Indeed, the mulakkaram had little to do with breasts other than the tenuous connection of nomenclature. It was a poll tax charged from low-caste communities, as well as other minorities. Capitation due from men was the *talakkaram*—head tax—and to distinguish female payees in a household, their tax was the mulakkaram—breast tax. The tax was not based on the size of the breast or its attractiveness, as Nangeli's storytellers will claim, but was one standard rate charged from women as a certainly oppressive but very general tax.

When Nangeli stood up, squeezed to the extremes of poverty by a regressive tax system, it was a statement made in great anguish about the injustice of the social order itself. Her call was not to celebrate modesty and honour; it was a siren call against caste and the rotting feudalism that victimised those in its underbelly who could not challenge it. She was a heroine of all who were poor and weak, not the archetype of middle-class womanly honour she has today become. But they could not admit that Nangeli's sacrifice was an ultimatum to the order, so they remodelled her as a virtuous goddess, one who sought to cover her breasts rather than one who issued a challenge to power. The spirit of her rebellion was buried in favour of its letter, and Nangeli reduced to the sum of her breasts.

PART TWO

STORIES FROM THE RAJ

WHAT IF THERE WAS NO BRITISH RAJ?

The appearance in recent years of a series of books on India and the Raj shows that the history of empire is once again in fashion. There is Jon Wilson's magisterial *India Conquered*, which investigates the manufacturing of British power in India, and Ferdinand Mount's *The Tears of the Rajas*, which explores its traumatic corollary. Shashi Tharoor delivers a withering review of colonial exploitation in *Inglorious Empire*, while Walter Reid, in *Keeping the Jewel in the Crown*, exposes British perfidy in the closing chapter of Pax Britannica. David Gilmour's *The British in India* is an apolitical social appraisal of the Englishmen who came to India—sometimes to escape scandal and prison sentences, sometimes to find spouses and fortunes—while Miles Taylor's *The English Maharani* situates Queen Victoria as empress of India, whose title and position appealed to colonialists and our early nationalists alike, with no manifest irony.

It's a slippery proposition, but what character might India have developed had the British never prevailed to begin with?

Would, for example, the south have existed as an autonomous unit, possibly under French influence? After all, by the mid-eighteenth century, the French had temporarily booted the English East India Company out of Madras and established a robust peninsular presence. The chief of Pondicherry was dignified by the Mughal emperor as a nawab and had managed to keep the Marathas at bay (including, in one instance, by plying the enemy commander's lady with alcohol). Tipu Sultan was a friend of the French, and had it not been for revolutionary convulsions in the 1790s that preoccupied his allies in their homeland, he might have received the assistance he needed to vanquish the British once and for all. More interestingly, Tipu entertained plans to educate a son in France, and given his interest in engineering, the fruits of the Industrial Revolution may well have found their way to Srirangapatna via Paris long before the British grudgingly allowed them to reach India's industrialists. Of course, as it happened, the French enterprise collapsed and the English claimed supremacy—it was they who wrote much of India's subsequent history.

It was the entrenchment of British power that made racism unofficial state policy; this could, perhaps, have been averted had Indians retained power, dealing with Europeans from positions of strength, confidently commissioning Western talent for indigenous purposes. After all, it was a German who commanded the Maratha troops at the Battle of Assaye, and in Kerala it was a Dutchman who modernised Travancore's armies under the celebrated king Martanda Varma. So too, in the late eighteenth century, as we have seen, the part-Kashmiri nautch girl turned Christian begum of Sardhana had tragic romances with a German, an Irishman and a Frenchman consecutively even as she became protector to the

The Courtesan, the Mahatma & the Italian Brahmin

emasculated Mughal emperor. Such exchanges were a two-way street, and could have continued had India retained its autonomy—just before the dawn of the Victorian age, Tamil devadasis performed in Europe before the French king, and Kalidas, as we saw earlier, won Western admiration when his Sanskrit *Abhijnanasakuntalam* was staged in London as the English *Sacontala*. Racism reversed this, but if the politics behind racism could have been avoided in the first place, things might have been happier, and our tale somewhat different.

Not everything, of course, would have emerged perfect even under sustained Indian rule—caste, for instance, would have remained a deep-rooted handicap to the dawn of any unifying sense of nationalism, and, ironically, it was British rule that allowed low-caste voices to emerge at last: it was a missionary education and access to Western texts, for instance, that galvanised Jyotiba Phule in his programme of reform. Politically, by the late eighteenth century, the Marathas dominated north India, from Lahore in the west to Bengal in the east, and, as we saw in a previous essay, a branch of Shivaji's family ruled in Thanjavur, deep in Tamil country. But while the Marathas might have united much of India politically, had the final Anglo-Maratha War in 1818 not culminated in their defeat, they would have had a long way to go before being able to claim the loyalty of India's diverse peoples. After all, it was raiding rather than governing that often animated them, and as the *Maharashtra Purana* notes in the context of Bengal, 'When they demanded money and it was not given to them, they would put the man to death. Those who had money gave it, those who had none were killed'—hardly a promising formula to inspire brotherhood and patriotism and pave the way for a shared tryst with destiny.

The irony, contested as it is, is also that it was a common hatred of the English that energised feelings of Indian unity. And that it was a foreign language that allowed Mohandas Gandhi from Gujarat to mentor Jawaharlal Nehru from Allahabad, collaborate with Tamil-speaking C. Rajagopalachari, and debate with the Bengali Subhas Chandra Bose. A firebrand like Bal Gangadhar Tilak recognised this value of English—though his nationalism was inflected with Hindu pride, when he set up an institution in Pune in 1880, it was the New *English* School and not a *gurukul*. Indeed, even V.D. Savarkar and M.S. Golwalkar published in English, without which large sections of their target audience would have been oblivious to their very existence. In fact, language would have been another interesting twist if the British had never reigned. English was imposed officially in 1837, before which it was Persian, now dead here, that served as the lingua franca of diplomacy across much of the subcontinent. As one 1858 report noted, Persian was 'for 600 years the language of justice ... the language of the Court ... [and indeed] it was much better known even than the English language is at present'. It was used in Nepal and in the early nineteenth century, it was employed as far south as Kerala. If English had never picked up, India's elite may still have been speaking to one another, across divides of region, religion and language, in an equally foreign tongue born in faraway Iran, though among the top layer of brahmins in temple towns, Sanskrit may have remained in place, serving as the language of philosophers and high-caste monks.

So, instead of the succession of East India Company rule by the Raj under Victoria Maharani followed by a successful nationalist struggle, Hindustan might have come into the twentieth century with a figurehead Mughal badshah, presiding over a Persian-speaking bureaucracy supervised by the Marathas, with diplomatic dealings with a French-influenced peninsula in the south. Like foreigners before them—from the Arabs and Jews to the Turks and Central Asians—the British, Germans and French would have been absorbed into our society, through inducements of marriage and employment. Indian philosophy and art would have proudly travelled beyond its frontiers, and ideas from the rest of the world would have received their usual welcome in India. Of course, this is all a grand hypothetical proposition, and like all such propositions, fraught with peril. But in a time when great attention is devoted to scrutinising the impact of the Raj in shaping modern India, one hopes to be forgiven for wondering what India might have looked like had the English never claimed dominion—what this strange and ever-fascinating land might have become had it never served as the jewel in a foreign monarch's crown.

ROWDY BOB
THE VICTOR OF PLASSEY

When, in 1757, Robert Clive prevailed at the Battle of Plassey in Bengal, he secured for himself a place as one of the great villains of Indian history. The wheels were set in motion for what would become British imperium in the East, but, for all its furious rapacity, even years later Clive saw no reason to regret what he had unleashed. Defending his actions in 1773 in the British parliament, he uttered words which have since become notorious. 'Am I not deserving of praise for the moderation which marked my proceedings?' he demanded. 'Consider the situation in which victory at Plassey had placed me. A great prince was dependent on my pleasure; an opulent city lay at my mercy; its richest bankers bid against each other for my smiles; I walked through vaults … piled on either hand with gold and jewels! By god, Mr Chairman,' exclaimed Clive, 'at this moment I stand astonished at my own moderation!'

One might have sympathised with the man's stream of thinking had his 'moderation' not cost Bengal rivers of gold

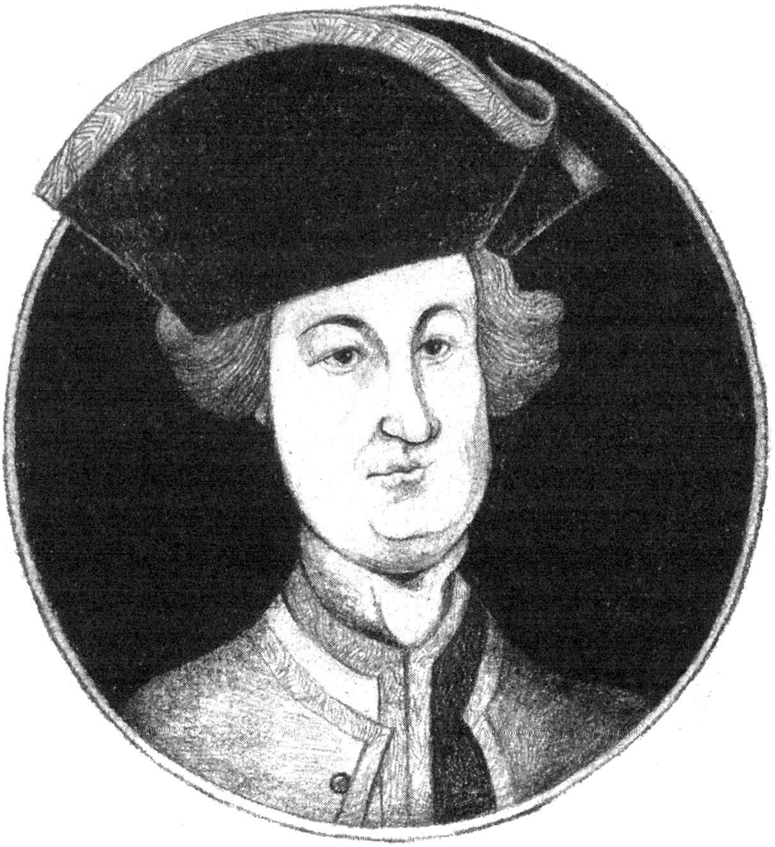

and silver already. An estimated 75–100 boats were deployed to carry the loot from Murshidabad to Calcutta after the victory of 1757, and Clive alone was granted not only a substantial cash reward by his freshly planted puppet nawab, but also a jagir that yielded £27,000 (a thousand times that sum in today's money) every year for the remainder of his complicated lifetime. It was an extraordinary achievement for this Shropshire boy who began life as 'Bob', and whose career, in the words of a biographer, first saw him serve as a 'glorified apprentice shopkeeper'. For here was a character who, long before he became a confirmed villain, was a typical specimen of eighteenth-century English middleclassdom, packed off by boat to India in his teens to either die or come back rich, plodding along on an annual £5 salary, and reduced in his misery to writing sad, lonely letters, all the while also complaining about the weather.

Clive was the son of an undistinguished lawyer, raised briefly by an aunt and her husband. When he was six, his uncle recorded that the boy was 'out of measure addicted' to fighting, with such 'imperiousness' of temper that nobody seemed able to tame his rowdy behaviour. As a biographer later wrote, he also 'formed all the good-for-nothing lads of the town into a kind of predatory army, and compelled the shopkeepers to submit to a tribute of apples'—a kind of protection money for not smashing their windows. Insolence travelled with him to India, and he often got into petty quarrels with his superiors—on one occasion, he disagreed with a man of the church and decided to give him a colossal whack in the middle of the street. He chewed paan and smoked the hookah, though the only wine he could afford was the kind that was mixed with plenty of water. 'I have not enjoyed one happy day since I left my native country,' he complained between days of clerical drudgery. His only consolation was writing, a practice, he reflected gloomily, 'invented for the comfort of such solitary wretches as myself'.

Change came to his monotonous, hitherto unremarkable career during the Battle of Madras in 1746, when this British settlement fell to French forces (it was subsequently returned after a peace agreement in Europe). Clive, all of twenty-one, and earlier written off mainly as 'a dunce, if not a reprobate', managed to escape from under the noses of his captors, face darkened and dressed in the clothes of his 'native' servant. Transferring from civilian service, he now elected to become a soldier, finding at last his calling. In a subsequent skirmish, he acquitted himself with courage and his superiors wrote to London: 'Mr Robert Clive, Writer in the Service, being of a Martial Disposition' was granted 'an Ensign's Commission'. Of course, he didn't shed his trademark impetuosity, though this was perhaps less dangerous than the other thing he acquired in the course of his military adventures in India: plain, old-fashioned gonorrhoea.

Venereal disease notwithstanding, as the years passed, Clive achieved considerable martial distinction—battles were won in Arcot, Kaveripakkam, Arni and elsewhere that allowed the man, even in his thirties, a special kind of celebrity. He was embroiled in the politics of the Carnatic, just as he was involved in the training of Indian troops for Western-style military practice. He cultivated spies, including an ill-fated prostitute, and began, at last, to earn an income that allowed him to indulge his love for an elaborate wardrobe (on one occasion alone he ordered 200 shirts along with other items, insisting that they 'must be of the best and finest you can get for love or money'). Marriage to a woman above his station followed, one who enjoyed being carried in palanquins and playing the harpsichord when she wasn't handling an unhappy series of pregnancies. When he returned to India in 1756 after a brief stint at home, he was senior enough to enjoy a gun salute, his victory at Plassey thereafter only confirming his importance in the order of precedence the Company established in India.

Laurels won here were not, however, the ones Clive wanted—India could be milked for cash, which like so many others he hoped, then, to invest in the pursuit of ambitions at home. By the time he went back in 1760, he had become enough of a personality to receive an audience with the king, and purchase more than one mansion for his use. But the hero of Plassey, despite his fame, was seen as a mere upstart, even if the Mughal Emperor titled him 'Flower of the Empire'. As Horace Walpole sniggered, 'General Clive is arrived, all over estates and diamonds. If a beggar asks charity, he says, "Friend, I have no small brilliants about me."' It was not an exaggeration. There is evidence that he purchased £25,000 worth of diamonds in Madras at one time, and remitted £180,000 home through the Dutch East India Company, £40,000 through his own English Company, besides a whole lot more with private bankers and friends. But new money gleamed a little too brightly, and there were quite a few men in London who lost no opportunity to look upon Clive and rub in their contempt with so many sniggers.

In 1764, confronting internal politics in the Company (it hardly helped that the mercurial Clive referred once to the chairman as 'this mushroom of a man'), he left for a third stint in India. To later biographers, this was a phase of great importance. As Lord Macaulay wrote, Bengal, which was seen by Company men simply as a land of endless riches to exploit, was placed on a sound administrative system, as

The Courtesan, the Mahatma & the Italian Brahmin

Clive made 'dauntless and unsparing war on that gigantic system of oppression, extortion, and corruption'. Even as he conveniently overlooked his own corruption and avarice in the previous decade, he replaced 'that gang of public robbers' who governed the province for selfish gain with 'a body of functionaries not more highly distinguished by ability and diligence than by integrity, disinterestedness and public spirit'. The result was that while his name came to stand 'high on the roll of conquerors', it was also fit for another list—that 'of those who have done and suffered much for the happiness of mankind.' What the Indians thought of Macaulay's generous estimation was, of course, irrelevant.

His 1773 trial—provoked by parliamentary horror at the Company's depredations, of which Clive was the principal mascot—saw the man defend himself vigorously. Thanks to his work, he had argued earlier, the Company 'acquired an empire more extensive than any kingdom in Europe, France and Russia excepted'. They had 'acquired a revenue of four millions sterling and a trade in proportion'. Now he reiterated that he 'was never guilty of any acts of violence or oppression ... such an idea never entered into my mind'. His defence was later reinforced by sympathetic minds like Macaulay. If at all Clive was cruel, this nineteenth-century imperialist wrote, it was because he knew 'he had to deal with men destitute of what in Europe is called honour ... men who would unscrupulously employ corruption, perjury, forgery, to compass their ends'. And so he had no option but to become 'himself an Indian intriguer'. In other words, if there was a hint of evil in Clive and his designs, it was because he was in a land of evil, surrounded by men much worse. 'There never, perhaps,' concluded Macaulay, 'existed a people so thoroughly fitted by nature and by habit for a foreign yoke.' And as the man who fastened that yoke on Bengal and India, what Clive rendered was public service.

In any case, the trial, which attracted a great deal of press, wound to an end and Clive was cleared soon enough. Peace and true respectability evaded him, however, for the rest of his lifetime. In 1774, a year after these embarrassing proceedings in parliament, he died suddenly, rumoured to have stuck a knife down his throat, though it may well have been an opium overdose. It was suicide, either way, and that 'audacity of his spirit' which so marked his youth had patently snapped, making way for something darker. In great secrecy, then, the man who inaugurated the Raj in India was laid to rest in an unmarked grave, his name associated forever since with greed, tragedy and scandal. And there his ghost would languish for generations before the Victorians resurrected his memory and invested it with respect. 'Clive committed great faults,' admitted Macaulay. 'But his faults, when weighed against his merits … do not appear to us to deprive him of his right to an honourable place in the estimation of posterity.' Of course, as usual, what the Indians thought of Clive hardly mattered.

THE BLOODY MONSOON OF VELLORE

On 17 July 1806, British authorities in colonial Madras rescinded a four-month-old order that had bathed the countryside in a monsoon of blood. A week earlier, soon after the moon rose on the night of 9 July, serving sepoys had mutinied in nearby Vellore. Over a hundred British officers were put to death, including the commander, as he emerged in his bedclothes to check what the noise was all about. The few Westerners who survived managed either by playing dead or hiding in a gatehouse. Even as a lone officer raced to Arcot for reinforcements, the mutineers forgot their principal purpose and succumbed to the attractions of plunder. When the Arcot troops arrived at eight o'clock, they discovered that rebels of this so-called first war of independence (long before the Great Rebellion of 1857) had forgotten to even lock the gates of the fort they had only hours before triumphantly 'taken'.

Retribution was swift—of the 1,500 Indian troops present, about 400 were killed immediately, some of them blown out of cannons, presumably to transmit the message far and wide. But the British themselves were terrified. Power in India was tenuously held to begin with, and if even their own troops could not be counted on, the Raj was on less than solid foundations. By the time news of the mutiny reached England, months had passed, and the horror of the Madras authorities was matched by dread in London at this 'disastrous event'. A commission of enquiry had already been constituted. As one officer later said, 'The natives of Hindostan are meek and submissive beyond any other example in national character.' What then caused these spineless men to stand up to the white master? The answer, the officer offered, lay in an old saying: 'If you prick them, they will bleed; if you insult them, they will revenge.'

But the provocation was, on the face of it, bewildering—it was a simple matter of uniform. In March that year, the Madras authorities had issued new dress regulations for consistency. Beards were banned, and moustaches standardised. A new turban was designed, with a feather, a leather cockade and a flat top. Superficially, these were simple innovations, but, as the British discovered belatedly, in India costume had much to do with custom, and dress was not merely an issue of dressing up. Appearance signified caste, and in a veritable whirlpool of identities, sartorial conventions were a matter of honour. As the enquiry concluded, 'Nothing could appear more trivial to the public interests than the length of the hair on the upper lip of a sepoy.' But to the sepoy himself, 'the shape and fashion of the whisker is a badge of his caste, and an article of his religion'.

This ought not to have been a surprise to the East India Company. As soon as the new turban (which was especially resented for resembling European hats) was introduced, some

The Courtesan, the Mahatma & the Italian Brahmin

soldiers had raised objections. For their pains, they were rewarded with 500–900 lashes. Some sensible commanding officers on the ground knew the risks—in Hyderabad, where rumour already presented Christians as requiring the heads of 100 natives to consecrate their churches, the officer in charge refused to execute the dress regulations. In Vellore, however, the orders were firmly enforced. The result was a conspiracy so outlandish in its initial rumblings that even when alerted on multiple occasions, the British pooh-poohed it instead of allaying the concerns that led, in the end, to tragedy and violence.

As London put it, 1806 became the first example of 'the Native troops rising upon the European, barbarously attacking them when defenceless and asleep, and massacreing [sic] them in cold blood'. Of course, admitting that this bloodbath was due to a misunderstanding about moustaches and turbans felt a little awkward, so a number of other instigations were paraded—there were arrears of pay, so there must have been resentment. Though there were no Christian missions nearby, missionary polemics must surely have provoked the sepoys, it was added. And most important of all, the real conspirators—despite lack of corresponding evidence—were the family of the dead, fearsome ruler of Mysore, Tipu Sultan (r. 1782–99), housed in Vellore fort.

This theory conveniently suited an old British prejudice that the 'main instrument of mischief were Mahomedans'—a point that would be made even more forcefully decades down the line, after the sensational events of 1857. Behind the smokescreen of offensive uniforms, the Muslim sepoys had wanted, the authorities claimed, to restore Tipu's line to power. As in 1857, when the rebels would resurrect the emaciated Mughal emperor, in 1806, too, during the few hours Vellore was in their control, the soldiers had named Tipu's son their leader. The wedding of Tipu's daughter, Noor-al-Nissa, the previous day had allowed them to set the rebellion in motion behind the general noise and activity. An old flag of the Lion of Mysore (purchased, incidentally, from a Parsi merchant in the local market) was also unfurled that fateful night—all this construed as 'proof' that the Mysore exiles were architects of the uprising.

As it happened, the Mysore party did have a role to play, but only insofar as stoking the fire in 1806 went—attendants in service with the princes had goaded already upset sepoys by calling them unmanly 'topiwallas' who had sacrificed their honour for firangi coins. The result was a combination of caste and religious pride, political vendetta and accumulated resentment against British haughtiness culminating in spectacular slaughter. Just deserts awaited: The Mysore men were packed into twelve ships and exported to Bengal, the women following by land in an arduous journey. Punishments were handed out to those mutineers who had not already been chopped to pieces. But even as the facade of control returned, the monsoon of 1806 in Vellore sent the first jolting intimation to the founders of the Raj that they were not, ultimately, welcome in India—and that what would become the jewel in the empire's crown came soaked in an ocean of blood, and in ferocious anger.

WILLIAM JONES
INDIA'S BRIDGE TO THE WEST

Not many in India today remember Sir William Jones, though at the time of his death in 1794, he enjoyed what a biographer calls 'one of the most phenomenal reputations of all time'. To some he was Persian Jones, the translator of the *Tariq-i-Nadiri*, while others, after he founded the Asiatic Society in today's Kolkata, called him, predictably, Asiatic Jones. To one not entirely enraptured crowd, he was Republican Jones, what with his 'seditious, treasonable, and diabolical' ideas about popular education and universal (male) suffrage. But as far as India was concerned, it was in his avatar as Oriental Jones that he became one of the sincerest interpreters of this land in the West. As *Gentleman's Magazine* reported soon after his death, 'Sir William Jones by unwearied industry, aided by superior genius, successfully explored the hidden sources of oriental science and literature and his attainments in this interesting branch of learning' made him 'the most eminent oriental scholar in this or perhaps any other age'.

To be sure, Jones was not devoid of imperial prejudice. 'I shall certainly not preach democracy to the Indians, who must and will,' he argued, 'be governed by absolute power.' As a British judge, he scoffed at any political conception of Indianness; it was only India's historical accomplishments he thought profoundly admirable, not its grimy, politically emasculated present. Like his contemporary, Warren Hastings, he agreed that it was essential that the British rule India, though this should be done, he argued, through India's own laws and customs and not by engrafting a Western system in this eastern land. For all that, in the end, India came to mean more than just business to him. 'I never was unhappy in England,' he once wrote, 'but I never was happy till I settled in India.' Part of it, admittedly, had to do with the splendid £6,000 salary that had attracted him here in the first place—Jones calculated that a decade in India promised stately retirement when finally, unencumbered by financial distress, he could pursue assorted intellectual interests.

This quest for financial stability was a consequence of Jones's background. He was born in 1746 to the daughter of a cabinetmaker and a seventy-one-year-old mathematician, whose peers included Sir Isaac Newton. His father died but the cabinetmaker's daughter gave him a good education—a worthwhile investment, given his prodigious appetite for learning. By thirteen, Jones was not only already familiar with Shakespeare but had also written his first poem, and by the time of his death knew, in varying degrees of fluency, a grand total of twenty-eight languages, starting with Greek, Latin, French and Italian. A desire to read the Bible in the original drew him to Hebrew, and an interest in Confucius led him to Chinese in due course. He thought Greek poetry 'sublime' but when he 'tasted Arabic and Persian poetry', his enthusiasm for Greek 'began to dry up'. Incidentally, one of the languages he knew 'least perfectly' was his native Welsh.

By his mid-twenties, Jones had authored several books and was recognised as an authority on the East—when the King of Denmark came on a visit to Britain, among those he specifically asked to meet was young William. But while accolades and a knighthood arrived in steady succession, the want of a dependable income brought inescapable pressures. Fresh out of his teens, he had served as tutor to the son of an English aristocrat, earning also some money working as a translator. But with the passage of years, and the creeping up of attendant pressures, demands for greater stability came to press against this Oxford man. 'I was surrounded by friends, acquaintances and relatives who encouraged me to expel from my way of life ... poetry and Asian literature.' They wanted him to 'become a barrister and be devoted to ambition'. He agreed, but managed to orient his legal interests towards the East, producing the forbiddingly named *Mahomedan Law of Succession to the Property of Intestates*.

Before he was thirty, it was becoming clear that Jones was leaning towards republicanism. He was close to Benjamin Franklin, then living in Paris, and it was in his house that he composed a controversial pamphlet innocuously named *The Principles of Government*. Through an imagined dialogue between a scholar and a peasant, the latter is educated (somewhat paternally) about constitutionalism through relatable parallels and told that he too can participate in affairs of the nation. The result was that Jones's publisher was sued for libel by the government. The scholar was not pushed into fear, though—where the first print was published anonymously, it was now printed again with his name clearly mentioned. Writing in 1782 to Franklin, Jones noted gloomily but not less idealistically that he had 'no wish to grow old in England; for, believe me, I would rather be a peasant with freedom than a prince in an enslaved country'. Naturally, any political ambitions he had in Britain now floundered.

It was in 1783, when not yet thirty-seven, that he came to India. He had applied for a post with the British Supreme Court in Calcutta as early as 1777, but his political leanings meant he was hardly in the good books of the government. Now, however, his name was confirmed—and this despite the scandal about his pamphlet—and so it was that Jones set out for India, aboard a frigate called *Crocodile*. But, in his typical fashion, he connected his pursuit of money with a pursuit of intellectual stimulation also. He drew up a list of sixteen subjects, ranging from the Mughal and Maratha political systems to the 'Music of the Eastern Nations' and 'Medicine, Chemistry, Surgery and Anatomy of the Indians', to investigate. And it took only a year-long glance at India's cultural riches, for him to constitute the Asiatic Society—the body that through the researches of a generation of Orientalists, reminded Indians of a figure we ourselves had forgotten: Emperor Ashoka.

But what struck Jones with the greatest intensity was language. 'Sanskrit,' Jawaharlal Nehru would later write, 'fascinated him ... It was through his writings and translations that Europe first had a glimpse of some of the treasures of Sanskrit literature.' It began with professional demands—Jones could interpret Islamic law without translators given his knowledge of Arabic and Persian, but Hindu codes of justice evaded him. To rectify this, a pandit was hired on a princely retainer of hundred rupees to give him lessons. Given his outcaste position, however, lessons with the brahmin had a prescribed protocol: they were conducted in a 'pure' room with white marble floors, cleaned every day with water from the Ganga, lest the pandit be defiled by his constant intercourse with a *mlechcha*. The student also had to sit for his lessons on an empty stomach, though occasionally a little tea could be consumed in the presence of the high-caste tutor. These efforts paid off and soon Jones built up a vocabulary of 10,000 words. And when brahmins in Benares refused to translate the *Manusmriti* for him, he simply produced his own *The Ordinances of Manu*, relied upon for generations thereafter as a classic.

Soon he felt a deeper affection for Sanskrit poetry. 'By rising before the sun,' wrote Jones, 'I allot an hour every day to Sanscrit, and am charmed with knowing so beautiful a sister of Latin and Greek.' It was the first time a familial bond was established between Sanskrit and the classical languages of European antiquity. And there were other dots of history that Jones joined through the medium of language. The Palibothra of the Greeks he connected to Pataliputra. Sadracottus, he discovered, was none other than Chandragupta. India's past came alive in a wider context, with its own philosophers and emperors. 'The Sanskrit language, whatever be its antiquity,' he announced to fellow members of the Asiatic Society, 'is of a wonderful structure; more perfect than the Greeks, more copious than the Latin, and more exquisitely refined than either, yet bearing to both of them a strong affinity, both in the roots of verbs and the forms of grammar, than could possibly have been produced by accident; so strong indeed, that no philologer could examine them all three without believing them to have sprung from some common source.'

But if there was one Sanskrit poet who gripped our polymath most, that poet was Kalidas. And through Jones's obsession, as we have seen before, Europe was transfixed with *Shakuntala*. Translated in 1789, Jones's *Sacontalá: The Fatal Ring* inspired Goethe to declare: 'I should like to live in India myself … Sakontala, Nala, they have to be kissed.' Friedrich Schlegel also came to consider *Shakuntala* the best example of Indian poetry. Interestingly, Jones did not merely translate—there was censorship also, given the moral predispositions of the West. Where Kalidas spoke of Shakuntala's 'breasts no longer firm', Jones accepted his remarks on ageing cheeks and shoulders but omitted the breasts completely to avoid embarrassing himself and his Western audience. In a way, Jones modelled a new Shakuntala—a prototype of European virtue, as opposed to the sensuous Shakuntala Kalidas described; an

Indian woman born of Western idealism rather than anchored in authentic Indian tradition. Indians too embraced this paragon of chastity over her erotically charged predecessor, much like so many Western slants came to be accepted as unquestionably (and 'purely') Indian.

By 1794, Jones declared a new mission. His desiderata featured Panini's grammar, the Vedas and the Puranas, and much more needed to be completed before he settled into a life of scholarly retirement. It was a tragic twist that within the year he was dead—the climate never agreed with him— and a grave was built for him at the Park Street cemetery in Calcutta where he still lies buried. 'The best monument that can be erected to a man of literary talents,' he once said, 'is a good edition of his works.' And so his widow published a collection dutifully, enshrining in it his legacy as the decipherer of India for the West. For a few years Jones's reputation was treasured in a place of respect, and he was read by everyone from Thomas Campbell to William Blake and even William Wordsworth. But within a few decades, British attitudes began to change—as the growing empire in India took a racist turn, Jones was dismissed altogether. His researches came to be seen as useless and frivolous; Shakuntala, far from admirable, was now painted preposterous. And India, this new generation of Englishmen decided, was not only never great, it never could be. The India Jones saw was a myth, all his work a fallacy. And for Indians, soon enough, the likes of Jones withdrew and the cruelties of the Raj became our reality.

THE GENTLEMAN REFORMER OF BENGAL

When Raja Rammohun Roy landed in England in April 1831, among those who disembarked with him were his servants, an adopted son rumoured to be his bastard from a Muslim woman, a brahmin cook and a milch cow. The cow and cook were essential to the enterprise—Roy had already been written off in Bengal for defying rules of caste and custom, and needed to demonstrate some degree of ritual conformity to support his venture across forbidden seas. But while adversaries at home resented him, in England he became a celebrity, received to cheers of 'Long Live Tippoo Saheb', with the police summoned in Manchester to moderate public enthusiasm. Roy, for his part, 'longed to see the country to whose keeping the destinies of his own had been entrusted—the country whose philosophy, liberty, and science had achieved their proudest triumphs', but the view on the other side was somewhat different. *The Times* hailed him as a poster child of the West's civilising mission, calling him 'a harbinger of those fruits which must result from the dissemination of European knowledge' in the exotic darkness that was the East.

There was good reason for such romanticisation. On the one hand, Roy came on a mission from Akbar II, the Mughal emperor who sought a more generous pension from the East India Company after it had reduced him to a cipher. On the other, Roy, whose works on Indian philosophy had earned him a reputation as Hinduism's Martin Luther, also wished to acquaint the British with his homeland. As he remarked, 'One of my objects in visiting this country has been to lay before the British public a statement, however brief, of my views regarding the past conditions and future prospects of India.' He was the emperor's envoy, but he saw himself also as an ambassador for India itself, as the urbane face of a reforming society that would soon rise to find its destiny. Of course, none of this stopped him from telling Victor Jacquemont that India cried for 'many more years of English domination' to arrive at this destination: 'Conquest,' he felt, 'is very rarely an evil when the conquering people were more civilised than the conquered' (a position not likely to win him any friends among India's hyper-nationalists today).

Indeed, it was such presumption that made him enemies, including in his household. Roy was born to the junior wife of a junior son in a brahmin line that had served the Mughal state. His father, with whom he disagreed uncompromisingly, had brought upon the family great ignominy by going to prison for failing to honour his debts. His formidable mother was even less pleased with Roy, when at 'about the age of sixteen, I composed a manuscript calling in question the validity of the idolatrous system of the Hindoos'. He went away from home very young, and in Patna upset Muslim leaders with his observations on their faith, while his *The Precepts of Jesus* rubbed Christian missionaries the wrong way when he presumed to pass comment on their hallowed shepherd. Some called him a lapsed Hindu and threw bones and garbage into his yard. Others created obstacles at work during the years he served the Company government, rising from *munshi* or language instructor to the post of head clerk at a British court—all this before he inherited a fortune and through that, financial independence.

Roy, most widely known for his campaign against widow burning and for founding what would become the Brahmo Samaj, was educated in Sanskrit, Persian and Arabic, and is rumoured to have ventured as far as Tibet in his quest for learning (a somewhat unlikely claim). He was suave and polished but acutely conscious that his recommendations on reform were seen as the toyings of a dilettante, the newspapers he published in English, Urdu, Persian and Bengali notwithstanding. As one biographer notes, 'Rammohan was an anomaly to many of his Bengali contemporaries. In his ... English language skills and European tastes, he was the image of the prosperous nineteenth-century Calcutta babu. Yet in private he hankered for distinction as a *shastric* scholar.' His *Tuhfat-ul-Muwahhidin* (A Gift to Deists) was seen as an effort to flaunt his Persian (badly), while his first Vedantic essay in 1815 invited scorn from traditionalists as far away as Madras. But he remained steadfast. 'For many years,' he said, 'I have never ceased to contemplate ... the obstinate adherence of my countrymen' to various 'superstitious puerilities'. And the only means to change this was to increase access to sacred books and their lofty ideas, even if the orthodox and rigid sneered at him on the way.

But local disdain did not mean unpopularity or hatred. Roy stood up to the colonial state when censorship was attempted, pointing out that every ruler must acknowledge his inability to do everything well, and be willing, therefore, to embrace criticism from his subjects: 'To secure this important object, the unrestrained liberty of publication is the only effectual means that can be employed,' argued Roy. Even as he railed against colonial policy, he explained Hindu scripture in English to that very same Western audience. Like William Jones, he persuaded them of the value India's past held even if its present was corrupted. There was conviction here—he refused, scandalously, to participate in his father's funeral rites because he thought them meaningless. He produced such texts as *Questions and Answers on the Judicial System of India* even as he expounded *A Tract on Religious Toleration*. He had a

curious mind, vision and clarity of expression, all united in a desire to serve as spokesperson for a more pristine Hinduism in a reinvigorated India. It alarmed his contemporaries, but also surprised others. As Bishop Heber declared with a pinch of racial condescension, this brilliant 'Asiatic' with his 'good English, good sense and forcible arguments', not to mention excellent ideas, was nothing short of 'a real curiosity'.

To a great extent Roy succeeded in his efforts—a fascinating intellectual movement was born through his and his contemporaries' efforts in Bengal, while his two years in England saw him impress individuals from King William IV down to Benjamin Disraeli. Lord Macaulay, otherwise no admirer of the Indian mind, waited hours one evening hoping to introduce himself to Roy, while Jeremy Bentham began a campaign to elect him to parliament. There was also a christening where the infant was named Thomas Rammohun Roy, and stories floated of a romance in Bristol. There was no doubt that Roy was immensely popular in English society, for he was also on the side of introducing Western education in India—Sanskrit schooling, he argued, 'would be best calculated to keep [India] in darkness'. As he wrote to Lord Amherst, the governor-general, Sanskrit was 'so difficult that almost a lifetime is necessary for its perfect acquisition'. This had been 'for ages a lamentable check on the diffusion of knowledge', and in any case 'the learning concealed under [its] almost impervious veil' was 'far from sufficient to reward the labour of acquiring it'. Educational reform was the need of the hour, therefore, and the language of such reform did not matter to him—tradition might offer security, but for progress change must actively, he felt, be welcomed.

The brahmin had no place in Roy's reformed Hinduism—'If in doubt,' he recommended, 'consult your conscience,' not your priest. He rejected brahmin domination, calling them 'self-interested guides, who, in defiance of the law as well as of common sense, have succeeded ... in conducting [ordinary people] to the temple of idolatry', hiding 'the true substance of morality'. Roy would have had even more to express had he not died in 1833 on a moonlit night. It took 120 days for the news to reach India but his message had already taken root: that Indians 'are capable of better things' and 'worthy of a better destiny'. Indeed as one obituary put it, despite the 'extreme interruption and inconvenience' his views caused him, Roy remained true to his convictions and that which he believed was right for the good of India and his fellow Indians. And, despite any flaws in his message and the human limitations of his character, for this alone he deserves to be remembered.

THE COLONIAL STATE AND INDIA'S GODS

In 1812, the fortunes—quite literally—of hundreds of temples in southern Kerala found themselves in the hands of a man who was born in faraway Scotland. It was one of those strange ironies of colonial rule in India, for Colonel Munro had originally come to princely Travancore as the East India Company's representative. Quickly, however, he was also elevated as minister by the ruling princess, a formula designed to give the British the power they desired while ducking actual annexation. Munro's goal, with his split loyalties, was to balance the government's books and ensure the company received regular tribute. And as part of his campaign to augment revenues, he took over 348 significant temples and 1,171 smaller shrines across the land, so that 62,000 gardens and 63,500 acres of cultivable land became state property overnight. Hereafter, sums were disbursed to the temples for their upkeep, but so valuable was the real estate seized that it still produced an enormous balance—an

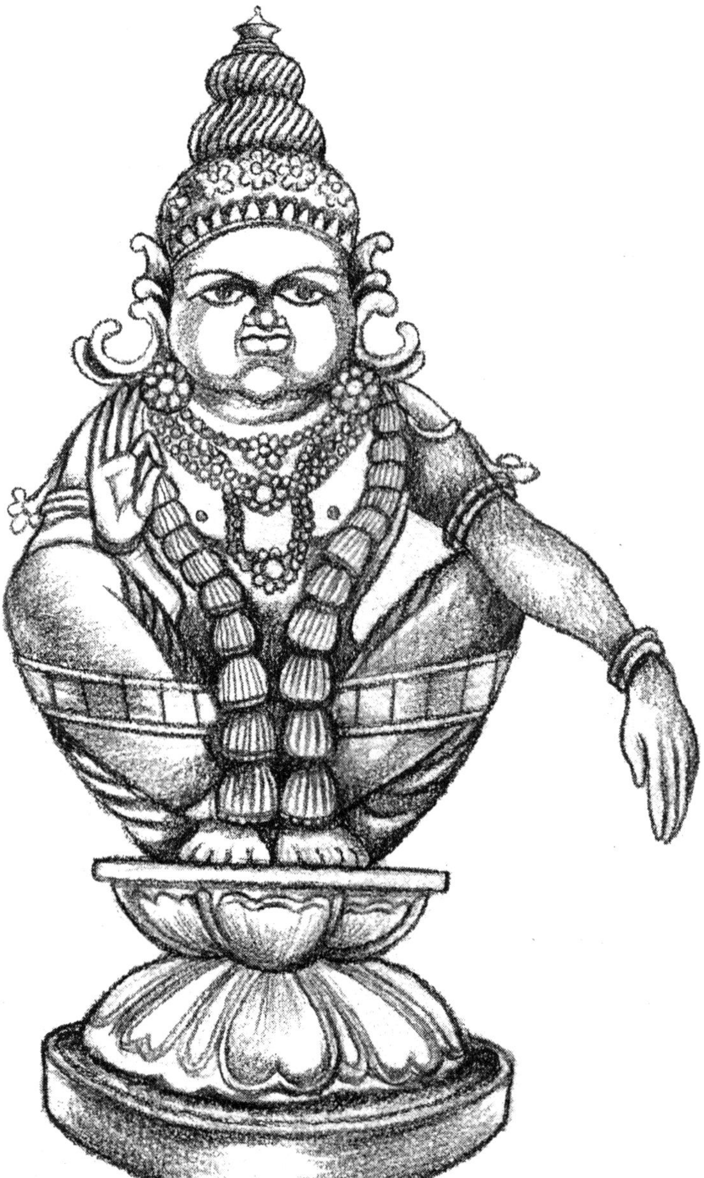

The Courtesan, the Mahatma & the Italian Brahmin

amount that could be used for other purposes, including to service political obligations to the company.

It was an act that birthed repercussions felt to this day, for some of Kerala's celebrated shrines—including Sabarimala, for example—remain under government control, provoking persistent questions about what business precisely the state has in institutions of faith. To be fair, Munro's action was not unilateral—temples, with their unregulated funds and powerful trustees, were a political threat to the emerging modern state on the one hand, while on the other, there were complaints that revenues were being embezzled; in some instances, trustees stole even the idols of their deities. In neighbouring Tamil provinces, too, the story was similar: the collector of Thanjavur, John Wallace, noted that temple custodians in his jurisdiction had piled up debt to the tune of ₹2 lakh (a colossal figure at the time). Like in princely Travancore, in British territories too, the company was embroiled without delay, then, in the business of religion. And here, too, profits followed: in 1846, after all expenses were deducted, officials of the Madras Presidency found themselves with ₹8 lakh in surplus from temples, a figure promptly diverted to the 'general education fund', while another lakh was 'expressly devoted' to a highway project between cotton-producing Tirunelveli and the port of Thoothukudi. Gods were now building roads.

To be clear, as political sovereigns, the company did possess certain prerogatives where these establishments were concerned. Hindu rulers reserved the right to intervene in the affairs of shrines should the need arise, and in eighteenth-century Madras, the Christian British often continued traditions instituted by previous powers, intervening when necessary. So, for instance, in 1789, when quarrels arose in the Thiruvallur temple and officials discovered that the brahmins in charge 'had mortgaged part of the property for their own private use', the company saw to it that the men were made 'answerable for the few things missing'. Devotees also, without means to stand up to influential trustees, approached the company, inviting the latter to proactively intervene in temple affairs. This led, in 1817, to the earliest official legislation in Madras on the subject, to ensure incomes from temple endowments were disbursed 'according to real intent and will of the granter' and not frittered away by untrustworthy trustees. It was a good step in theory, though in about two decades, the company found itself involved in as many as 7,600 temples—a state of affairs it had not quite expected when it set out to uphold tradition.

As it happened, despite financial gains, this was an uncomfortable position for the company. Missionary propagandists, for instance, lambasted British officials for promoting 'idolatry': by protecting temples, organising festivals, supervising repairs and settling disputes, the company had become the primary trustee for assorted Hindu deities. As one reverend complained in 1831, 'When we point out to [the Hindus] that idolatry is not the worship of god ... they ask, "How can you say so? Who keeps our pagodas in repair?... Do you not do it yourself? If you do these things, where is the reasonableness and propriety of saying idolatry is sinful?"' In fits and starts and under growing pressure, then, the British attempted to extricate themselves from this knot. While in Travancore the Hindu ruler clung on to the temples, in Thanjavur over 2,000 shrines were returned to locals, and bigger temples were placed in the hands of committees, panchayats and in some cases, 'influential' individuals. This, predictably, led to its own politics, featuring caste competition, sectarian rivalries and much confusion, made worse by flawed legal interventions through the nineteenth and twentieth centuries.

In the end, what the colonial regime began, secular India inherited, and this peculiar mix-up of government with temples continues to this day. For the British, the issue eventually became one of several complications to negotiate in the subcontinent—from the start, the company ruled through bureaucracy and centralisation, essential instruments for a foreign power in an alien land. One-size-fits-all rules were put in place despite contradictions, which in independent India raise valid questions that the colonial power wasn't obliged to answer. In Sabarimala, for example, this was one of the arguments posed by critics of the 2018 Supreme Court judgement—that different temples have different features which cannot be guided by a singular principle. Certainly, there is room for a new framework to preserve the individuality of India's countless shrines—a new vision with an accommodative mechanism—though some overarching principles must still prevail. After all, even before the days of Colonel Munro and the British, Indian sovereigns intervened in temple affairs. Now, the constitution is supreme, and while diversity should be respected, this paramount document must necessarily be obeyed.

WHEN A TEMPLE WAS BESIEGED IN AYODHYA

On 6 December 1992, when a howling mob tore down the sixteenth-century Babri Masjid in Ayodhya, a nation watched in horror as governments of the day stood by, pleading helplessness. Decades have elapsed since that shameful event, and many more may pass before anything close to a real—and sensible—resolution is reached for what is essentially a festering wound. But if in living memory Ayodhya has gone down as a symbol of the worst manifestation of communal politics in contemporary India, there is an episode in its past that could be construed as the inaugural chapter of this ugly narrative, pitting Hindu against Muslim, man against man. And unlike recent times, many years ago it was a *temple* that attracted the attentions of a fanatic crowd, their actions becoming linked in several ways to the larger discussion around the Ram Janmabhoomi agitation.

The Courtesan, the Mahatma & the Italian Brahmin

The story resides in the mid-nineteenth century. The Nawabs of Awadh, who seized sovereignty in the region as agents of the Mughals, never actually enjoyed absolute power in their princely dominion. As was the case with Muslim rulers across the subcontinent, authority was, in fact, exercised in conjunction with old and new Hindu elites. In pre-Mughal Deccan, for instance, its sultans utilised brahmins and Marathas as their intermediaries with the masses, just as in Awadh the nawabs were served by kayasthas who operated their administration, and by legions of Hindu warrior ascetics (or Nagas) who waged war against their enemies. As the splendour of the nawabs grew, so too did the wealth and influence of these classes—the frenetic building of temples in Ayodhya in the eighteenth century, for example, had a great deal to do with the wave of prosperity enjoyed by the

Hindu aristocracy under a thriving nawabi court, which also patronised pilgrim activity, revitalising the worship of Rama.

It was the second nawab, Safdarjung, who, in return for military services, presented to a group called the Ramanandi Nagas money for the construction of a shrine to Hanuman at a spot about 700 metres from the Babri Masjid. In due course, a Hindu nobleman enabled the expansion of this structure into what is today called Hanumangarhi, described as a temple-fortress, and which in the nineteenth century possessed gifts from the Awadh crown that brought it a phenomenal ₹50,000 in revenue (worth many times that sum at today's value). Scholars like Hans Bakker and Peter van der Veer note that Babri itself is believed to stand on the site of an eleventh-century Hindu shrine that was demolished and converted into a mosque by a Mughal general. Furthermore, old temple columns were said to have survived (though there is controversy on this subject), unwittingly also becoming pillars for the cause of 'restoring' the premises to its original use. In any case, the irony was that far from splitting men into irreconcilable enemies, till the mid-nineteenth century, Hindus and Muslims worshipped at Babri in peace. Each enjoyed custody of different parts of the compound and there was enough general harmony for this practice to carry on.

The first communal conflict that Ayodhya witnessed occurred in the mid-1850s. On the face of it, this was a Hindu–Muslim feud. As we learn from *The Anatomy of a Confrontation*, a collection of scholarly essays edited by Sarvepalli Gopal, and other sources, Shah Ghulam Husain, a Muslim firebrand, claimed that Hanumangarhi stood, in fact, on the ashes of a mosque that dated back to Emperor Aurangzeb's reign—in other words, just as Babri is supposed to stand on the ruins of a temple, this Hindu shrine occupied

The Courtesan, the Mahatma & the Italian Brahmin

a space that earlier housed a mosque. Husain's call to 'reclaim' the mosque was answered by enough men to result in a violent clash soon afterwards. The Muslim party was not just repulsed; we read how the Hindus took the skirmish into Babri next door, which Husain's fighters had used as a base. In the course of events, seventy men were killed on the Muslim side. An attack on Muslim civilians and plunder of their property followed, with reprisals after some Hindus decided to make a grand display of slaughtering pigs on the day the seventy fallen Muslims were buried. It was, simply put, provocations galore and blood and violence everywhere.

While this was superficially a Hindu–Muslim conflict, in reality matters were more complicated. Muslims in Awadh comprised about 12 per cent of the population; the vast majority within this minority was Sunni. The nawab, however, was of Shia persuasion, and the cream of courtly patronage was distilled in favour of the Shia super-minority. That the reigning nawab, the colourful Wajid Ali Shah (about whom we will read more in a subsequent essay), was also an enthusiast for Hindu traditions, in addition to the court's general collaboration with Hindu elites, provoked the 'arch villain' Ghulam Husain and his 'vile', 'disreputable' followers to plot their attack on Hanumangarhi. This was, in other words, not only a move against the Hindus but also a Sunni rebellion against an unorthodox Shia nawab. While Husain's plot was a failure, his place was soon taken by another zealot, the maulvi Amir Ali. And this man went as far as declaring a jihad to occupy Hanumangarhi and re-establish the mosque that was supposed to have existed within.

Interestingly, the claim that there was a Muslim place of worship in Hanumangarhi may not have been incorrect, even if it was inaccurate in the vocabulary of its expression. While a committee constituted by the nawab found that there was never a mosque within the fort, it is likely that the Muslims were building on an earlier tradition when they enjoyed access to the shrine. Before the Ramanandi Nagas turned it into their military seat, the deity in the temple was worshipped by Hindus as Hanuman and by Muslims as Hathile, one of the five saints (*panch pir*) of Sufism—Hanumangarhi, in other words, was a shrine that attracted everybody. It was not a full-blown masjid, but by preventing Muslim access to the shrine at some point, those in charge of Hanumangarhi inadvertently allowed grievances to mount. This, in turn, culminated in the imagined memory of a 'mosque' that required reclaiming, even if this meant shedding blood and sacrificing lives—an example of how extreme piety can quickly transform a shadow from the past into incontrovertible 'fact'.

In any case, when Amir Ali refused to accept the decision of the committee, the stage was set for battle. Armed with fatwas from Shia as well as Sunni clerics that declared Ali's jihad unlawful, the nawab's forces under British command intercepted him on his way to Ayodhya. Several hundred rebels lost their lives and their obstinate leader fell on the battlefield. Hanumangarhi was retained by the Hindus, while in Babri the British erected fences to separate the mosque from the platform where Hindus offered worship. What is curious, however, is that some date the first claim that the masjid sat on the spot of Ram's birth to the mid-1850s—precisely the time when Muslims claimed Hanumangarhi was 'originally' a mosque, and Hindus, in their counter-claim, reminded them of a temple upon which Babri is supposed to have been built.

The matter may never be satisfactorily resolved. So perhaps the best lesson we can learn from the last time a mob went to destroy a place of worship in Ayodhya, before the tragedy of 1992, is that at least on that occasion, those in power did not stand by idly; that, instead, they did their duty and protected the temple from destruction, something that cannot be said of those who watched quietly as a mosque was razed a hundred years later by a terrible, monstrous mob.

A FORGOTTEN INDIAN QUEEN IN PARIS

She lies buried amidst sepulchres that house the remains of many who are still famous. There is Jim Morrison on the premises, the American rock legend whom trains of tourists come to pay homage to, like pilgrims bearing flowers. Edith Piaf, the waif who sang her way to greatness, finds her peace nearby, as does Frederic Chopin, the composer whose pickled heart waits in Warsaw but whose body dissolves in the French capital. Benjamin Franklin's grandson rests here, and in the vicinity is a man believed to have been sired by Napoleon. Oscar Wilde's sculpted grave competes with Marcel Proust's neat bed of stone, and many more still are the artists, writers and persons of esteem who crowd the hillside cemetery that is Père Lachaise in Paris. And amongst them all, under a platform of rugged rock, lies this tragic Indian woman. Her name and cause have been largely forgotten, but since 1858, she has been here, longer than many of her revered neighbours. Tourists walk by with cameras, oblivious to her unmarked

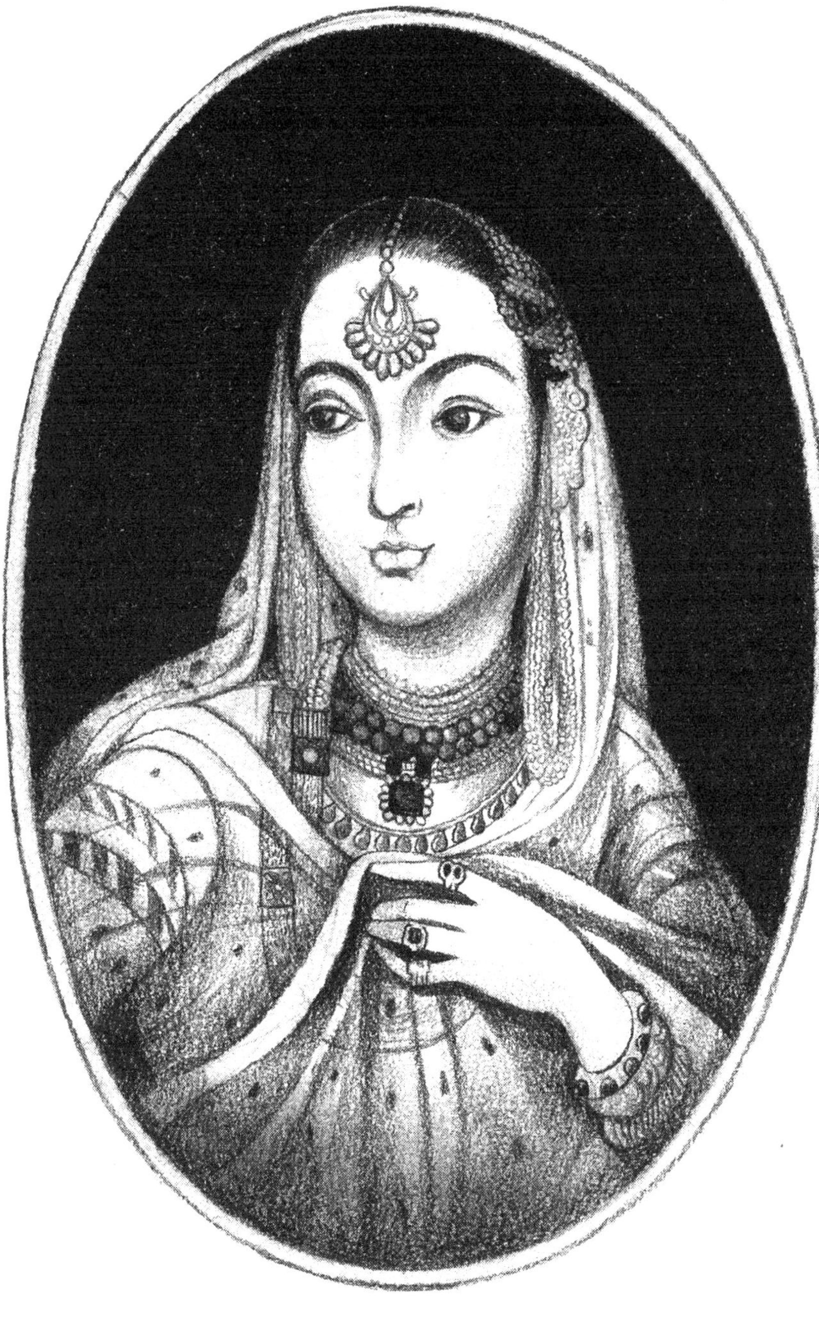

square existence. But every now and then, there is a stray visitor who arrives on a quest: to locate the final resting place of that remarkable woman, the last queen of Awadh.

I was that visitor in the winter of 2017, when I trekked up Paris's most famous graveyard to look for this forgotten tomb. The lady appears in yellowed old books by several names. She was to some Malika Kishwar, while others knew her as Janab-i Aliyah, Her Sublime Excellency, mother to the ruler of 'Oude', Wajid Ali Shah. In 1856, when the British deposed the nawab from his ancestral seat in Lucknow, his family departed for colonial Calcutta with all the money they could gather and what dignity they had left. But while the son (a 'crazy imbecile' in the eyes of his oppressors) prepared to fade quietly into history, the mother was determined to win back that which was her family's by right. That very year, this woman who knew little beyond her sequestered palace, set foot on a ship, determined to sail to England so she might speak—woman to woman—to the English queen in person. After all, declared the middle-aged begum, Victoria was 'also a mother'; she would recognise the despair her people had unleashed, and restore to the House of Awadh territory, titles and its rightful honour. And so proceeded Malika Kishwar, her health already in decline, braving cold winds in a foreign land, to plead the cause of royal justice.

The mission was doomed from the start. Her advisers were many, and much was the money they sought for the privilege of their counsel. The results, however, were nowhere to be found. As the historian Rosie Llewellyn-Jones records, Kishwar discovered quickly enough that Queen Victoria, in her grand 'circular dress', had little power to bestow anything more than polite conversation on her and her Awadhi line— when an audience was granted, they spoke about boats and

The Courtesan, the Mahatma & the Italian Brahmin

English mansions, not about imperial treacheries and the unjust transactions in Lucknow. In the Houses of Parliament, things got worse. A prayer prepared at long last was dismissed on spurious bureaucratic grounds: the begum was to submit a 'humble petition', words that she failed to use in the document laid on the table. While her son reconciled to British imperium, the mother was obstinate in battle. So, when she wished to travel, they sought to dragoon her into acknowledging their suzerainty—if Malika Kishwar and her ménage wanted passports, she would have to declare herself a 'British subject'. The begum refused to do anything of the sort, prepared, at best, to be under 'British protection'. And legal quibbles aside, the Great Rebellion of 1857 compounded matters—there was now no prospect of relinquishing even a fragment of British power when the hour called for a demonstration of obdurate strength alone. Awadh was lost forever.

The tide having turned, in 1858, the begum decided to return at last, defeated and unhappy in the extreme. But while in Paris, she fell ill and died on 24 January. The funeral was simple, though there was yet some dignity and state—representatives of the Turkish and Persian sultans gave the Indian queen the regard the British denied her and her line. A cenotaph was constructed by the grave, but it has long since fallen to pieces—when decades later, the authorities at Père Lachaise sought funds to repair the tomb, her exiled son decided from Calcutta that it was simply not worth his pension, while the colonial state was even less inclined to honour a difficult woman lying several feet underground in an alien European country. And so, since that time, in a graveyard full of magnificent memorials, the queen of Awadh has remained, a shell of broken stone sheltering her from the weeds and overgrowth that alone have made a claim upon her and the story that she tells.

Others of her suite also suffered. A younger son travelled with her, Sikandar Hashmat by name. He died in England, and was carried to join his mother in her unmarked grave. A grandson's infant child was also buried within, turning the tally in Paris to three. But it was in London that one more of the delegation fell, this one a baby princess, born to Sikandar Hashmat from his Rajput wife on British shores. I walked around a dull little place called Kilburn to look for this grave. And there, in a cemetery, after an hour amidst tombs set in the soggy English ground, I found a memorial to the child: Princess 'Omdutel Aurau Begum', who died on 14 April 1858, a few months after her grandmother who was once a queen. But Omdutel, all of eighteen months, enjoys a minor triumph where her royal grandmother had none—lying by a pathway in that cemetery in Kilburn, her grave at least bears her name. The begum, on the other hand, has become to the passing tourist a plinth on which to rest, smoking a cigarette and gazing at a horizon full of the dead, till a stranger might appear to tell how beneath them are the remains of a fascinating woman—pieces of one of history's unhappy tales.

THE STORY OF WAJID ALI SHAH

In 1874, *The New York Times* dispatched a correspondent to India to survey the life of a fabulously wealthy man. Once he had been an even wealthier monarch, but by the time the journalist arrived, he had already spent decades in vastly reduced conditions, having lost his territories and squandered much of his money. From a kingdom the sise of Scotland, Wajid Ali Shah now reigned over only an estate in Calcutta. The sheer number of followers cramped into his premises, however, gave some impression of pomp—the grounds hosted over 7,000 people, including prostitutes, household guards and dozens of disgruntled begums, not to speak of a menagerie of monkeys, bears and 18,000 pigeons. 'The Ex-King of Oude's mimic kingdom', the *Times* called the establishment, and that is precisely what it was: a pale imitation of vanished glories.

Wajid Ali Shah was a creative, difficult and interesting man. Born in 1822, he wore his hair in ringlets and dressed in robes that coyly exposed his left nipple. His early years were unremarkable but for his interest in music, dance and poetry—and for the ample proportions of his royal person. By the time he succeeded to the throne of Awadh in 1847, a state carved out of the crumbling Mughal empire, he had already produced works such as the *Darya-yi-Ta'ashshuq* (The River of Love) and the *Bahr-e 'Ishq* (The Ocean of Affection). His plays were sensational productions that took months to put together, and every now and then the Shah threw grand parties—the Yogi Mela of 1853 saw his gardens opened to the masses, with everyone instructed to dress in saffron. In 1843, he directed a play on the Hindu deity Krishna, with four of his wives playing milkmaids and prancing around on stage.

Predictably, the heavily starched, studiously avaricious British were displeased. 'The Heir Apparent's character holds no promise of good,' it was noted. His 'temper is capricious and fickle, his days and nights are passed in the female apartments and he appears to have resigned himself to debauchery, dissipation and low pursuits'. This, of course, made for a wonderful excuse for annexation, so that even when the Shah made efforts to govern his kingdom well, producing an administrative manual called the *Dastur-i-Wajidi*, the British preferred to dismiss him as an imbecile. Less than a decade after his succession, when he was told in 1856 that his kingdom would be absorbed into British territory, the Shah cried, 'Why have I deserved this? What (crime) have I committed?' There was no clear answer, but one hint lies in the fact that the East India Company owed him large amounts in debt. Why bother repaying a loan when liquidating your moneylender was a more comfortable option?

Some of the blame did lie with the Shah. He loved gun salutes from the British, but when it came to actually protecting his honour by fighting the annexation of his kingdom, it was his elderly mother who made more of a real (if abortive) effort by travelling to London (as we saw earlier). While the old lady died in an alien country, her son agreed to become a pensioner of the East India Company. Once Wajid Ali Shah commanded 60,000 soldiers, but now he was reduced to a life of domestic frustration and chauvinistic rage. There was a time when he saw himself as a modern-day Krishna, a hero whose brilliance attracted women by the hundreds. But as his biographer Rosie Llewellyn-Jones notes, 'For all his passionate love poetry, Wajid Ali Shah may have been one of those men who enjoy the pursuit and capture, but do not actually like women very much.'

Perhaps this stemmed from when he was sexually abused by a nanny at the age of eight, or perhaps there were other reasons. About one wife he wrote: 'Day and night I would loiter around her like one possessed.' But in 1849 he was dismayed to learn that what he got in return from this darling was gonorrhoea. He liked dark women, and an African wife was cheerfully named Ajaib Khanum (Strange Lady). Another consort, Sally Begum, a descendant of a Mughal prince from his Anglo-Indian wife, was five years his senior, while of the eight women he divorced at his mother's insistence, one, the redoubtable Begum Hazrat Mahal, stayed on in Lucknow and waged war against the British in 1857; this lady too had more spirit than her ex-husband.

Having settled in Calcutta, Wajid Ali Shah got down to practical matters. In the next two decades, he divorced fifty of his remaining wives, but in 1878 when he tried to get rid of twenty-seven more in a single shot, the British responded with embarrassment—he could not simply shed begums, he was informed. The man responded with exasperation: 'But the women are old and ugly!' When asked who should care for them, quick came his reply: 'The Government.' By 1880, the principal queen was 'living in adultery' with someone else, possibly from sheer desperation—the king was a miser and thought a monthly allowance of ₹90 to his oldest son was perfectly generous when his own income was ₹12 lakh every year. The British, in turn, hadn't quite counted on the man living so long and costing them grand amounts in pension.

When in September 1887, the Shah finally died, there was a general sense of relief not only among the authorities but also in his camp. 'His ladies were nearly as numerous as his animals,' the governor general's wife recorded. 'They [depart] at the rate of seven or eight a day… the slaves of an hard-hearted old man who cared more for his cobras and his wild beasts than he did for them.' The Shah had once been heir to a kingdom and to a large fortune—a decade after Awadh's annexation, it was found that the British still owed the ex-king £2 million. He had reigned in style and patronised the arts. He was an inheritor who, were he not entrapped by prejudice and by colonial machinations, might have gone down as the creator of an even greater legacy. His downfall, however, turned him into an unhappy tyrant bent on preserving a miniature copy of his past—a past that

The Courtesan, the Mahatma & the Italian Brahmin

came at the cost of depressing those who stood by him when calamity struck, and who only too late learnt that Wajid Ali, the Shah, had long predeceased Wajid Ali the embittered pensioner.

VICTORIA MAHARANI AND INDIA

On 1 November 1858, Queen Victoria formally extinguished the fires of the great rebellion of the preceding year with a historic proclamation. Two pages of grandiloquent text was all it took to inaugurate a new chapter after the 'mutiny', and possession of India was transferred from the bloodied hands of the East India Company to the custody of the British Crown. Everything was infused with the moral legitimacy of a maternal sovereign, her words offering a world of guarantees, from territorial integrity for princely states to freedom of religion for the masses. Writers on all sides descended into ecstasies about this 'Magna Carta of Indian Liberties', though bureaucrats in actual command prevented too liberal an interpretation by the queen's new subjects. But for all that, the proclamation generated a sweep of goodwill across the board—a clean slate for colonial officers, and hope for India's earliest generation of nationalists. And in the meantime, Queen Victoria herself was transformed, becoming India's own Victoria Maharani.

The Courtesan, the Mahatma & the Italian Brahmin

The process was a fascinating one, despite its unequal politics. From the very start, the queen had shown interest in matters Indian, often revealing a broadness of mind that horrified the men who sternly operated her government. As Miles Taylor argues in *The English Maharani*, if the queen was magnanimous, it 'always came from belonging to the winning side'. But even as she collected baubles and gems from the subcontinent, there was an awkward sincerity to her politics. The proclamation itself was a document with which she was not satisfied: she wanted a firm statement that Indians would be 'placed on an equality with [all other] subjects of the British Crown', a proposal parliament watered down to a vague line on her 'obligations of Duty' towards India. Elsewhere, she won—while an earlier draft loosely committed to the 'relief of poverty', Victoria revised this to promise Indians 'peaceful Industry', 'Works of Public Utility', and a government 'for the benefit of all Our Subjects' whose prosperity, contentment and gratitude would be the tests of its success.

Of course, what followed was revealing. To successive viceroys appointed in India at the head of an extractive state, the queen's proclamation of 1858 was held up as a mirror of shame. As late as the 1890s, Dadabhai Naoroji's campaigns in Britain cited the promise of 1858, while in 1908 Mahatma Gandhi referred to the proclamation to demand rights in South Africa. The proclamation became the standard against which the Raj could be judged, and everyone, from dethroned princelings to ordinary souls fighting property disputes, appealed to Victoria's words—and often directly to her—asking the British to live up to its meaning. Indeed, even the introduction of income tax was lambasted as flouting guarantees in the proclamation. So the men in

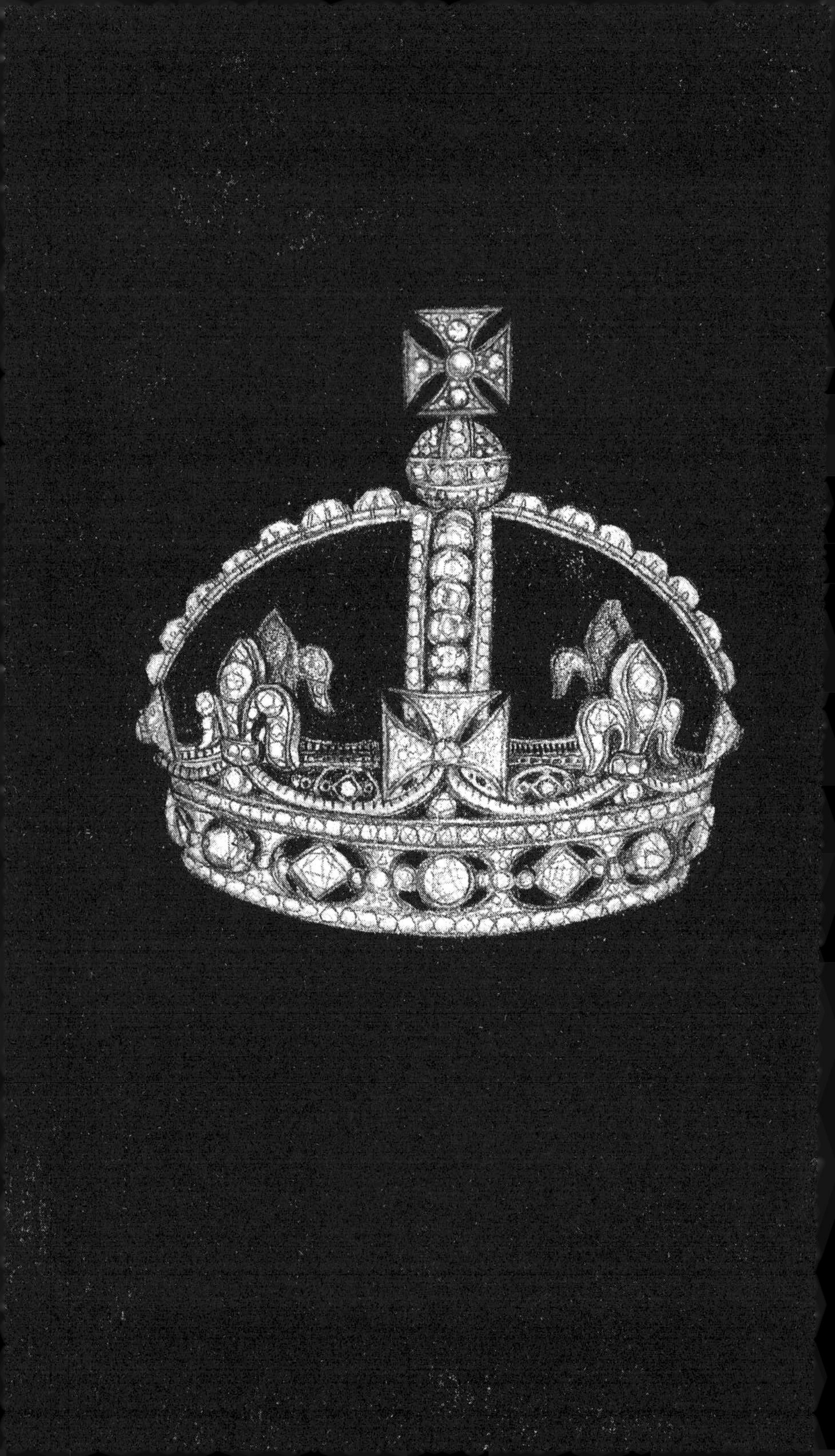

charge found a typically British solution to play things down: a protocol was evolved to determine which petitions actually reached Victoria's desk and, to quote Taylor again, soon 'the Government of India [was] transformed from postman to the sovereign to censor of the royal mail'.

Interestingly, for Victoria, India opened up something new on a deeply personal level: renewed relevance. 'Denied a political role at home' by constitutional convention, Taylor argues, 'she found it instead in her Indian dominion'. From the 1840s, for instance, she corresponded privately with viceroys, and although this still offered a lopsided picture, it eliminated some filters installed by officialdom in London. While reports of atrocities against British women during the 1857 rebellion appalled her, she soon suspected sensationalism in the press, and asked for evidence. And she revelled in the adulation that came from India's elites—whose nationalism at this stage did not sit in opposition to loyalty to the queen—as they composed poems comparing her to Hindu goddesses. Her affection for her Hindi *munshi* is, of course, well known (the letters they exchanged were destroyed after her death), and even from afar India came to mean something special for her in a way it did not for others in her establishment.

Naturally, Victoria also grew jealous of her position. During the celebrated 1875–76 tour of the country by her son and heir, Edward VII, she was determined to ensure that the masses did not mistake him for their sovereign. Much to his irritation, she made it clear that he was the viceroy's guest and not her representative. She would not even permit the prince to read out a message on her behalf to her Indian people. In fact, when the tour became a massive success, the queen chose to orchestrate a sensational event of her own to surpass it: the assumption of the title 'Empress of India'.

It was another matter that the innovation was received with borderline hostility in Britain itself, for powerful sections in the House of Commons were appalled by this gaudy claim of imperial status. The queen was furious, but the episode also highlighted the utility India held personally for her—her daughter, married to the German crown prince, was set to one day become an empress, and Victoria could not imagine being outranked by her offspring. Her son, meanwhile, used the occasion to pay his mother back in her own coin: he wrote to the prime minister that he had no desire to be styled His Imperial Highness, and was quite content as a Royal Highness.

In the end, Victoria represented something for everybody in connection with India, becoming a bridge between competing ideologies and identities. The British deployed her to contain the earliest stirrings of Indian nationalism; to Indian nationalists, her proclamation allowed for calls for reform to be issued, couched in a language of loyalism. For Victoria herself, India offered both an empire and queenly purpose, carving out for her an unparalleled position that no British monarch after her was quite able to emulate—or imitate.

THE ABSENT QUEEN OF LAKSHADWEEP

In 1781, finding herself in a tricky spot with the English East India Company, an Indian woman sent a courier to the Ottoman sultan bearing a plea for assistance. Abdul Hamid I was inclined to help and, summoning the English ambassador in Istanbul, expressed hope that 'the Beebi Sultan, the Queen of Malabar' would be treated sympathetically by his countrymen. It was a generous gesture, certainly, but like most gestures did not translate into any tangible advantage for his supplicant. In 1783, on the contrary, since she had allied with the wrong side during the Company's war against Tipu Sultan, her fort in Cannanore in Kerala was invaded, and her palace plundered. Plunder, that is, in addition to the ₹2.6 lakh she was compelled to pay as indemnity, of which a lakh, she discovered, was off the books to satisfy the personal (and secret) avarice of certain officers. A treaty was signed with both sides promising, somewhat ambitiously, to uphold it 'as long as the sun and moon shall last'. Six years later, these exalted celestial bodies were brushed aside abruptly as the two parties went to war once again; and this time, the lady lost her fort forever.

The woman in question, Junumabe II, belonged to the Arakkal family of Cannanore that had controlled the Lakshadweep islands from at least the sixteenth century, though of course no ruler ever actually condescended to visit their little kingdom, parked as they were across the water on the Indian coast. The origins of the house are obscure. One tale connects them with a legendary Malayali monarch who converted to Islam and sailed for Mecca—an eternal flame was maintained in the Arakkal Palace in memory of this 'uncle'. Another story features a Hindu princess who, the Dutch said, 'was made pregnant by a prominent Moor or Arab', spawning a Muslim royal line that followed Hindu matrilineal succession. The firstborn ruled regardless of sex as the Ali Raja; if it was a girl, she had the additional honorific of 'Bibi'. Yet another origin myth shows their ancestress in chaster light—she was drowning when a Muslim youth dived in to her rescue, but having been touched by a stranger in a compromising, watery situation, she took him and his faith as her own. A final story erases all royal links and simply points to a noble family that transferred its allegiance to Islam many centuries ago, and over time rose to princely status.

Either way, a local rajah from the mainland called the Kolathiri granted this Muslim line the sovereignty of Lakshadweep in return for adequate tribute. 'In its palmy days,' one scholar notes, 'the House administered its own laws, maintained its own currency and exercised powers of inflicting capital punishment over its subjects.' These subjects are believed to have gone in boats from Kerala to populate the islands a long time ago, some claiming descent from high-

The Courtesan, the Mahatma & the Italian Brahmin

caste Hindu clans. At a certain point, a saint revered locally as Munbe Muliyaka sailed in and persuaded them to embrace Islam, though the religion actually practised was a blend of Quranic principle and Hindu custom. It was the Portuguese who first disturbed the independence of the islands, and in the resultant bloodshed, the islanders sought the protection of the Kolathiri—the very Hindu ruler who would transfer the suzerainty he thus gained to the progeny of the drowning woman. This new royal family grew wealthy by cultivating commercial networks as far away as Arabia and Persia, and their approach to the islands now in their possession was also driven by calculations of profit and loss—a policy that led to great discontent in Lakshadweep.

It appears that the islands were viewed, from the comforts of the palace in Kerala, more as a cash cow than as a community to which its rulers also had certain obligations. In the 1760s, for instance, the Ali Raja introduced a coir monopoly under which islanders were prohibited from selling their goods to outsiders. The prices approved by the Arakkal treasury for coir were, however, vastly lower than the market rates. There were other rules too, some of them ridiculous enough to infect the air with a mood of rebellion. 'Except jaggery', we are told, 'all the minor products of the islands' (including tortoise shells) were monopolised. Cowries, for instance, were purchased dirt cheap from Lakshadweep and sold at a 400 per cent profit by its absentee princes in markets elsewhere. With tobacco, the arrangement was 'particularly scandalous', the Bibi reaping profits of up to 1,000 per cent. Agents of her government who were stationed on the island made things worse—their measly annual salaries meant they too were anxious for cuts. If a bovine were killed, the agent was entitled to a quarter of its meat. If a new boat was to be launched, the Bibi's men could seize it if they were denied their illicit fee.

In the 1780s, the cluster known as the Amindive islands revolted and pledged itself to Tipu Sultan. And when that ruler was defeated, control of these islands passed to the English as spoils of war. The Bibi, though, retained Minicoy and the Laccadive cluster, paying tribute to the Company now—during negotiations, she claimed her revenue from these was only ₹20,000, while a British investigation revealed that she drew nearly six times that figure in actual income. Her tribute was settled grudgingly at ₹15,000 a year. The islanders, however, continued to clash with their overseas royal government, and, by the middle of the nineteenth century, several years of tribute was in arrears—in 1869, it was discovered that Arakkal had, in fact, lost control over most of the islands and no longer had any revenue from them. A 'phantom sovereignty' remained in force, while the British took matters into their own hands. If Arakkal wanted the islands back, the Bibi was informed, she would have to improve her style of government—and, of course, settle the pending payments. Neither of these, everyone knew, was actually feasible.

Decades passed in this fashion, till in 1908 the impasse was broken. Imbichi Ali Raja, the then Bibi, agreed to surrender sovereignty over Laccadive and Minicoy in return for an annual *malikhana* (pension) of ₹23,000—an amount that is still paid to the family. A seven-gun salute appears to have been granted, along with British recognition of the title 'sultan' for heads of the dynasty. As for the islanders, these events generated hope of a better, or at least fairer, regime. And to a certain extent, conditions were created, if not of prosperity, of fewer exactions. After all, in shaking off the autocracy of a princess in Kerala, the islands were only placing themselves under the very different variety of tyranny that came with becoming subjects of the British empire. And any real promise of progress would have to wait for some more decades till the colonial government withdrew, and a democratic state handed over the destinies of Lakshadweep, at last, to its own people.

THE ENGINEER AND HIS RICE BOWL

In 1877, at the height of the Great Famine that devastated the south, a distinguished Englishman, recently knighted for services rendered to the British empire, yet again took a vociferous stand against the policies of his queen's government in India. For years he had railed against imperial overzeal for the railways—a sophisticated scam that funnelled out Indian resources while delivering unconscionable profits to faraway investors—and now he was vindicated. For 'we have before our eyes', he noted, 'the sad and humiliating scene of magnificent [rail] Works that have cost poor India 160 millions, which are so utterly worthless in the respect of the first want of India, that millions are dying by the side of them.' The railways certainly brought grain to starving masses, but the costs were so disproportionately high that nobody could afford to buy them—official profiteering perverted even the delivery of famine relief.

The Courtesan, the Mahatma & the Italian Brahmin

Sir Arthur Cotton had made a career of crossing the line where India was concerned, taking stands that irritated his superiors even as they earned him much local admiration—two districts of Andhra Pradesh hold an estimated 3,000 statues of the man. He was, of course, as much an imperialist as his peers, but it was not a desire to bring glory to Great Britain that motivated him. Instead, this tenth son of the tenth son of a regrettably named Sir Lynch Cotton had experienced a religious awakening as a young man in 1826. Thereafter, he felt his mission was to work 'for the glory of God ... and the benefit of men', and with familiar racial condescension, he decided that the men in question were poor brown Indians. His self-righteousness, however, was wedded to sincerity—having taken up the Indian cause, Sir Arthur never gave up, describing himself as 'a man with one idea' that could make a difference in India: irrigation.

Sir Arthur was a military engineer who caused his colleagues great consternation by refusing to be awed by steel and steam. He had no dispute with the railways but it made no sense to him that extortionate technology should be imposed on a landscape where the basics had been entirely neglected. He was also somewhat naïve—he once argued against the term 'collector' since it suggested that the sole interest of revenue officials lay in extracting money, when surely they were also responsible for that other thing called development. The architects of the Raj, of course, were under no such delusions—the collector was there precisely to collect, and Sir Arthur's lifelong mistake lay in hoping that India's wants would also somehow feature in those essentially exploitative calculations masquerading as government policy. Naturally, he was thwarted by 'administrative jealousy', and many were the sneerers who called him a 'wild enthusiast' with 'water in his head'.

Still, Sir Arthur was tireless. In 1827, after inspecting the second-century Kallanai dam near Thanjavur, he regretted that 'this work, which had a population of perhaps one hundred thousand and a revenue of £40,000 dependant upon it, had not been allowed £500 to keep it in repair.' He personally rode out to persuade his superiors to correct this, only to be rebuffed. 'Government,' he was told, 'could not squander such sums as this upon the wild demands of an Engineer.' 'Is it surprising,' he asked in dismay, that 'the natives thought us savages?' Nevertheless, he kept up his interest in irrigation—learning from furloughs in Australia, as well as travels in lands as diverse as Egypt and Syria—till finally he was able to leave a real imprint along the eastern coast of India; something his daughter called 'The Redemption of the Godavari District' through, as his brother chuckled, 'The Cheap School of Engineering'—also known today by that Hindi word *jugaad*.

The British, Sir Arthur thought, brought 'disgrace to [their own] civilised country' by their 'grievous neglect' of India. He decided to make amends. When the Godavari project was sanctioned in 1847, he asked for six engineers, eight juniors and 2,000 masons. Instead, he was allotted one 'young hand', two surveyors, and a few odd men. Yet he persevered. 'To save on masonry work', Jon Wilson writes, 'he copied the method of construction' used by the Cholas. 'Cotton created a loose pile of mud and stone on the riverbed, which he then covered in lime and plastered with concrete, instead of building up entirely with stone.' The whole project was finished at a third of the cost initially estimated, till 370 miles of canals [339 of which were navigable] irrigated some 364,000 acres of land, transforming a dry expanse into the 'rice bowl' of Andhra Pradesh. And waterways, the Englishman demonstrated, were a doubly rewarding alternative to rail transport, simultaneously nourishing the farmlands of rural Indians.

In the end, however, Sir Arthur couldn't prevail over the railway lobby. Between 1885 and 1887, the railways cost £2.84 million while the irrigation budget stagnated at a measly £6,130. As late as 1898, the year before his death, it was stated that rail absorbed 'so large a measure of Government attention, [that] irrigation canals, which are far more protective against famine ... are allowed only one-thirteenth of the amount spent on railways each year'. It was easier, Sir Arthur sniffed, to propose a £4 million railway project over a £40,000 irrigation scheme. He had no dearth of ideas, however, offering a pan-India river-linking project, and bombarding his bosses with notes and suggestions till they finally established, almost out of sheer exhaustion, a Public Works Department—the ubiquitous 'PWD' of today. And after collecting his shiny knighthood, he continued to cheerfully lambast the Raj for its neglect of India, receiving a more profound honour instead from ordinary peasants, who, to this day, remember Sir Arthur less as a representative of British dominion and more as a local saviour.

THE MAN BEHIND MODERN HINDI

In 1757, on the eve of the historic Battle of Plassey, a merchant called Amir Chand alarmed the notorious Robert Clive with a fresh demand. 'Omichund', as the English knew him, had served the East India Company, assisting in their shaky relationship with the Nawab of Bengal. Now, as war looked inevitable, he also made himself indispensable, helping hatch that infamous plot by which the nawab's commander, Mir Jafar, was to betray his sovereign and join ranks with the Company. At the last minute, however, Omichund put forth an ominous clause—he wanted ₹30 lakh for his services, failing which he would (regretfully) divulge the scheme to the nawab himself. Clive was upset. But he was also shrewd: two copies of the pact with Mir Jafar were prepared. The counterfeit carried Omichund's clause, while the actual agreement said nothing about his reward. And when everything was over and the English had prevailed, the old merchant was summoned and simply told: 'Omichund, the red paper is a trick, you are to have nothing!'

It is said that Omichund died a broken man. It may have been so, for two of his sons left Calcutta to do business in Varanasi, where prosperity returned to them soon enough. But it would be some generations before one of their line could redeem the reputation of their perfidious ancestor. To be sure, this great-grandson, Harishchandra, often referred to as Bharatendu (Moon of India), was not a vengeful nationalist—before he died in 1885, many were the occasions when he hosted gatherings to demonstrate affection for the Raj that betrayed his forebear. But even as he sang of 'the Western rays of civilisation' and the 'progressive policy of the British nation', Harishchandra's contributions to the development of Hindi carved for him a place in the eyes of posterity. He might have composed panegyrics when births and weddings took place in Queen Victoria's household and tried his best to meet the visiting Prince of Wales, but it was also his pen that helped propel a movement to transform a neglected language of mixed origins into a mass cultural campaign that culminated in that famous cry, 'Hindi, Hindu, Hindustan'.

Harishchandra began life in 1850 in a combination of tragedy and grandiosity. He lost his parents young but grew up so rich that all his life his greatest difficulty was how not to mismanage more of his money. He founded and edited one of India's first women's journals, *Balabodhini*, but to his own wife all he offered was neglect. If an object caught his eye—a camera perhaps, or a new perfume—he required it at once. 'This money,' he laughed, 'has eaten my ancestors; now I am going to eat it.' But even as he reduced life to an oscillation between debt and extravagance, he also left behind a mark that endures to this day. His *Kavivachansudha* (founded 1868) and *Harishchandrachandrika* (founded 1873) emerged as iconic platforms for literary exchange in northern

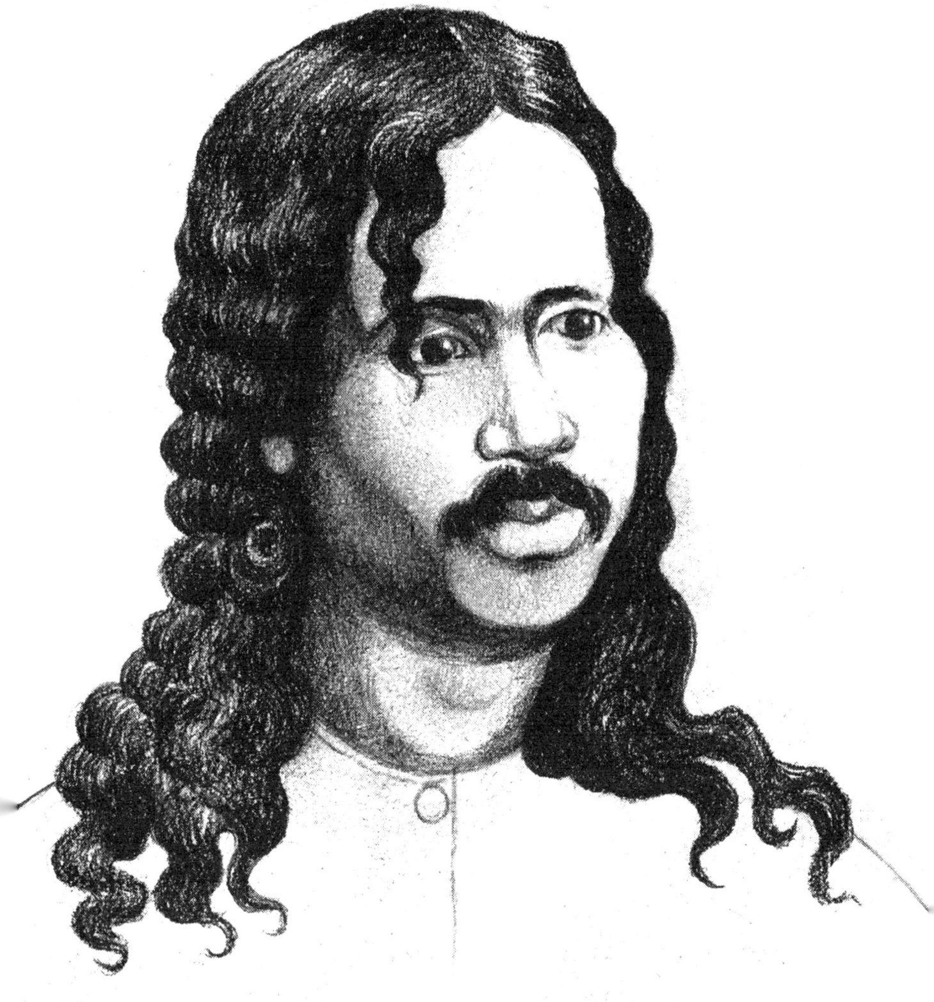

India. Featuring Dadabhai Naoroji's drain theory as well as news from the local Dharma Sabha, it was through these publications that Harishchandra, as the scholar Vasudha Dalmia notes, 'veritably created literary Hindi' even as he gently voiced his support for Hindu consolidation. He became a catalyst for a vernacular nationalism that would achieve full force in the following century, simultaneously rising as the 'Father of Modern Hindi Literature and Hindi Theatre'.

If modern Hindi is today well entrenched, where it comes from is an issue that still provokes debate. As Harish Trivedi writes, 'Hindi was commonly perceived to be an underdeveloped and underprivileged language, fragmented into several competing dialects, backward and dusty by association with its largely rural constituency'. The British recognised Urdu, instead, as the north's language of government. Since it was spoken primarily by elite Muslims, this stirred resentment among others who competed for jobs but did not know Urdu. As Harishchandra argued, thanks to this official bias, Muslims enjoyed 'a sort of monopoly' where employment was concerned, which was not only 'injustice' but also 'a cause of annoyance and inconvenience' to masses of Hindi speakers who also happened largely to be Hindus. His rival and contemporary, Raja Sivaprasad, similarly insisted that the use of the Urdu script meant that for large numbers of common folk, government papers and documents were as alien as 'hieroglyphics'. The matter was not black and white, but the message carried resonance. Both languages were cousins derived from the same roots—one was truer to Sanskrit, while the other had gained much from Arabic and Persian. Now they increasingly became rivals.

But this movement also coincided with an urge to make new literature—something modern and suited to emerging feelings of cultural and political nationalism. Much of the poetry in Hindi was in the Brajbhasha and Awadhi dialects, traditionally considered prestigious but thought to be encumbered by an excess of devotion and piety. Khariboli, the dialect spoken around Delhi and present-day Uttar Pradesh, on the other hand, was an open vessel for literary innovation. 'The progress of one's own language is the root of all progress,' Harishchandra argued, and page after page in his magazine was devoted to plays, poetry, satire and essays, all of which combined to create a new corpus for speakers of an increasingly standardised Hindi. Khariboli was swiftly invested with pride and disseminated widely through Harishchandra's energy and enthusiasm. Only he could have pulled it off—wealthy, flamboyant, and with personal networks stretching from British officials to Bengal's reformers, he was noticed in the right circles. That he also centred his activities in Varanasi, a city of special significance for Hindus in a time of political consolidation, further legitimised his ventures.

In 1885, not yet thirty-five, Harishchandra died, by now less convinced of the Raj and its goodness for India. But what he had helped launch assumed a life of its own, becoming the Modern Standard Hindi of today in the course of a few decades. By 1893, a Nagari Pracharini Sabha emerged to lobby for official recognition of Hindi and Devanagari—the request was granted in 1900. By 1910, the Hindi Sahitya Sammelan was born, of which Gandhi remained a member longer than he was of the Congress. Gandhi, in fact, went to the extent of advising south Indians that the 'Dravidians being in a minority... they should learn the common language of the rest of India'—a patronising remark that inspired C.N. Annadurai to quip that by this fallacious logic of numbers, the best candidate for national bird in India was not the minority peacock but the majority crow.

But change was already in the air. Poets and writers raised to think of Urdu as the language of culture invested increasingly in Hindi. As Premchand wrote in 1915, 'Urdu will no longer do. Has any Hindu ever made a success of writing in Urdu, that I will?' This 'Hindi Renaissance' was infused with nationalism and some even drew links to 1857—seeds of a standardised Hindi were sown, they claimed, when speakers of various dialects united for the 'First War of Independence' and recognised themselves as one people.

Harishchandra did not live to see the fruits of his work—but for many, by helping Hindi rise to its feet, he more than paid off his ancestor's debt. Omichund may have erred by siding with the British, but by creating a vehicle for cultural and national aspirations, Harishchandra earned only honour.

THE RAILWAYS AND INDIA

In 1857, soon after the sepoys rose against the East India Company in a burst of volcanic fury, the *Delhi Gazette* carried a proclamation issued in the name of the Mughal emperor, Bahadur Shah Zafar. Popularly called the Azamgarh Proclamation, this was authored most likely by a junior member of the imperial household, though its contents are not remotely less fascinating on this account. Besides predictable denouncements of the 'tyranny and oppression of the treacherous' English, the document was also a manifesto that sought to win support from influential quarters, offering—like political manifestos today—a cascade of promises. Thus, for instance, the rights of zamindars were guaranteed, just as attractive pay was guaranteed to soldiers. More interestingly, among promises made to the commercial classes was one that speaks much of the age in which the mutiny took place. For it was pledged to men of trade that when the *badshahi* regime was restored, they would enjoy 'gratis' the use of 'government steam-vessels and steam carriages for the conveyance' of their all-important merchandise.

As it happened, the rebels scattered and the Mughal emperor fell. But on his journey to Burma (now Myanmar) in a bullock cart, Bahadur Shah Zafar did witness the construction of railway lines on which would ply the 'steam carriages' that only yesterday were being offered free in his name. While rebel leaders discerned advantages in this new mode of transport for purposes of trade, they were hardly alone: Ten years earlier, *The Times* in London had claimed that while 'there may be no diamonds [left] at Golconda', there was 'the worth of a ship-load of diamonds in the cotton fields of the Deccan'. All that was needed to exploit this plentiful land was a reliable network. Then, of course, the mutiny confirmed for the British the military advantage that the railways offered, as loyal armies could in future make their way at record speed and contain any threat of rebellion. This, perhaps, was among the reasons that agitated Gandhi when he beheld the welding of India's geography with steel and steam. He declared ominously that this was all for 'bad men [to] fulfil their evil designs with greater rapidity'.

Leaving the Mahatma's suspicions aside, the railways in India roused many, from Rudyard Kipling to Rabindranath Tagore, Florence Nightingale to R.K. Narayan. Talk of its introduction in the subcontinent began in the 1830s and, ironically, the concerns raised were endless. One question was of viability: would 'the Hindoos', with their caste and religious taboos, embrace the railways, or would they boycott it resolutely? In the event, 'the Hindoos' nodded approval: pilgrimages that took weeks could now be covered in days, even if by means of the devil's contraption. Others argued that the fire carriage was at best a vanity project—India's destiny lay in waterways, insisted Sir Arthur Cotton, whom we encountered in a previous essay. Yet another set of people welcomed the steam engine for its political potential. 'If India is to become a homogenous nation,' wrote Sir T. Madhava Rao, the nineteenth-century statesman, 'it must be by means of the Railways [and]... the English language.' (Good for him that he lived then, for today he would be labelled anti-national.)

The dawn of the Indian railways (now the fourth largest in the world, transporting billions, and with over a million employees), like new technology in general, inspired opportunity while also birthing subversion. As the scholar Arup K. Chatterjee writes, the railways could become 'clandestine spaces for experimentation' where 'vegetarian looking businessmen' tasted chicken and mutton: removed physically from their everyday universe, days and hours spent on the track offered a window into something new, something that was usually taboo. To Europeans in India, meanwhile, the way the railways functioned offered a 'nominal provincial Europe' on wheels, where the food, cutlery, decor and everything else reminded them of home. There could also be disease and horror—to quote Ira Klein, 'plague [too] rode the rails'. In 1947, similarly, the railways conveyed death across the border, as photographs recorded their role in the appalling tragedy of India's partition.

The British, of course, presented the railways as proof of their civilising mission—this, when it was an elaborate commercial enterprise delivering obscene profits to English investors at the expense of the Indian peasant. The railways also allowed for architectural experiments: buildings like the erstwhile Victoria Terminus in Bombay projected colonial splendour, visually stamping India with the presence (and threat) of British supremacy. To the dismay of the architects of empire, however, the railways also ended up transporting that inconvenient thing called nationalism. Soon, even the Mahatma was able to Indianise the railways, using it, as Chatterjee notes, to collect donations just as much as to demand Swaraj, every station and every third-class carriage a platform for his invigorating politics. Revolutionaries, meanwhile, could disrupt rail lines, and even such small things as travelling ticketless or pulling the chain became acts of civil disobedience. What began as a (lucrative) civilising mission ended up embodying Indian resistance.

In the end, the story of the railways in India is one of splendour as well as shock, elegance as well as embarrassment, opening up many worlds in which its carriages and engines served as both witnesses and participants. In its early avatar, it was a symbol of colonial oppression. But like with foreign ideas that were seized by Indians for their own domestic purposes and intentions, the railways quickly won local imagination, becoming integral to the shaping of India's national character. The Father of the Nation might well have continued to suspect the railways even as he used it, but there is no doubt that its steel frame occupies a place of importance in the tale of the Indian people: one that bridged far and diverse provinces, even as it connected everyone from Bahadur Shah Zafar to the Mahatma himself.

THE PHULES AND THEIR FIGHT

When Jyotirao Phule (1827–90) embarked with his partner, Savitribai, on their journey to promote radical (and necessarily painful) internal reform, he had already smashed the social shackles that came with being the son of a greengrocer and the grandson of a gardener (*mali*) in orthodox Pune. This was a boy who received a rudimentary education in Marathi, found himself married before thirteen to a bride of less than ten, and who then resumed his education in a Christian mission school at the insistence of a Muslim neighbour. While 'correct' behaviour would have been to quietly keep stock of pulses and vegetables and pursue his family profession, Phule digested Thomas Paine's *Rights of Man* and *The Age Of Reason* and charted a course of his own, asking all those inconvenient questions that reason sparks in sensible people.

Jyotirao must have been an unusual man at the time for transmitting the ideas he absorbed to his wife—indeed, not only did he tutor her in private, he supported her when she embarked on a teachers' training course in Ahmednagar, far away from home. They were on either side of twenty when the they ventured into female education in 1848, dismissing the resultant conservative hysteria as 'idiotic beliefs'. 'There was no school for girls that could be called 'indigenous' at that time here,' Jyotirao told a government commission later. And so 'I was inspired to set up such a school' where 'My wife and I worked... for several years.' Activities had to be briefly suspended for some time, but soon after they were resumed in the form of not one but three girls' schools in 1851, the Phules offered a remarkable 237 candidates for examination—an event so sensational that, according to Hari Narake, as many as 3000 people gathered to witness the proceedings. As a newspaper correspondent reported in the summer of 1852, 'The number of girl students in Jotirao's school in ten times more than the number of boys studying in the government schools... If the Government Education Board does not do something about [the inferior quality of its own schools] soon, seeing these women outshine the men will make us hang our heads in shame.'

All this was revolutionary enough, but Jyotirao, who drew inspiration from George Washington and dedicated his most significant book—*Gulamgiri* (1873)—to 'the good people of the United States' for eliminating slavery there, went on to establish a school for untouchables with Savitribai. And this in a city where, until recently, the government of the brahmin Peshwas required the low-born to move around with brooms tied to their waists so that the ritual defilement they brought into town could also be brushed away after every polluting step. The consequences of such radicalism were dire. As Jyotirao himself stated in an 1853 interview, his father threw his wife and him out of his house in response to their controversial activities. Conservative angst manifested in petty ways too: when, for instance, Jyotirao was draped at a public felicitation with a ceremonial shawl, many insisted that the son of a *mali* did not deserve such an honour, no matter what his personal or professional achievements.

Yet, recognition came steadily to the Phules: *The Poona Observer and Deccan Weekly* noted how their work was 'the beginning of a new epoch in the history of Hindu culture,'. The couple themselves did not rest on encomiums: As Jyotirao, aged only twenty-five, declared after he was honoured by the Government of Bombay, 'What I may have done towards furthering the cause of educating native females is indeed too little and falls far short even of the demands of duty as one of the sons of the beloved land.' A lot more energy and enterprise were needed to make a lasting difference, and prioritising the girl child, the Phules were convinced, was the secret to the reform of social structures and the Indian family. That said, public events where he appeared also served as platforms for Jyotirao to disseminate his radicalism even if he did not have the wherewithal to scale up his activities to the extent he desired. In 1853, for example, he lambasted the brahmin orthodoxy for its stand against female education, stating that, 'In their opinion, women should forever be kept in obedience, should not be given any knowledge, should not be well-educated, should not know about religion, should not mix with men, and they bring out extracts from our Shastra in which women are so deprecated, in support of these idiotic beliefs, and ask whether anything written by the great and learned sages be untrue!'

Every inch a contrarian, Jyotirao was clearly willing to take on his largely high-caste opponents even in the intellectual realm, without mincing words or concealing his indignation.

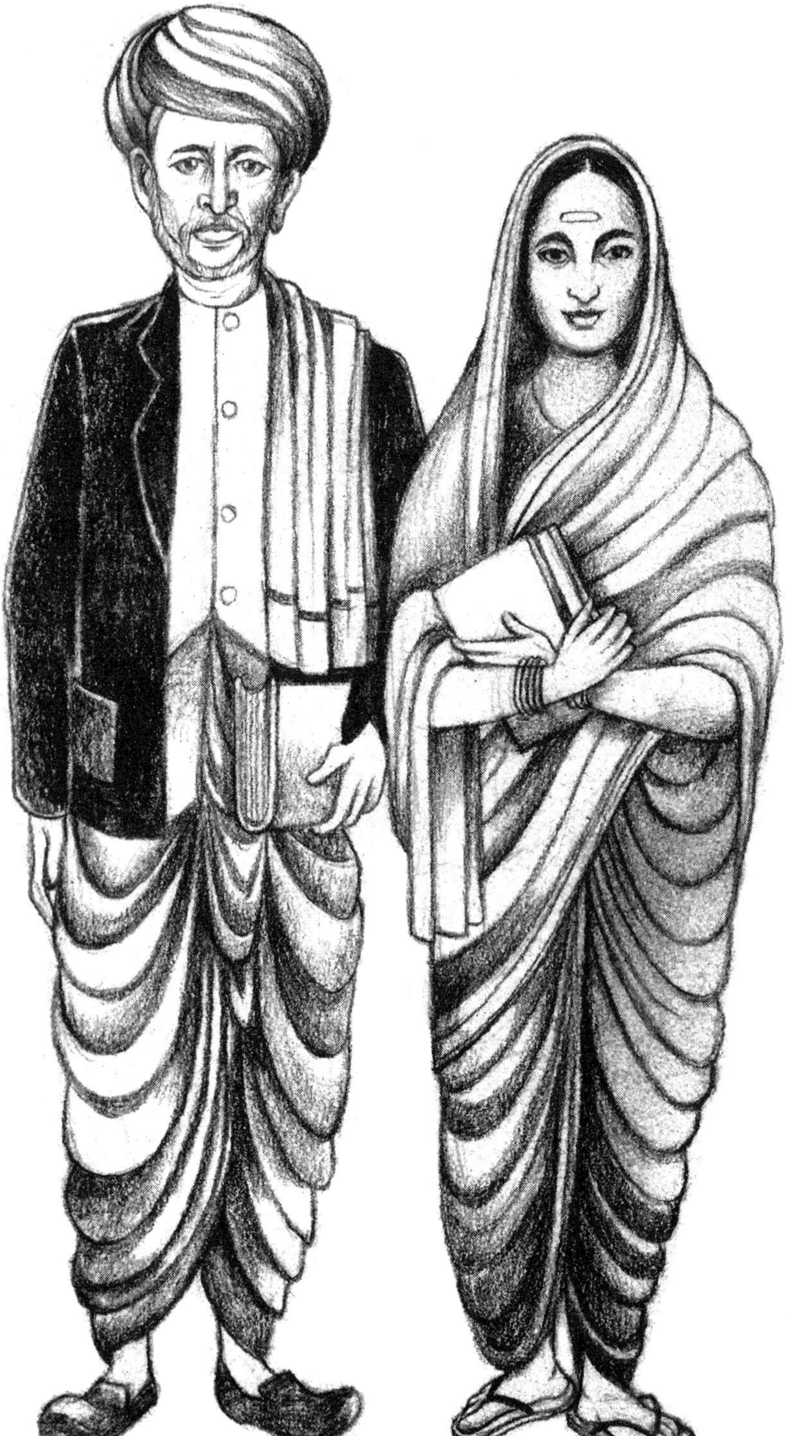

The Courtesan, the Mahatma & the Italian Brahmin

He dusted up in the dialect of the poor (which was thought crude) tales of the Maratha king Shivaji's valour, casting him as a protector of peasants and upholder of the rights of the weak. His irate respondents reacted with the more enduring construction of Shivaji as a protector of sacred cows and Sanskritic high tradition. Jyotirao didn't care and carried on with his criticism. When brahmins claimed that they were high because they were born from Brahma's mouth, Jyotirao enquired if the creator also menstruated from that area, before deploying Darwin to demolish his scandalised interlocutors.

Because Jyotirao was a man, and an influential man with access to the British, it was Savitribai who often faced physical retaliation for their work. This came in the form of being pelted with dung and stones while she walked to their schools, for example. She remained undaunted, inspiring her husband and countless others.

There was, for instance, an incident in a village outside Pune, where an untouchable girl was made pregnant by her upper-caste lover. Lynching was proposed—the boy for disgracing his family's honour and the girl for being disgrace itself—when Savitribai appeared. 'I came to know about their murderous plan,' she wrote to her husband later, with a palpable sense of accomplishment, '[and] rushed to the spot.' And there she 'scared [the mob] away, pointing out the grave consequences of killing the lovers under the British law'.

Naturally, many grumbled that with his tributes to the West and reliance on new freedoms enshrined in colonial law, Jyotirao was an unpatriotic lackey, and his partner an equally hopeless proposition. But as it happened, the Phules merrily exasperated the British too. In 1888, the colonial authorities extended to Jyotirao the honour of an invitation to dine with Prince Arthur, Duke of Connaught. Jyotirao accepted, only to horrify his Victorian interlocutors by arriving in peasant's garb, a torn shawl his chief accessory (well before Gandhi made a similar statement by going to meet the King of England in a loincloth). He proceeded to lecture Queen Victoria's son that he must not mistake his dinner companions that evening as representative of India—it was the voiceless poor who were the soul of the land. On another occasion, when the local municipality sought to demonstrate loyalty to the Governor of Bombay through an extravagant 1,000-rupee present, Jyotirao alone among thirty-two members opposed the idea, insisting that the money be spent on something more worthwhile than fanning the already inflated vanity of yet another Englishman. Something such as education.

Sharp in his attacks on hypocrisy within Indian society, Jyotirao was equally upset with the colonial tendency to privilege Indian elites even in Western institutions. What 'contribution', he asked, 'have these [elites] made to the great work of regenerating their fellowmen? How have they begun to act upon the masses? Have any of them formed classes at their own homes or elsewhere, for the instruction of their less fortunate or less wise countrymen? Or have they kept their knowledge to themselves, as a personal gift, not to be soiled by contact with the ignorant vulgar? Have they in any way shown themselves anxious to advance the general interests and repay the philanthropy with patriotism? Upon what grounds is it asserted that the best way to advance the moral and intellectual welfare of the people is to raise the standard of instruction among the higher classes? A glorious argument this for aristocracy, were it only tenable!' In other words, while the elites sought Western education and rights for themselves, they did not seem motivated enough when it came to empowering their own traditional inferiors. They too, essentially, were guardians of their own privilege.

The Courtesan, the Mahatma & the Italian Brahmin

When Jyotirao died, a few years after he suffered a debilitating heart attack, many thought the nuisance had finally withdrawn to the proverbial grave (he was cremated, though he originally wanted to be buried). Savitribai, however, continued to infuriate the elders, breaching convention yet again by not only appearing at her dead husband's cremation, but by also lighting the pyre. She died seven years later, following the great plague of 1897—after facing financial crises and a number of other personal and professional difficulties—but across western India and beyond, she is still remembered through the rousing anthem she left:

May all our sorrows and plight disappear
Let the brahmin not come in our way
With this war cry, awaken!
Strive for education
Overthrow the slavery of tradition
Arise to get education.

It is no wonder, then, that hundreds of books have since been written on the Phules of Pune, whose tireless fight did not focus merely on the political, but unhesitatingly exposed the rot within traditional social structures—the nerve centre of Indian culture, and a place that few before or after them had the courage to try and question.

THE AMMACHIES OF TRAVANCORE

In 1912, a magazine in London carried a feature on the wife of an Indian maharajah. 'Whenever a stranger goes to Travancore, one of the largest and most picturesque native States,' it began, 'they always tell him not to address her as "Your Highness". They think this word is too dignified to apply to her. No doubt she is the Ruler's spouse; but that does not make her the Maharani or even the Rani. She is only Ammachi, just the mother of His Highness' children, and they believe that word is good enough to express her relationship to the man who is autocrat of more than 2,950,000 people, inhabiting [over] seven thousand square miles of territory, yielding an annual revenue of about £700,000.'

Visitors to Kerala often found themselves fascinated by the matrilineal system that governed succession among its leading dominant castes. For here, to put it simplistically, a family did not consist of man, wife and children but of man, sister and her children. In the royal family too, much to the disbelief of outsiders, the wife of the maharajah was not his queen—she could only be addressed as 'the consort' and had no claims to being a 'Highness'. There was, however, a maharani, the difference being that she was either the sister or niece of the ruler, and it was she who produced heirs to the throne through a male 'consort' of her own. Power always descended from uncle to nephew and not father to son, and no maharajah had ever inherited the throne from his father, and no son of his could ever claim anything more than a glamorous bloodline.

Similarly, the husbands of the Maharanis of Travancore had no official standing at court and as late as the 1920s, when the ruling queen granted her husband precedence over her chief minister at a banquet, it caused a minor scandal—one could be married to royalty, but one remained a subject. If she went out, it was essential that her consort followed in a separate car, and if by some breach of protocol he travelled with her, it was essential he sat *opposite* and not next to his wife. At feasts in the palace, the maharani was served four varieties of *payasam*—her husband received two. Most tellingly, perhaps, the partners of the princesses of Travancore were not permitted to sit in their presence, and had always to address their wives as 'Highnesses', never by name. When the aforementioned maharani had earlier decided to 'modernise' things and permit her husband to take a seat and to drive with her, her uncle, the maharajah, 'much disapproved' of such radical innovations.

If this was the status of the men who married the Maharanis of Travancore, the female consorts of its maharajahs were in a similar boat. When in the 1860s Theodore Jensen, a Danish painter, arrived in Thiruvananthapuram to do a portrait of the ruler and his consort, he was baffled to discover that they would not give him joint sittings even though the painting was to show them together. As Samuel Mateer, a contemporary missionary, noted, 'The Ammachi… is not a member of the royal household, has neither official nor social position at court, and cannot even be seen in public with the ruler whose associate she is.' When the maharajahs' daughters were married, the fathers did not attend the ceremonies—they were his offspring but they were not his matrilineal kin. And when a maharajah died, his children were not permitted at the funeral. So too, when the consort of a Maharani was on his deathbed, he was removed from the palace. They could have been married for decades, but a consort always remained a mere consort and could not defile the palace by dying there.

This was both on account of matrilineal conventions as well as due to reasons of caste. The wife of the maharajah, in particular, was never his social equal. The Ammachies were chosen from the Nair community, which was the most important non-brahmin upper-caste in Kerala. But its members did not wear the sacred brahminical thread and were, therefore, a rank below the Maharajahs of Travancore, who had acquired the thread and a social upgrade in the eighteenth century. Food cooked by his consort could never be touched by a maharajah (though fried items and pickles were exceptions—and it is very likely many princes cheated). Indeed, as late as the 1940s, wives of royal men were not entertained at feasts. As a member of the family would recall:

The whole family would assemble for this ritual [feast] but not the Ammachies. They couldn't come anywhere near us when a meal was being eaten and if by accident they did, then the whole meal had to be sent back—because if anyone below caste set foot in the room while the meal was in progress, it would have to be cooked again. Dinner was always a bit more relaxed because that was after sunset, when everything is more relaxed.

For all this, however, the wives of the maharajahs were not concubines. They were legitimate spouses whose status, in the patriarchal system, is most comparable to morganatic wives, i.e. women married to high-born men on the understanding that they could not inherit their titles and estates. Often the Ammachies were strong, accomplished women and their lives with the maharajahs moving romances. One maharajah in the 1850s hosted a durbar in honour of Queen Victoria to satisfy his British overlords. But once the formalities were over, he hastened to join his ailing consort, who died that very night, leaving him distraught. In 1882, another prince, upon the death of his wife—the woman with whom he could not be seen in public, whose food he was prohibited from touching, and to whom he could never grant more than aristocratic status—wrote: 'The loss is an irreparable one and it is more than I could bear with all my fortitude.' He didn't marry again for nearly twenty years.

In 1885, when the then maharajah lay on his deathbed, 'he sent for his Consort and children, and they came before him in the evening very late. He beckoned his daughters to approach close to the cot, and the light not being very bright, he bade his Consort trim the flickering lamp, in order to enable him to see his daughters well, and he gazed on them for a while and wept. His Consort and children also wept; but he told them that God would protect and help them, and asked them to take leave. His Consort, his son, and daughters prostrated themselves at his feet, according to oriental custom, and took their last farewell. On the same night his Consort and his eldest daughter took ill, being overcome with grief.' Part of the concern might also have been that this particular Maharajah had left them little money—his predecessor had ensured that his wife was extremely well taken care of, and this allowed him to depart somewhat in peace.

History has erased the Ammachies from memory on account of the fact that their sons never succeeded to power—at least the consorts of the maharanis fathered monarchs and could therefore claim some celebrity, unlike the wives of maharajahs, who disappeared into the shadows after the lifetimes of their royal husbands. Kalyani Pillai, the wife of the maharajah who ruled from 1860 till 1880 was a poet of talent, with interests in art, culture, music, and more, emerging as one of the earliest patrons of Raja Ravi Varma, the painter. An exquisitely good-looking woman, hers are also some of the earliest portraits Ravi Varma did. She was also a very confident woman, this daughter of the chief minister of neighbouring Cochin state, who had been married once before she met the maharajah. Visitors to court called on her, and she scandalised the orthodox by taking English lessons and inviting missionaries to read the Bible with her in her palace. If an 1868 photograph is any proof, she was also probably the first Malayali woman to wear a sari. After her husband's passing, however, an associate noted that 'she is very thin and delicate looking, and has lost much of her beauty... She seems so friendless and lonely that I feel sorry for her...' When she died in 1909, few outside Thiruvananthapuram remembered the remarkable lady once celebrated as Nagercoil Ammachi.

The Courtesan, the Mahatma & the Italian Brahmin

Then there were consorts such as the one who features in that London magazine from 1912. 'She has a light complexion and is short and very stout', possessed as she was of 'an excess of adipose tissue' in a culture where every additional pound was seen as 'a sign of prosperity'. This lady too had been married before she was espoused by the maharajah, the difference being that her husband, a palace employee, went on to achieve tremendous notoriety as a corrupt influence behind the throne. Soon the maharajah became putty in his hands, the consort retreating to an upstairs suite in her palace where she painted landscapes, while the 'former husband of the Maharajah's present wife' became the real power in the state. When this penultimate ruler of Travancore died, his consort was forgotten too, though not her ex-husband, whose scandalous career continues to animate popular talk.

The last Maharajah of Travancore never took an official consort. While there were rumours that his mother, who was the real force behind the throne, and his long-time minister had an 'unholy pact' to keep him under their thumb and prevent a third influence on him, the official line was that the maharajah disapproved of the very matrilineal system that had vested him with power: The idea of his wife being only the consort and his children being excluded from the privileges of his dynasty were most repugnant to him. Instead he lavished his attention on the offspring of his royal sister, who remembered that after signing over Travancore to the Indian Union in 1949, he went straight to the girls' room and resumed a story he was telling them from one of the great Indian epics.

But the story of the consorts does not end with the bachelor maharajah who died in 1991. The final chapter is yet to close, for living in Bangalore in an old colonial-era house on Richmond Road is the last of the male consorts who married a princess of Travancore. He was twenty-one when, in 1938, the daughter of the maharani spotted him from her palanquin during a procession. Before he knew it, he had been elevated as her consort. Independence followed a decade later and the world changed—the princess and he chose to give up their titles and begin a new life away from the kingdom her ancestors ruled. She passed away in 2008, but her husband still lives in their large, old house, as the final of those consorts who married into what was once the House of Travancore.

MACAULAY
THE IMPERIALIST WE LOVE TO HATE

Thomas Babington Macaulay (1800–59) enjoys the unique situation of being that one British imperialist whom Indians of most political shades love to hate. Only infrequently is he remembered in the land of his birth, but in India, even the Internet generation has heard of Macaulay thanks to a controversial quote widely ascribed to him. And like most things widely ascribed in the Internet age to historical figures, this one too is a fabrication, intended to outrage thin-skinned sensibilities while reinforcing right-wing conspiracy theories. 'I have travelled across the length and breadth of India,' Macaulay allegedly declared, 'and I have not seen one person who is a beggar, who is a thief, such wealth I have seen in this country, such high moral values, people of such caliber, that I do not think we would ever conquer this country unless we break the very backbone of this nation, which is her spiritual and cultural heritage, and therefore I propose

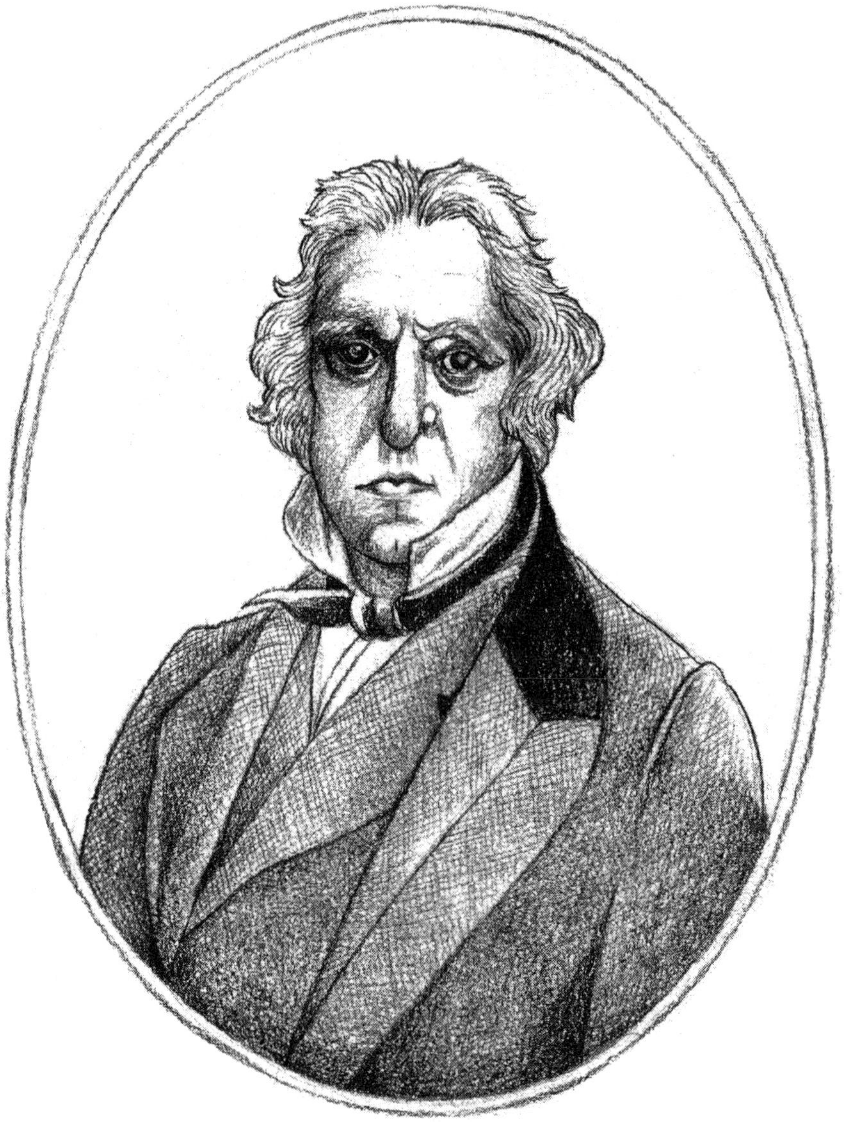

The Courtesan, the Mahatma & the Italian Brahmin

that we replace her old and ancient education system, her culture, for if the Indians think that all that is foreign and English is good and greater than their own, they will lose their self esteem, their native culture, and they will become what we want them, a truly dominated nation.'

Like most human beings, Macaulay was a man who said and did a number of contradictory things, some of which seem wholly unpleasant in retrospect. And while he did institute a new (enduring) education system in India and introduce the language in which we transact national business (English), we can be sure that he would never have endorsed the backhanded compliments which feature in that patently spurious quote. On the contrary, he despised all things Indian and spent his career admonishing Orientalists enamoured of Sanskrit and other subcontinental charms for wasting their time on 'a people who have much in common with children' (and therefore begged imperial supervision). Indian music, for instance, Macaulay dismissed as 'deplorably bad'—the only point of debate was whether it was instrumental or vocal music that was worse. The Hindu gods, all thirty-three million of them, were 'hideous, and grotesque, and ignoble'—Ganapati, for instance, was essentially 'a fat man with a paunch', and 'In no part of the world,' he claimed, 'has a religion existed more unfavourable to the moral and intellectual health of our race.' Even the higher variety of mortal Indian lacked sophistication according to him—a glance at the furniture in the Mysore maharajah's drawing room horrified Macaulay into comparing His Highness to 'a rich, vulgar Cockney cheesemonger'. But most preposterous of all was his hatred of tropical fruits—to him the mango was about as appetising as 'honey and turpentine'.

Macaulay was a consequence of his times, both in terms of his racism and his conviction that Britain 'ruled only to bless'. But before he became the scheming imperialist of Indian contestations, Macaulay was a young parliamentarian who campaigned for Jews to be able to sit in the House of Commons. He was the parvenu idealist who penetrated the aristocracy and fought to abolish slavery. Ruin, he warned, was the fate of those 'who persist in a hopeless struggle against the spirit of the age'. It was also he who declared that, 'If men are to wait for liberty till they become wise and good in slavery, they may indeed wait for ever.' It was another matter, of course, that he buried these principles in India—as we saw with his defence of Clive earlier, Macaulay did not believe the same moral compass applied to people who belonged to different cultures. Or when their characters left much to be desired.

'The physical organisation of the Bengalee is feeble even to effeminacy,' he wrote infamously. 'His pursuits are sedentary, his limbs delicate, his movements languid. During many ages he has been trampled by men of bolder and more hardy breeds.' This certainly upset many in Bengal, but to be fair, it wasn't like Macaulay was taken very seriously back home either—his *History of England* may have been a bestseller, but Marx thought him a 'systematic falsifier of history', while J.S. Mill declared that despite his superior air, he was 'an intellectual dwarf'.

And yet, Macaulay made history in India. He came to this land with prejudice in his mind, condescension in his pen—and because he was offered a salary ten times what a political career in London provided, with a generous supply of servants. He championed unpopular changes: The Indian Penal Code was the result of his labours and remains the backbone of India's legal system, despite its many un-Indian provisions. The Indian Civil Service too, from which are descended today's bureaucrats, was designed by Macaulay. But it was his *Minute On Education* (1835) that cast his name in stone. Till Macaulay's arrival, the East India Company supported what it deemed traditional Indian education in Sanskrit and Persian (i.e. education for an Indian elite who were largely brahmins and other high castes). Activists in Bengal, including the likes of Rammohun Roy, were already clamouring for access to Western schooling, and Macaulay was, to them, a godsend. 'Does it matter in what grammar a man talks nonsense?' he thundered. 'With what purity of diction he tells us that the world is surrounded by a sea of butter?' It was not the business of government to watch students 'waste their youth in learning how they are to purify themselves after touching an ass, or what text of the Vedas they are to repeat to expiate the crime of killing a goat' as was the case, he argued, with existing Sanskrit education.

Instead, Macaulay decided, Indians must learn mathematics, geography, science—and they would learn it in English. Far from singing praises of Indian culture, he saw it as British destiny to bring modernity to India—where a few decades earlier William Jones had immersed himself in Indian literature, Macaulay spent his time in Calcutta reading classics from Greece and Rome. 'It may be,' he hoped with patronising transparency, 'that the public mind of India may expand under our system till it has outgrown that system; that by good government we may educate our subjects into a capacity for better government; that, having been instructed in European knowledge, they may, in some future age, demand European institutions.' And whenever that time came, 'it will be the proudest day in English history'.

The result was that Macaulay succeeded in replacing brahminical education with Western institutions, throwing open schools to all Indians. They could recite the Vedas at home if they so wished, but at school, children would absorb the fruits of European modernity. Nativists resented Macaulay but there were others who embraced his policy—after all, the likes of Jyotirao Phule, son of a gardener, could never enter Sanskrit schools but were welcome in English institutions. They felt no shame in being painted 'Macaulayputras' when the alternative was demeaning drudgery in service of the upper castes, who only appeared less haughty than Englishmen because they were brown and looked more familiar.

'Too clever by half, too certain of what is truth, what falsity,' as a scholar put it, Macaulay's behaviour may also have had a great deal to do with his personal life and character. Very likely sexually repressed, he was obsessively attached to his sisters—the marriage of one resembled, for him, a personal calamity, and his death before sixty was hastened very likely by dread brought on by the imminent departure for India of the other. Studiously proper in his personal manners at first, he was bullied at school and grew into a stout little adolescent—indeed, even as a grown man he was lampooned in the British press as a 'shapeless little dumpling'. His statistician father expected better from Macaulay, and produced a catalogue of his faults and weaknesses. 'Loud-speaking, affected pronunciation in reading, late lying in bed, neglect of cleanliness': these were some of the crimes for which he was pulled up. Cambridge, however, liberated him and as the writer Zareer Masani notes, here he was 'at the centre of a scintillating intellectual circle ... [spending] days and nights reading, sharing and debating poetry, philosophy and politics'. So when Macaulay the Elder called him out for being too fond of novels, a supposedly undignified habit, Macaulay the Younger had enough courage to respond that he didn't care for criticism from men who were 'mere mathematical blocks... beings so stupid in conversation, so uninformed on every subject of history, of letters and of taste... To me,' he concluded in triumphant rebellion, 'the attacks of such men are valuable as compliments.'

India was merely one remunerative chapter in Macaulay's life as a writer, parliamentarian and public intellectual in England—he came here not so much out of choice but because his father's financial debacles placed great pressure on him to support the family. But having set foot in this country almost by accident, and despite his mulish character, he left behind a complicated legacy that still affects government, education, and the law in India. He famously wanted to create a class 'Indian in blood and colour, but English in tastes, in opinions, in morals and in intellect'. To them, he grandly proposed, the British could bequeath the gift of modernity so that they might educate their inferiors and bring light to India. Even before he set eyes on Indian shores, he was clear about this—in 1831, he was convinced that in a generation there would 'not be a brahmin in Hindustan who will not eat beef'. Little did he know that Indians have a unique capacity to absorb what is offered by the world, and to Indianise it altogether—the class he created, far from venerating the British in gratitude, turned instead against them. Its heroes united and forged a new Indian nationalism, using English and Enlightenment ideals to hold up a mirror to the oppressions of their colonisers. One wonders what Macaulay would have made of such Indians, from M.G. Ranade down to M.K. Gandhi. But of one thing we can be sure: whichever way the 'civilising' project in India went, Macaulay himself would never concede he made a mistake.

FOOTBALL AND NATIONALISM IN INDIA

In 1314, the mayor of London issued a proclamation banning a particularly rowdy sport that had captured the imagination of large numbers of the city's residents. There was, he announced, a 'great noise' in town caused by this 'hustling over large balls', and so, 'on pain of imprisonment', the game was outlawed in the name of King Edward II—and, of course, god. The whole business concerned what we recognise today by the innocent name of football, but at the time it was considered a monstrous affair, as men kicked about an inflated pig's bladder from one village to another. No rules existed, and the upper classes sneered at this disorderly pastime of their inferiors, oblivious that centuries down the line, 'ffooteball' fever would infect the entire world, birthing an industry so profitable that even god might be forgiven for reconsidering his position.

As with the English language, when the British transported football to India, they didn't expect the 'natives' to match them at it. Records suggest that it was in 1721, in Gujarat, that western traders first began to play cricket, while the earliest extant report of football appears over a century later, in an 1854 newspaper. This second sport, however, was inaugurated on India's eastern flank, in Bengal, when the (white) 'Gentlemen of Barrackpore' played against the (white) 'Calcutta Club of Civilians'. Football, by now, was acquiring a distinct shape and structure, with formal rules and codes. That these rules varied from place to place did not matter—the Victorians had realised that this was a 'masculine' exercise for boys as they grew into men, besides serving as an outlet for dangerous hormonal energies. Controlled aggression in an authorised environment appeared to impart lessons in discipline, obedience, honourable victories and dignified defeats. And so, slowly, football became respectable.

It was another matter that the British were not particularly dignified in the manner in which they passed on the sport to Indians. They had their exclusive clubs in various cities, besides the teams of army regiments. But even after the 1880s, when Indians formed their own clubs in Bengal—Shobhabazar, Aryans, and so on—the establishment thought little of locals and their sporting capabilities. 'By his legs you shall know a Bengali,' declared one journalist in 1899, asserting that the typical Calcutta male's legs were either hopelessly thin, or else 'very fat and globular ... with round thighs like a woman's.' 'The Bengali's leg', simply put, was 'the leg of a slave' (Macaulay would have approved). And this at the end of a decade when Bengali clubs had already started to win small victories against British teams, and just before Mahatma Gandhi was inspired to establish in South Africa his 'Passive Resisters Soccer Club'.

What really announced India's arrival on the football scene, however, was the contest between the Mohun Bagan Athletic Club and the East Yorkshire regiment for the legendary Indian Football Association (IFA) Shield in 1911. The team was representative of emerging middle-class Indian aspirations—one member, the sports historian Ronojoy Sen records, was a clerk, while another was an employee of the Public Works Department. A third was a veterinary inspector, but all of them were products of the English education system, with a growing consciousness of their identity as Indians. They played barefoot, partly because a pair of boots in the early 1900s didn't cost less than ₹7—an average schoolteacher's monthly salary. It was no surprise, then, that when Mohun Bagan made it to the finals, against all odds, the football maidan attracted some 100,000 visitors, including from as far away as Bihar, Orissa and Assam.

As it happened, the Indians won both the trophy and much prestige. 'May god bless the Immortal Eleven of Mohun Bagan for raising their nation in the estimation of the Western people,' rhapsodised the *Amrita Bazar Patrika*, noting that this victory demolished the old jibe about Bengalis being 'lamentably deficient' in physical prowess. Besides reasserting the Indian male's masculinity, the victory of a barefoot team against a privileged English set also rang resoundingly of nationalism—as the scholar Partha Chatterjee notes, the win in 1911 came at a time when Bengal was electrified by armed resistance against the Raj, not to speak of agitation challenging the partition of the province by the Viceroy, Lord Curzon, six years earlier. If sport had helped discipline Englishmen to grip the world in the Victorian era, football shattered imperial arrogance as Indians reclaimed their pride at the close of the Edwardian age.

Of course, expectations of football sparking a righteous nationalist fire did not pan out quite so romantically. As with cricket in Bombay, where Parsis played against Hindus who played against Muslims, in football too, differences and disagreements reared their heads. In 1911, the Mohammedan Sporting Club enthusiastically celebrated the victory of their 'Hindu brethren' against the British, but by the 1930s the mood had chilled. There was the leading 'Muslim club' and then there were 'Hindu clubs', for whom rivalry went beyond sport. Among the Hindus, there emerged an additional problem of regionalism—the East Bengal Club was formed mainly on account of a grievance that West Bengalis looked down on easterners. In other words, where two decades earlier nationalism had electrified the sports arena, football was afflicted now by the poison of communalism and its divisive cousins.

It might have spelt wholesale disaster, but luckily, a change in political winds transformed the horizon. With the Second World War and the advent of independence, sport for the love of sport—and not as a vehicle of nationalism or communal pride—slowly began to become possible. And in 1947, with those very legs once written off as resembling those of slaves, Indians turned around and gave the British a proverbial kick off the field they had for so long sought to dominate. New problems emerged—of poor infrastructure and state indifference—which plague sport to this day in India. But by then Indians had already embraced football, doing their bit to transform an old game that once featured a pig's bladder into an enduring obsession of their own.

MANUBAI
THE RANI BEFORE THE BATTLE

Manubai Tambe was a woman of formidable spirit, long before she was lost to a nationalistic fog of myth and legend. Better known by her more elaborate name, Manikarnika, she was a sharp judge of horses. She wrote official letters in Persian and during the rebellion of 1857 famously led men—and women—into battle. Round of face, she was taller than most of her peers, and is said to have favoured simplicity, unlike the bejewelled depiction chosen by today's film directors. 'She bore,' an Englishman later recorded, 'all the outward signs of a powerful intellect and an unconquerable resolution.' But if there was one thing that ruined the impression she left, it was her voice: as her legal adviser bemoaned, when the Rani of Jhansi began to speak, substance of great intelligence was conveyed in a sound that could only be described as 'something between a whine and a croak'.

Lakshmibai, a name bestowed on her after her marriage (and one which she would make famous), was not born royal. Her father, Moropant, was a retainer of the Peshwas of Pune, serving the latter even after they were deposed by the British. It was in Varanasi that the future rani was born to this brahmin, though the auspiciousness of the setting was dulled somewhat by the loss of her mother. Moropant gave his daughter both affection and the confidence born of education: she read, she rode, she fenced, and she saw to it that her male playmates treated her as an equal. Many are the tales woven around her fascinating personality: once, it is said in a story that survives in multiple iterations, the Peshwa's adopted son refused to take her along on his elephant. Years later, when she was granted three wishes at her wedding, she expended one of them to courier to this old friend the present of a particularly mighty elephant.

It was as a child-bride that the heroine of 1857 first arrived in Jhansi. The Newalkar family in power here were minor royalty of recent vintage. A late eighteenth-century creation of the Peshwas, their loyalties were ceded in the early nineteenth century to the East India Company. 'Maharajadhiraj Fidvi Badshah Jamjah Inglistan' (Devoted Servant of the Glorious King of England) was the title Lord Bentinck bestowed upon them in 1832, transforming the line from subedars to maharajas. And it was when Lord Dalhousie withdrew favour in 1853 that their fortunes were reversed. In 1851, meanwhile, young Manubai had given her husband an heir, but the baby did not survive. Two years later, when the rajah followed his child to the grave, there was nobody to occupy his place. With that the stage was set for the drama that now cements Lakshmibai's memory: as the 'Jezebel of India' in unkind Victorian eyes and as a patriot in the Indian imagination.

The annexation of Jhansi, as is well known, was opposed by the rani. It so happened that from his deathbed, her

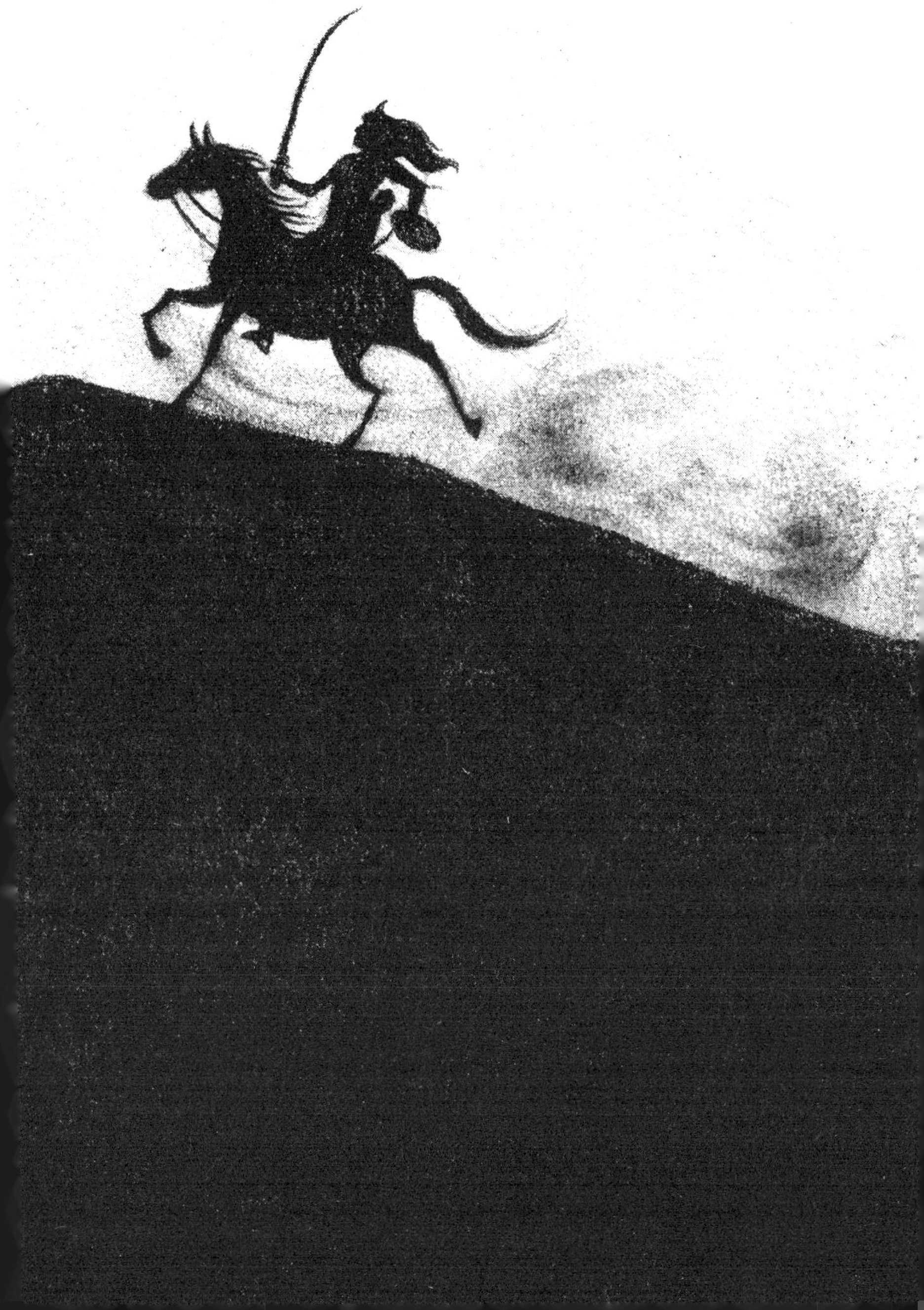

husband—a bibliophile whose love of drama sometimes saw him appear on stage, according to the scholar Joyce Lebra-Chapman—had adopted a relation as his heir. The British, of course, decided there was no compelling reason to recognise any of these proceedings: They had upgraded provincial officers into princelings, and they reserved the right to demote them now. Interestingly, this was despite popular sentiment: their own local representative had expressed confidence in the young widow (she was 'highly respected and esteemed' and 'fully capable' of ruling in her husband's place), while another argued that since adoption had been recognised in a neighbouring state, there was no reason to deny the privilege to the Newalkars. The rani herself, meanwhile, petitioned the governor general, arguing her case logically, highlighting portions from consecutive treaties to show the latest British decision to be what it truly was: an injustice.

In an April 1854 letter, Lakshmibai appealed to Dalhousie to remember 'How loyal the Rajas of Jhansi have ever been; how loyal are their representatives; how strong are the inducements that they should continue to be loyal in the future.' Her husband had not, she pointed out, any warlike characteristics, and Jhansi's military capabilities were limited to 'five thousand rusty swords worn by people called the army'. 'Helpless and prostrate,' she ended, 'I once more entreat Your Lordship to grant me a hearing.'

Of course, she was exaggerating her helplessness and the impotence of her armies, but at this stage she was willing to plead with Dalhousie—if only he had relented, in 1857, she might even have stayed loyal, like other princes, to the British. However, the governor general dug his heels in, leaving Lakshmibai to protest the 'gross violation' of previous understandings, warning that this would cause 'great disquietude' among India's nobility, with lasting repercussions on the future of the Company and its designs.

Dispossessed, at first the rani declined the British offer of ₹60,000 per annum but was soon persuaded to accept the settlement. In the years that followed, there was much bickering and haggling—over the late raja's debts, which were deducted from her allowance; over the continuation of the pension to Lakshmibai's adopted son, which the British were against; over a temple; and even such issues as cow slaughter. When the rebellion broke out, at first the rani was undecided—in a letter dated June 1857, she hoped the rebels would go 'straight to hell'. Even months later, by which time the local British presence had been destroyed through a massacre, Lakshmibai was uncertain. It was only early in 1858, when many of her old friends, including the aforementioned Peshwa's adopted son, Nana Sahib, became confirmed leaders of the rebellion and she herself was being viewed with suspicion, that she made her final choice: a choice that saw her ride out bravely on horseback towards tragedy, and enshrined her in India's national history.

POWER, PREJUDICE AND CURZON

Studying the feud between its moderate and extremist factions, in 1900, Lord Curzon wrote to his superiors in London of his belief 'that Congress is tottering to its fall'. What would become the grand old party of Indian independence was still in its early infancy at the time, but already had become something of a nuisance for the Viceroy. Relishing the sight of dissensions exploding from within into the public domain with all its chaos and clamour, Curzon added with smug delight how 'one of my great ambitions while in India' was to assist the Congress to 'a peaceful demise'. He spent six years investing precisely in this ambition, only to withdraw frustrated—the Congress took a deep breath and resurrected the freedom struggle. And the viceroy's own career went down the wrong path, smashing what were once prime ministerial ambitions into a chapter remembered in India only with rejection and dismay.

The Courtesan, the Mahatma & the Italian Brahmin

As viceroy, Curzon ruled India with self-appointed purpose. That it was the wrong purpose altogether is another matter, but his conviction was unparalleled. He always had a sense of his own importance, and made every effort to flaunt it. At Oxford, his peers came up with the doggerel: *My name is George Nathaniel Curzon/I am a most superior person/My cheek is pink, my hair is sleek/I dine at Blenheim (Palace) once a week.* It didn't help that he had a most disagreeable habit of passing judgement everywhere he went. On a trip to Canada, he sniffed about how there were few well-bred passengers on board, and the 'social status of the remainder is indicated by the aristocratic names they bear—Tulk, Tottle, and Thistle'. Funnily, he married a blacksmith's descendant called Leiter, a match perhaps less repulsive after the small matter of a not-too-small dowry was discussed with the bride's millionaire father.

It was India, though, that truly made Curzon—and unexpectedly so. 'From nobodies,' his American wife exclaimed, 'we have jumped into grandeur.' Only thirty-nine when he was propelled into his viceregal mission, Curzon couldn't stand the demands of the 'native' elite for a share of power and a fraction of respect. India's maharajahs and nawabs he dismissed as 'a set of unruly and ignorant and rather undisciplined schoolboys', while the Congress was a 'microscopic minority' of jobless lawyers, completely divorced from reality and with a propensity for grandiloquent speeches. 'You can as little judge of the feelings ... of the people of India from the plans and proposals of the Congress party as you can judge of the physical configuration of a country which is wrapped in the mists of early morning, but a few of whose topmost peaks have been touched by the rising sun.' This Curzon declared before he set eyes on a single Congressman.

He did, however, show empathy for ordinary people, partly because in those days ordinary people didn't ask inconvenient questions. When British soldiers raped a Burmese woman, he was horrified by the conspiracy to protect them—the entire regiment was expelled to Aden, 'the worst spot I could find' after his seniors vetoed stricter action. When a planter flogged his Indian servant to death and escaped a harsh sentence, Curzon appealed for real punishment. 'I will not,' he wrote, 'be party to any scandalous hushings up of bad cases ... or to the theory that a white man may kick or batter a black man to death with impunity because he is only "a damned nigger".' The English, he argued, must set an example in India by their 'superior standards of honour and virtue'. While he personally went about setting examples, other Englishmen continued to kick Indians, calling Curzon a 'nigger-lover'.

Good intentions aside, Curzon was also the kind of man who centralised power and reigned over mountains of paper. 'The Government of India,' he mourned familiarly, 'is a mighty and miraculous machine for doing nothing.' His solution, was not to empower Indians, but to pile up more on his own imperial plate—on one occasion, he set out to catch a chicken-thief when accounts did not add up in the stately kitchens of his palatial establishment. He couldn't quite understand why the Indian education system—designed by men of his ilk like Macaulay—was so focused on manufacturing a 'rush of immature striplings' interested 'not to learn but to earn'. He made half-baked but well-intentioned attempts to develop a research-oriented university system and emphasise technical education, though in implementing these wonderful ideas he again forgot to involve those brown people for whose benefit they were intended in the first place.

What most offended everybody, however, was Curzon's notorious partition of Bengal. He had already carved the North-West Frontier Province out of Punjab, and had plans for Berar, Orissa and other provinces as well. As the cradle of Indian nationalism, however, Bengal was unique. Despite mastering the principle of *divide et impera*, London warned Curzon not to proceed because 'the severance of old and historic ties and the breaking up of racial unity' would backfire on the Raj. But he went ahead anyway—and lived to regret it. The partition, to begin with, settled the internal doldrums of the Congress, rallying all factions against this single cause. Curzon, who in 1904 began a second term, was recalled within twelve months into a future with no more spectacular prospects, while his partition itself was eventually reversed. By the time of his death in 1925, he was reduced to complaining how not enough people were visiting to check on his welfare. 'I must be entirely forgotten,' he lamented, 'or have no friends left.' Both were partially true.

There is, however, one thing for which Curzon deserves lasting credit: his genuine interest in preserving India's monuments, a responsibility 'scandalously neglected' till then. When some complained that he was protecting 'pagan' structures, he reminded them that as sheer manifestations of human genius, to him 'the rock temple of the brahmin stands precisely on the same footing as the Buddhist Vihara and the Mohammedan Masjid as the Christian Cathedral'. Personally touring swathes of land, climbing up hills and down ruins, Curzon ensured that the Archaeological Survey of India began to do its job. And for all his prejudices, this one contribution was enough for Nehru, no great admirer of friendless, resentful Curzon, to later remark: 'After every other Viceroy has been forgotten, Curzon will be remembered because he restored all that was beautiful in India.' That, one hopes, would give Curzon's soul some gratification even though he went to the grave abandoned and alone.

WHEN SAVARKAR JUMPED SHIP

A little after 6.30 a.m. on 8 July 1910, V.D. Savarkar made more than a ripple in history when he plunged from *The Morea* into the Mediterranean Sea. The ship, on its way east with this high-profile prisoner, had docked at Marseilles when Savarkar expressed a desire to use the toilet. Two 'native constables' stood guard outside, but before they knew it, their charge had shot the door bolt, deciding to seek personal liberty via the porthole. Even as Constable 'Amarsing' and his colleague took off after him—sensibly choosing the land route—Savarkar swam to the quay and climbed into Marseilles harbour. He was quickly apprehended, of course, and this sensational attempt at escape soon became part of the Savarkar legend. But what he inadvertently provoked in the process was a diplomatic headache for Britain and France, the Hindutva ideologue's brief, wet moments on French territory opening up a can of legal worms that took months to settle.

Though *The Morea* and its precious cargo set sail from Marseilles the very next day, by 18 July the affair was being discussed at the highest levels of state. The French envoy in London set forth his government's view that 'As the prisoner had reached French soil... questions of international law were involved' in the matter. In other words, the moment Savarkar set foot, it was argued, on the sovereign territory of France, his British-Indian keepers no longer enjoyed legal rights over him—and certainly not the right to apprehend, seize and cart him back to a foreign vessel. Since Savarkar was already out of hand and en route to India, the request of the French government was simple: until the matter was settled between the two nations, the prisoner should not be tried for the charges that had provoked his arrest in London in the first place. If the French had any say in the matter, Savarkar should first be left to them to handle.

The British authorities were puzzled by the French claim, and, by 29 July, the Home Office, India Office and Foreign Office were all involved in the bureaucratic nightmare. Among those in the loop, interestingly, was a certain Winston Churchill, then Home Secretary, whose note emphasised that 'Great Britain should maintain an attitude of dignity and of dispassionate submission to the law of nations (i.e. international law). 'The petty annoyance,' he added, 'of a criminal escaping may have to be borne.' Curious as it is to picture Churchill inadvertently promoting the cause of 'Veer' Savarkar, he was stoutly resisted by paladins in the India Office. Unlike their colleagues, the India hands insisted that while a pious commitment to international law was admirable, it was 'of the utmost importance from a political point of view' that Savarkar should be tried. There was, to them, no question of returning him to French soil.

The Courtesan, the Mahatma & the Italian Brahmin

A somewhat topsy-turvy solution suggested, then, was to have Savarkar tried as scheduled, to suspend the sentence when delivered, hand him over to the French thereafter, and finally have him extradited to India to serve the sentence—all this involving Savarkar being given a two-way ticket to sail overseas and back simply to satisfy legal requirements. But the charges against him being what they were—a veritable catalogue including 'Waging and abetting the waging of war against the King', 'Collecting arms with intent to wage war against the King', 'sedition', 'abetment to murder', and more—it was decided to explore all possibilities to retain him in India while the matter was resolved. Churchill might have wanted to preserve British dignity in the face of French legal incandescence but, for the colonial authorities in India, Savarkar was the 'head of a widespread conspiracy, the threads of which it was essential to unravel' through trial.

As both the French and the British got into the matter, there appeared two versions of what had transpired in Marseilles. The French asserted that once Savarkar appeared on the docks, it was a gendarme who caught him—he claimed to have chased him 'about 400 metres' before catching up. He then walked ten metres with Savarkar in his physical custody before the Indian policemen showed up. Constable 'Amarsing' and his colleague, however, said that while the gendarme's action was crucial, he had appeared from the left while they were closing in on Savarkar, and that they arrived moments after the Frenchman had the prisoner by the arm. Savarkar himself may well have been conscious of a legal opportunity to obtain asylum, for he appealed to the officer to take him to a local magistrate. Instead, he was marched back to the ship and guarded even more closely till he got to India.

Pressed immediately after by the French press, which raised issues of law and national pride, the authorities in Paris came

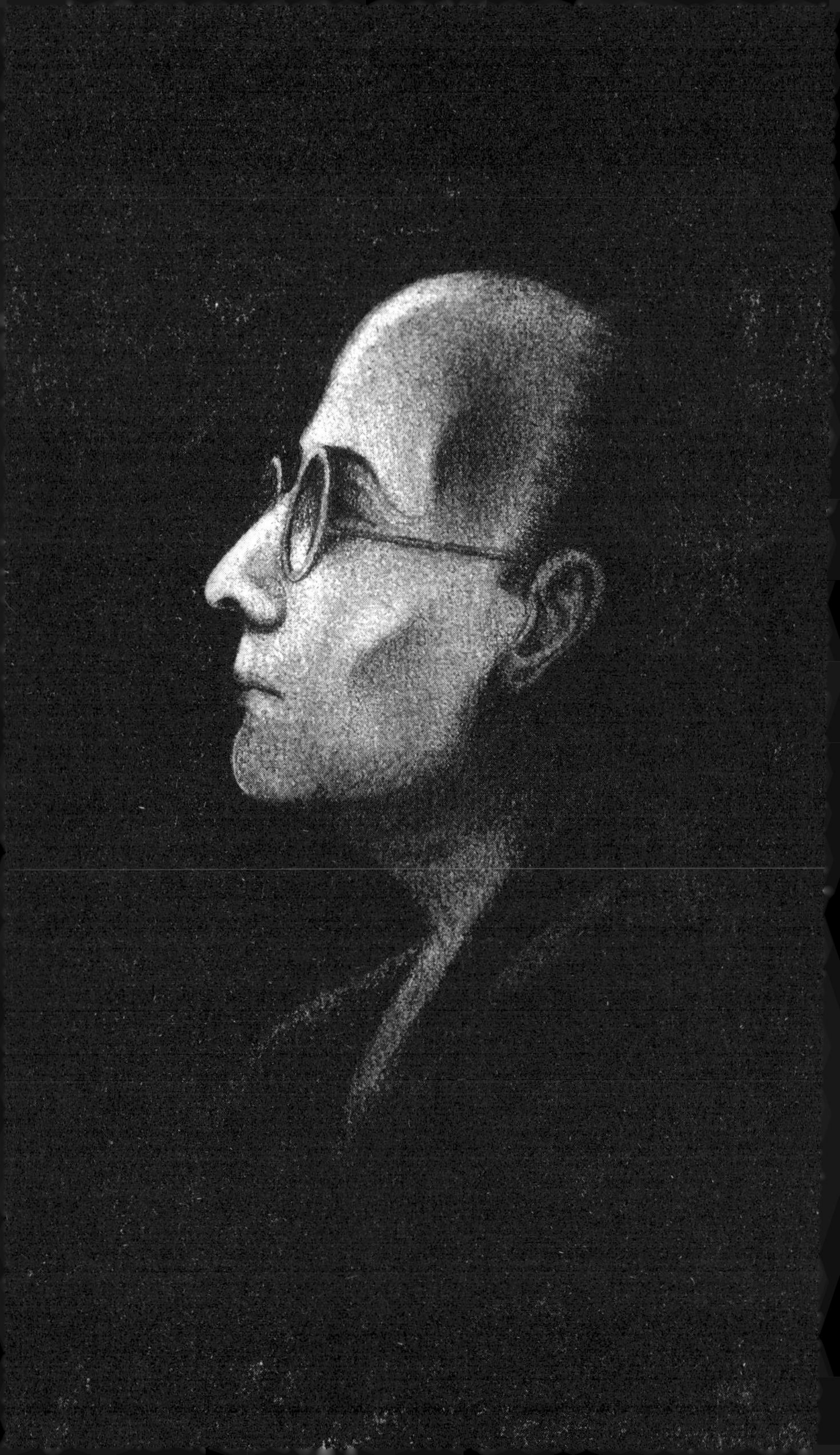

to regret the actions of the otherwise efficient gendarme. In London, the claim that the French had any kind of right over Savarkar was, meanwhile, rejected. The French, it was accurately argued, were informed in advance of Savarkar's presence on the ship, and the gendarme had been posted precisely to prevent his escape—that he succeeded in doing what he was meant to do merely confirmed Savarkar's position as British prisoner and could not be construed as creating a right of asylum even by the most generous reading of the case. 'His Majesty's Government,' it was firmly communicated by September, 'are therefore unable to admit that they are under any obligation to restore Savarkar to French territory.' He was now in India, and that was where he would remain.

The matter did not end there, however. In October 1910, it was decided by the French to take the dispute to the Permanent Court of Arbitration, and in February the next year the court ruled in favour of Britain—while there was an 'irregularity' in Savarkar's arrest, London's logic made sense to them. Perhaps, if the gendarme had handed over Savarkar to his superiors instead of taking him back to the ship, the story might have been different. But in the circumstances as they were, the British prevailed. And so—even as the French erupted in righteous protest—the matter finally came to an end, and the fifty years Savarkar was sentenced to serve began. Fifty years, that is, till he composed his infamous mercy petitions and obtained an early release, which, of course, is another story.

SAVARKAR'S THWARTED 'RACIAL DREAM'

In November 1940, V.D. Savarkar presented a most fascinating proposition in a newspaper called the *Khyber Mail*. Authored under his usual pseudonym of 'A Mahratta', the architect of Hindutva went beyond his familiar arguments about 'Hinduness' and nationalism here, highlighting instead a political framework in which these concepts could achieve fruition. Ostensibly, this was a rejoinder to a 'spineless' statement by Mahatma Gandhi that the Nizam of Hyderabad was a potential candidate for emperor of united India when the British left. But Savarkar's 'virile antidote' to Gandhi's 'inferiority complex' is not less puzzling. The thrust of his argument painted India's rajahs ('defenders of Hindu faith and honour... the reserve forces of Hindudom') and not the nizam as the road to the future. And if, he argued, Hindus in British territory and the princes joined forces, they could offer a sparkling alternative vision for India, establishing a nation that was a veritable 'racial dream'.

Like much of Savarkar's writing, this essay too features a good deal of anti-Muslim polemics. The 'academical' view offered was that if it came to civil war, Hindu military camps would spring up spontaneously in the princely states, from Udaipur and Gwalior in the north to Mysore and Travancore in the south. 'There will not be left a trace of Muslim rule from the Seas in the South to the Jamuna in the North,' while in the Punjab Sikhs would keep at bay the Muslim tribes of the west. Independent Nepal (of all countries) would emerge 'as the Defender of the Hindu Faith and the commander of Hindu forces', mobilising 'Hindu rifles' to 'spit fire and vengeance in defence of Hindu Honour'. Indeed, Nepal might even make 'a bid for the Imperial throne of Hindusthan'. Its march into India would be reinforced, of course, by Hindus across the board, and at the end of the day they would together consecrate a Hindu *rashtra* with its own suzerain, ready to inherit 'the Sceptre of Indian Empire' as it fell from colonial hands.

The Hindutva family of organisations understandably perceived a community of interests with the princely states for a long time. The latter were, as the scholar Manu Bhagavan observes, viewed as 'portals to a pure, ancient past', 'sites of India's imagined past of purity', and 'the foundation on which the future nation' could be launched. In 1944, in a letter to the ruler of Jaipur, Savarkar openly declared the Hindu Mahasabha's policy of 'standing by the Hindu states and defending their prestige, stability and power against the Congressites, the Communists, [and] the Moslems'. 'Hindu states,' he concluded, 'are centres of Hindu power' and naturally, therefore, would become instrumental in the realisation of Hindu nationhood—not democratic assemblies or notions of secular government. Meanwhile, if not spirited support, the princes certainly provided a degree of encouragement to Savarkar and his supporters—several Hindu Mahasabha meetings were hosted in their states, including in highly advanced Mysore and Baroda, and the organisation found ample support among the orthodox in princely territory, where British influence was less direct and feudal power more sustained.

What, however, were the chances of the princes uniting around Savarkar's vision? They certainly did possess networks of blood and kinship that could, in theory, link them. Travancore in Kerala 'belonged' to Lord Padmanabhaswamy—a deity whose idol was made of salagram stones from Nepal. The Maratha dynasty in Baroda shared political roots not only with the rulers of Indore and Gwalior in the centre and north but also with the descendants of Shivaji's house who survived in Tamil Nadu. Mysore was ruled by Kannadigas, who eagerly sought Rajput brides. To this combination could also be added senior Indian statesmen of the time who thought the Congress vision of India a disaster, and were equally willing, therefore, to consider an alternative plan. As late as July 1947, for instance, the redoubtable statesman, Sir C.P. Ramaswami Iyer (who considered Gandhi a 'dangerous sex maniac' and Jawaharlal Nehru 'unstable') was convinced that if power went to the Congress, 'civil war ... within six months' was inevitable, culminating in the division of India between 'half a dozen principalities'—and Sir C.P. was considered 'one of the cleverest men in India'.

The Courtesan, the Mahatma & the Italian Brahmin

In reality though, most Indian rajahs were more interested in sustaining their decadent lifestyles and reaffirming loyalty to the Raj than in plotting grand designs for India's independence. Many of them were known not for their virile nationalism but for their boudoir passions. They certainly owned 40 per cent of Indian territory, but over 454 of the 565-odd states were made of less than 1,000 square metres; only a few dozen collected revenues over ₹10 lakh, and even fewer owned armies that deserved the name. The greatest of the states, Hyderabad, was inconveniently Islamic, while Kashmir, held by Dogra Rajputs, was majority Muslim. Add to this mass agitations within the states, encouraged by the Congress, and the heady picture of brave princes rising to inaugurate an age of Hindutva looked hopelessly remote.

In the end, history didn't quite play out in the way Savarkar and his confederates theorised. Nehru proved perfectly stable, the Hindutva cause was damaged after Gandhi's murder, while Sardar Patel integrated most principalities with the carrot of money and status and the stick of armed intervention. Despite obituaries and shrill prophecies of danger, India became a secular democracy, and not a Hindu rashtra. And, in perhaps what might have caused the father of Hindutva to recoil in horror, it was not the Nepali dynasty of Savarkar's 'academical' premise that soared to power in New Delhi. Instead, another family emerged to play a formidable role in shaping India's destiny: one bearing those very names—Nehru and Gandhi—that he viewed with such intense antipathy. What Savarkar envisioned in 1940 was a 'Future Emperor of India'; what India got in a decade instead was a people's constitution, defended by men and women who brooked no kings and shunned all empires.

THE CHAMPION OF TUTICORIN

When Mohandas Karamchand Gandhi arrived in Madras in 1915, among those seeking a private audience with him was a man called V.O. Chidambaram Pillai. Gandhi, already a hero after his political work in South Africa, had several demands on his time and suggested, therefore, a quick meeting. His correspondent was not pleased. 'I am afraid,' he wrote back dryly, 'that my conversation … will take more than the allotted "a few minutes".' Cloaking sarcasm as an apology for 'having intruded upon your precious time', Pillai grandly withdrew his request. Now it was the Mahatma's turn to be puzzled. He insisted on seeing the man, making equally sarcastic amends by requesting his time at 6 a.m. 'I cannot reach your place before 6.30 a.m.,' Pillai declared, but finally, they did meet: the champion of Tuticorin and the Mahatma-in-waiting.

What ensued was a long and somewhat frustrating exchange between the two leaders—one whose political career was on the ascendant and the other who not only found his

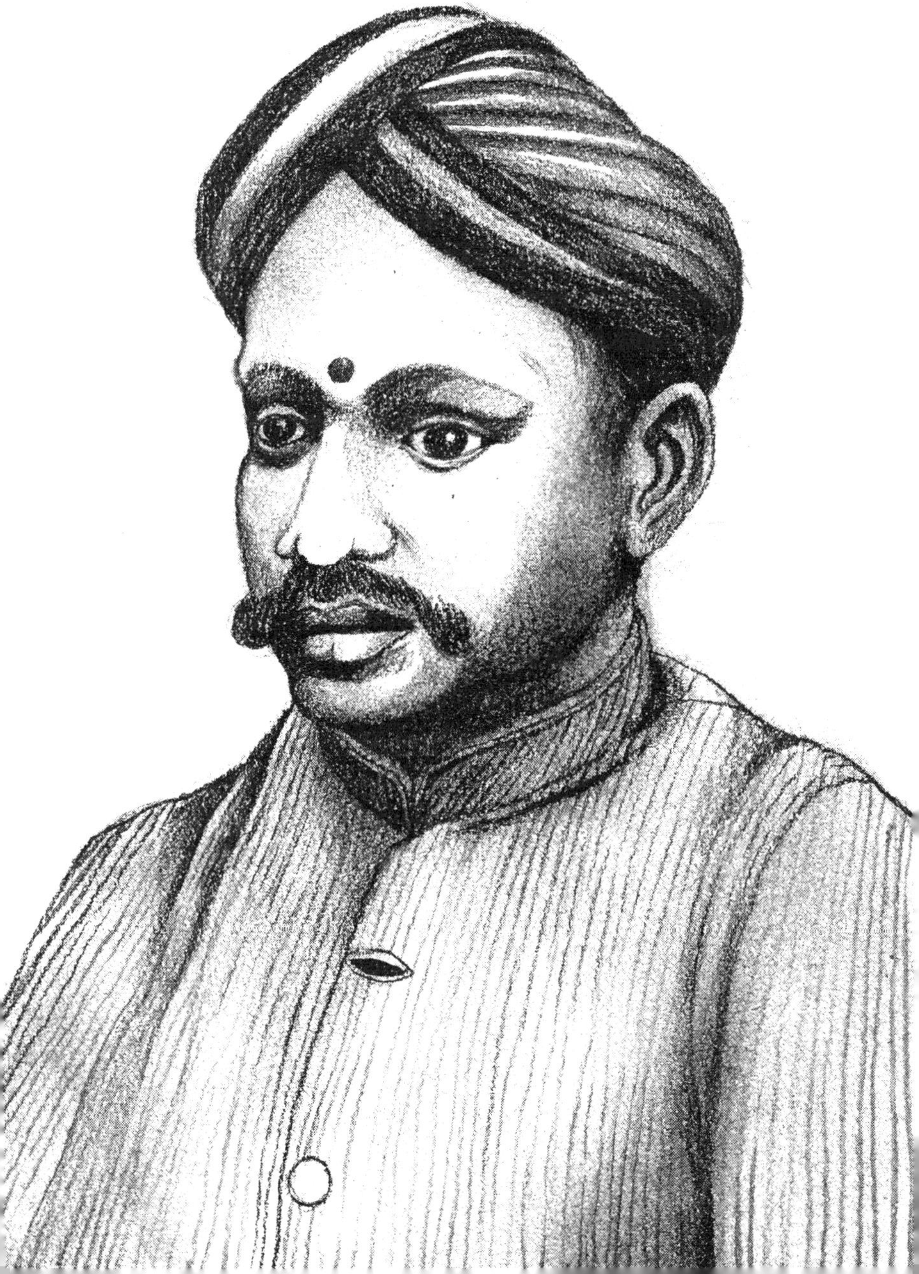

best years behind him but was also penniless. Sympathising with the man's predicament, Gandhi offered to help Pillai with money, and the latter readily accepted. But the amount was a long time coming. 'Don't you know at least approximately the total amount given... by your friend?' asked Pillai at one point. 'If you know it, can you not send me that amount or a major portion of it... so that it may be useful to me in my present difficult circumstances?' 'Not yet,' snapped the Mahatma abruptly. In the end, it took about a year, but 'Sriman Gandhi', as the former called him, did succeed in arranging ₹347 for Pillai, who was not only delighted by this satisfactory end to their strange, chequered exchange but also somewhat lighter of debt.

Pillai, who seemed to almost harass Gandhi with letters in 1915, was unrecognisable from the man who once handled lakhs of rupees and was a celebrated shipping magnate. Born on 5 September 1872 in Ottapidaram in Tamil Nadu, he had followed his lawyer father's instructions and become a pleader in 1894. But if Pillai Sr was pleased, it didn't last—father and son soon found themselves on opposite sides of a touchy case, and the latter demolished in court not only his esteemed parent's arguments but also the former's pride. It was decided that Pillai should move elsewhere for peace to exist between them, and so, in 1900, he transplanted himself permanently to Tuticorin. Influenced by Bal Gangadhar Tilak, he embraced swadeshi activities (firmly siding with the Extremist faction of the Congress, as opposed to the Moderates with their talk of patience and constitutionalism). It was in 1906, however, that the cause which would define his life came to him, putting him on a path that would bring pain as much as it would acclaim, accumulating honour but also inviting unhappiness.

At the time, Tuticorin was an established centre for

shipping, with thousands using its harbour. But the entire industry was in the hands of British companies that were, unsurprisingly, in bed with the colonial government to cement their mutual interests. It was not astonishing, then, perhaps, that the city was also a nursery for sustained nationalist activity. Or as one report put it, in the Madras Presidency the 'only district from which any suspicion of anti-British feeling is reported is Tinnevelly district, and there only in the town of Tuticorin'. So, when in October 1906 Pillai opened the Swadeshi Steam Navigation Company, there was a great deal of condescension, followed by a ballooning of anger and suspicion. After all, as A.R. Venkatachalapathy writes, in most places across the country at this time, the idea of swadeshi as popularised by the Congress 'was limited to such tokenisms as making candles and bangles'. In Tuticorin, however, it took 'the spectacular form of running nothing less than a steam shipping company'—a project that was not merely a business enterprise for its founder, but also a statement of nationalist pride in the face of unjust colonial disdain.

Scholars have investigated the systematic destruction in the nineteenth century of Indian shipping, so that by the 1850s, India's shipbuilding industry was practically history. Even with the advent of steam engines and advanced technology, while efforts were made by Indian industrialists and entrepreneurs, most attempts floundered into oblivion. Of the 102 companies floated in India between 1860 and 1925, only a handful became successes. 'The failure of India's shipping,' we are informed, 'was not caused by the non-existence of her marine engineering industry ... Nor did shipowners demonstrate a lack of managerial skills or experience specific difficulties in manning and running their fleets ... The basic cause of the lamentable position of Indian shipping ... was the formidable opposition they encountered from the major British companies operating in Indian waters'—companies that enjoyed a practical monopoly, to which they would brook no challenge or competition.

Given these circumstances, Pillai's attempt was truly novel, and his ambitions high—though Swadeshi's services were restricted to Tuticorin and Colombo only, the company aimed to 'popularise the art of Navigation' among 'Nations of the East', to employ 'Asiatics', to open dockyards, and do whatever it could to revitalise India's maritime traditions. Many prominent Indians invested in the venture, while local merchants were persuaded to ply goods on the company's hired steamer, the *Shah Allum*. 'This,' one newspaper report recorded, 'has naturally aroused the jealousy of the British Indian Steam Navigation Company.' The authorities, for their part, 'have not always been impartial. The impression that the white Civilian (i.e. government official) is likely to favour the white trader is gaining ground.' The principal rival company in the area engaged in rate wars and even offered free umbrellas to passengers, but Pillai and his enterprise did not fold. He was offered a princely ₹100,000 to sell the company, but this too failed to distract him—after all, Swadeshi was about a principle, and not merely about personal profit.

Initial attempts having failed, Pillai's rivals escalated their attack. Intense pressure was brought to bear upon the owner of the *Shah Allum*, who then withdrew it from Swadeshi. Undeterred, Pillai acquired ships from abroad and sailed into Tuticorin flying flags emblazoned with *Vande Mataram*. The British authorities, along with the rival company owners, threw all they could his way, not least of which was bureaucratic harassment, but Pillai's energy saw him through—that is, till two years later, politics furnished an excuse to smash

The Courtesan, the Mahatma & the Italian Brahmin

his commercial successes as well. In early March 1908, the acting collector of the area, RWDE Ashe, ordered Pillai, who was planning a public meeting to celebrate the release from prison of the Bengali nationalist Bipin Chandra Pal, to leave the city—this, after they had already had a run-in over a workers' strike in which Pillai was involved. He refused, and was arrested on a preemptive basis. The result was that by 13 March things got out of hand—mobs set fire to public buildings, made bonfires of state records, and for days Tuticorin witnessed riots, with four people losing their lives. Pillai was awarded twenty years in prison—the British judge held him 'morally responsible' for the deaths, and charges of sedition and worse were slapped against him and some others.

Pillai appealed the decision and eventually, the Madras High Court reduced the sentence to a maximum of four years. But while Pillai languished under a particularly sadistic jailor, his company collapsed, his family was bankrupted, and his friends disappeared, out of fear as much as reasons of self-preservation. Collector Ashe, meanwhile, went down as the last colonial officer to be assassinated in India during the freedom struggle. He had taken an aggressive interest in containing nationalist activity in Tuticorin—and this meant directly targeting Pillai's company and all that it represented. Indeed, to this day he is held responsible for the failure of the company, and when he was murdered in 1911 as part of a revolutionary conspiracy, Pillai wasted little sympathy on him. As he recalled, 'One day in the night at twelve, hearing the many loud calls of "Mr Chidambaram Pillai", I woke up. At the entrance to the cell the prison's junior sub-assistant surgeon enquired after me and asked, "Do you know collector Ashe?" "I know him too well!", I replied. "How?" "He is the cause of my being locked up here and the death of the swadeshi shipping company [sic]." "Yesterday someone shot him dead at Maniyachi rail junction and killed himself too." "You have given me good news, may you live long!" I said. "You will not get released at the Coronation [of the new British king emperor] this year," he said. "Even if I am not to be released forever, that's fine," I replied.'

As it happened, Pillai was freed, but by the time he emerged in 1912, he was not only poor but also forgotten. Prohibited from returning to Tuticorin, he moved to Madras, set up a shop there, getting by tutoring college students. Though a judge called Wallace restored his legal licence (to thank whom Pillai named his son Wallacewaran), his career was essentially over. During the next many years and decades, Pillai existed on the margins of the freedom struggle, frustrated and unhappy, and altogether disillusioned—he was one of those heroes who fell by the wayside, ignored even by his erstwhile colleagues. It would be 1949 before he was brushed up and restored to public memory. Soon after independence, India's first and only Indian Governor General, C. Rajagopalachari, came to Tuticorin to flag off a shipping service to Colombo—the first vessel was dutifully named the SS *V.O. Chidambaram*. Statues of the forgotten hero were installed and flowers and garlands were heaped to honour his legacy; in 1961 there was even a feature film produced which told his life story, called *Kappalottiya Thamizhan* (The Tamilian Who Launched a Shipping House). It was all too late though—in 1936, Pillai had already died in penury, surviving his last days selling his law books and ruminating on all that he had once been—a once famous lawyer and businessman destined to drown in an ocean of disappointment and sorrow.

THE COMPLICATED
V.K. KRISHNA MENON

Setting out for London in 1924, V.K. Krishna Menon found himself in the awkward position of being the son of a very rich father with very empty pockets. 'I telegraphed you yesterday that I wanted money', he wrote to his sister, weeks later, hoping again 'to get 100 pounds from Father'. The old man, of course, had no intention of subsidising his son's journey towards potential self-destruction. For at twenty-eight, Krishna Menon looked every inch a disappointment. He was sent to Madras to qualify as a lawyer but returned to Calicut, a bedazzled theosophist. He was raised to take over his father's legal enterprise, but all he talked about was Annie Besant and the imminent earth-shattering advent of a supposed 'World Teacher'. Now, to add to his erratic peregrinations, he was off to London for a diploma in education, planning to become, of all things, a simple schoolteacher.

Krishna Menon's was a family that thought modesty overrated. His father was a legal luminary in British Malabar and the son of a local raja. They paraded elephants (Sanku, Sankaran and Gopalan were favourites) and saw Queen Victoria's passing as tragedy unparalleled. His mother was the daughter of Koodali Nair, master of tens of thousands of acres, and played chess when she wasn't enjoying her ample inheritance. Of the eight children born to this proud and handsome couple, Kunjikrishna, as our protagonist was originally named, was from the start considered somewhat limited. Where a sister pursued French and Latin and upheld her family's imperious standards by discarding a husband, young Krishna was busy being sensitive and gentle, insisting on feeding his pony milk and oats from the breakfast table.

The unworthy heir who left India's shores in 1924, however, was far from the domineering, vain man who returned in 1952, cloaked in Cold War suspicions. The British saw in Menon Jawaharlal Nehru's 'evil genius', while the Americans were more colourful when they branded him a 'poisonous bastard'. In the 1950s, Menon was difficult to miss on the world stage: even a US president noted this 'boor' who thought himself so superior. Much of this reputation was accumulated from the 1930s. A decade into his stay in London, British intelligence was already tapping Menon's phone and reading his letters. In the 1940s, they feared he was both a prescription drug addict and a closet communist, warning Nehru that plans to appoint him India's high commissioner would not be 'well received' in their quarter.

Menon's journey from aspiring schoolmaster to the 1962 cover of *Time* magazine as an international mischief-maker is fascinating. Soon after he arrived in London, he upped his ambitions and acquired a string of qualifications. He studied under Harold Laski at the London School of Economics and wrote a thesis on psychology at University College London. On the eve of his father's death in 1934, he at last even became a lawyer. Breaking from his theosophist mentors, he became the face of the India League, and chief lobbyist for Indian independence in Britain's political circles. He cultivated links with the Labour Party, and, in the midst of all this, helped launch Penguin, the publishing house, only to quarrel and withdraw forever. In the late 1930s, the prospect of a parliament seat too appeared, but his 'double loyalty' meant plans for a political career in Britain were ill-fated from the onset.

In 1935, the dissolution of a complicated romance left Menon suicidal and he became more dependent than ever on astrology and medication. Still, when Nehru came that year to Britain, it was this complicated Malayali who was anointed local spokesman of the Congress. Nehru later dismissed views that his friend held great sway over him, but what is certain is that Menon's meteoric ascent after India's independence owed much to his access to the first prime minister. It was no wonder, then, that from the start, the man made enemies in the Congress—while they were parked in jail during the freedom struggle, it was argued, Menon served the London borough of St Pancras for fourteen cushy years as councillor. While they suffered kicks and blows, he was faraway on foreign shores.

His stint till 1952 as high commissioner was controversial. His arrogance, a defence mechanism to conceal lifelong insecurities, left him unapproachable. Worse, British intelligence saw in him (mistakenly) a Soviet pawn who might slip secrets through a mysterious mistress. When the Indian army sought jeeps for use in Kashmir, Menon embarrassed Nehru by delivering second-hand goods that were unserviceable. The prime minister tried to cajole him into leaving London—he was offered a vice-chancellorship, the embassy in Moscow, even a cabinet position—but Menon refused. At last, he was persuaded to represent India at the UN, where, while advocating non-alignment (a word he took credit for and a concept he claimed to have co-authored), he drove paranoid Americans wild with suspicion.

Menon was abrasive, but he got India noticed. He punched above his weight and strode the world stage with regal confidence. By 1956, this 'thoroughly dangerous man' was in the Union cabinet, but his role as defence minister culminated six years later with the debacle in 1962, where India was humiliated by China at its northern frontiers. He spent the rest of his years giving lectures, arguing cases in the Supreme Court, and quarrelling with a niece's husband over his traditional 'right' to name her children. Sometimes he gave long, ponderous interviews to foreign journalists, who alone seemed to think he remained a personality of tremendous influence.

The Courtesan, the Mahatma & the Italian Brahmin

'Krishna Menon was essentially an extremely lonely man,' wrote a relation, and his was a life that married emotional instability to political petulance. But for all that, the dangers of his influence were overrated. As he himself said in an interview, 'I was neither a buffoon nor a Rasputin.' He was merely Krishna Menon, who did some good but invited plenty of trouble.

THE SEAMSTRESS AND
THE MATHEMATICIAN

In the Madras suburb of Triplicane, there once lived a seamstress called Janaki. Respectfully addressed as Janaki Ammal, to her came many with saris to mend and blouses to stitch. But there was more to the old lady than tailoring. She was, for one, a pious brahmin who chanted mantras and went often to the temple. She gave to charity and educated a number of grateful children. Though in her youth she was cheated of a prodigious sum, she acquired skill enough to run a chit fund for the housewives of her neighbourhood. Upstairs, she lived in a little place, and downstairs, she conducted business. But for all the decades of her self-supporting life, she kept with her also a tin trunk, full of crumbling papers that concealed the most poignant memories. For in a different time and a different space, Janaki of Triplicane was married to a 'somebody'. And before she became a seamstress, she had been wife to a man who scaled the very heights of cerebral greatness.

The Courtesan, the Mahatma & the Italian Brahmin

It is not known what, as a ten-year-old, Janaki made of Srinivasa Ramanujan, who arrived in her Tiruchirapalli village to wed her in the summer of 1909. His train was delayed and her father was furious. Yet, once tempers were soothed and insults forgotten, the mathematical prodigy and this young girl from the country were married. To look at, the bridegroom was uninspiring: Smallpox had devastated his face, and a classmate described him as 'fair and plumpy', built like 'a woman'. At twenty-one, there was little to commend him to the top league of prospective husbands: Five years ago, he had dropped out of college, and a second attempt at university had also ended in depressive despair. His energy was electric, though, and his mathematical abilities astounding. But he had no patience for other subjects and spent his days doing humdrum accounts and failing hopelessly as a part-time tuition teacher.

Raised by a masterful mother, and awkward around his disapproving father, Ramanujan took some years to find his bearings. In 1912, employed as a clerk at the Madras Port Trust, he finally crawled out of poverty, renting a house where he was joined by Janaki. While he solved sums on discarded packaging paper and engaged with the city's mathematics professors, the young girl watched from the side and learnt what it meant to be a brahmin wife. He was a sensitive man, full of fears of rejection but bursting with godly devotion. 'An equation for me,' he declared, 'has no meaning unless it expresses a thought of god.' Of course, little of this was discussed with his teenage wife—he never saw her alone, and, when she slept, it was with her watchful mother-in-law. Janaki cooked, and Janaki cleaned. And then, one day, she heard that her husband had been invited to that alien country people called Great Britain.

The decision to go was not easy: Ramanujan had been corresponding with the celebrated G.H. Hardy and in Cambridge his name was already a sensation. But what sensible brahmin boy with a government job could toss aside everything to scramble after an abstract world of numbers? Finally, the gods were consulted—the family went on pilgrimage, and divine sanction was received in a dream that came to his shrewd mother. Janaki, all of fifteen, mustered up all her courage and asked to sail with Ramanujan. But this was dismissed as outrageous—he was going to achieve great things, and she would only distract him from his god-mandated purpose. Besides, where his mother could not go, his wife could not be allowed either. And so it was that, a week before he departed, Ramanujan said goodbye to his family, packing them off home before he cut off his tuft of hair and wore for the first time the garb of a Western gentleman. When a photograph arrived showing her son like this soon afterwards, it took his mother some time to recognise him.

For five years, Janaki didn't see her husband. At first, she served her mother-in-law, but soon there was mutiny in the kitchen. Letters addressed to her were intercepted by the older woman, and young Mrs Ramanujan built up the pluck to ask direct questions. Our genius himself, while making history, was living a life of personal misery—there was tuberculosis, social awkwardness, a suicide attempt, and all the inconveniences of the First World War afflicting life in Great Britain. In 1919, with much distinction under his belt but his health in pieces, Ramanujan returned at last to India. He asked for Janaki to come and greet him, but his mother 'forgot' to let her daughter-in-law know: It was from newspapers that the wife of this freshly minted Fellow of The Royal Society discovered that her husband had finally come home.

Ramanujan did not live long, but the year he and Janaki spent together had its moments of tender affection. She cared for him, and he told his mother to retreat—if only, he regretted, he had taken Janaki along, he might not have felt so lost on foreign shores. Their marriage, hitherto unconsummated, was at last given a semblance of substance. He remained orthodox—they moved from a house called Crynant because 'cry' was inauspicious. He approved of Gometra because it could be read in Sanskrit as 'friend of cows'. His tuberculosis, of course, cared little for auspicious addresses, and his mother blamed Janaki's stars for bringing upon her son the terrible eye of Saturn. When Ramanujan died on 26 April 1920, he took with him whatever trace of warmth survived between the two women feuding by his bedside.

A widow at barely twenty-two, Janaki spent most of the following decade in British Bombay with her brother, learning English and acquiring the skills of a seamstress. In 1931, she returned to Madras, beginning a new life, working to supplement her meagre pension from the Madras University, and eventually adopting a boy, who cared for her till her end, six decades later. Occasionally, great scholars from abroad came to see Janaki, seeking answers to questions left behind by her legendary husband. But she only had memories and gentle words to offer. As this seamstress of Triplicane said to one of them, the chief thing she remembered about her beloved Ramanujan was that he was always surrounded by sums and problems.

AN UNSENTIMENTAL MAN OF ACTION

Sir Mokshagundam Visvesvaraya was a thin man with a big head. He had a long, sharp nose, surpassed by an even sharper intellect. The offspring of a Telugu brahmin family, he was born on 15 September 1861 in a Karnataka village called Muddenahalli. His parents were of modest means, but learnt quickly that English education was a passport to social mobility. Their second-born did not fail them—a diligent student, Visvesvaraya grew into an unsentimental man of action, leaving for greener academic pastures in Bangalore soon after the untimely death of his father. He did have to earn his keep: while an uncle gave him breakfast and meals, board and college fees came from a wealthy local family. It was in the service of this household that the future 'Bharat Ratna' launched his career, giving private tuition to prosperous children long before he won his knighthood and came to be called India's Father of Economic Planning.

The 101-odd years 'Sir MV' lived were full of work and unceasing activity. He wrote books and gave countless speeches. He worshipped fact alone, caring little for oratorical wit or the charms of rhetoric. The keystones of his existence were routine and grinding discipline—the story went that he wore a three-piece suit (plus turban) even for a walk in his garden. When he spoke, his words came pregnant with substance, and he travelled the world—from America to Japan—commenting on everything from urban drainage to women's employment. He loved statistics with a passion: when he published *Reconstructing India* in 1920, he peppered it with facts and figures so diverse that it remains an encyclopaedia that tells us, among other things, how India a century ago had 19,410 post offices.

Such rigour served Visvesvaraya well. Soon after he acquired his Bachelor of Arts degree, he went to Pune to qualify as an engineer. He worked in the Deccan and served in Sindh, developing irrigation channels and building filtering systems. By his late thirties, he had superseded as many as eighteen seniors in the jealous ranks of officialdom, retiring in 1908 when he realised he would never be made, on account of the colour of his skin, that special thing: chief engineer of an entire British province. While touring Italy later that year, he received an invitation from the Nizam of Hyderabad. And so Visvesvaraya commenced the next part of his career, designing infrastructure in the prince's capital before transferring his services to the maharajah of his native state of Mysore.

At first, Visvesvaraya was chief engineer in India's most advanced princely realm, till in 1912 his ruler elevated him to the dignity of *dewan* (chief minister). Some muttered that handing the administration to an engineer was akin to

The Courtesan, the Mahatma & the Italian Brahmin

placing a woodcutter at the helm of government, but the technocrat shook the place up, marching the state ahead by characteristically systematic leaps and bounds. He set up Mysore University, and pumped money into the Krishna Raja Sagara dam; he established the Bank of Mysore and set in motion what would become the iron and steel works in Bhadravati. From developing the sandalwood soap industry to promoting silks from Mysore's looms, Visvesvaraya soon proved himself the force behind a thriving state. And without much ado, six years later, following a quarrel with the maharajah on the issue of reservations, Visvesvaraya resigned. Indeed, a popular story tells how he went to the palace in an official car to hand in his papers, but when he returned, it was in his private vehicle.

By now Visvesvaraya, who among other things was a M.I.C.E. (Member of the Institution of Civil Engineers), was ready for even bigger challenges. He had views not only on economics and governance, but also on social policy and national enlightenment. In *Reconstructing India* are ideas that even today resonate with Indian thinkers. 'If bureaucracy prevails,' he warned, for instance, 'industries will not prosper.' Without modern industry—which meant progressive education, social reform, and, crucially, women's empowerment—the nation itself would not prosper. The state had to guide the process but also recognise its limits: the 'people require help and backing,' he argued, 'not control and direction.' Page after page presented Visvesvaraya's vision for India, one in which caste retreated before 'a saner social system' and nationalism meant a love for the country that was not divorced from mundane civic awareness.

By the 1920s and 1930s, Visvesvaraya was already an elder with a voice that mattered. He sat on the board of the

Tata Iron and Steel Company and served as president of the Indian Science Congress. He lambasted the British for their economic exploitation of the subcontinent, even as he lectured his countrymen against making fatalistic philosophical excuses. In 1934, he argued even with Gandhi—the Mahatma did not share Visvesvaraya's faith in large-scale industry, noting that 'we hold perhaps diametrically opposite views' on which path would deliver the country to its destiny. 'I could never persuade myself to take up a hostile attitude toward … one with your brilliant achievements,' wrote the south Indian to the Gujarati sincerely. But he still believed that alongside the village and its cottage industries, India needed steel plants and factories, to transform itself and shine in the twentieth century.

Though they respected each other, Visvesvaraya had disagreements with Jawaharlal Nehru too. On one occasion,

The Courtesan, the Mahatma & the Italian Brahmin

he admonished the future prime minister publicly. He was also a strong advocate of meaningful federalism, where the centre's 'intervention in provincial affairs [is] reduced to the lowest possible minimum'. Nehru, on the other hand, empowered the capital and would [or could, according to some] not grant the states real autonomy. But between them emerged a constructive engagement, and the old man's letters were always welcome on the prime minister's desk. Visvesvaraya, by now, had risen from legendary mind into an object of sheer wonder. Nearing his hundredth birthday, when asked about the secret of his longevity, he remarked in a matter-of-fact fashion: 'Death called on me long ago but found me not at home and went away.' It returned on 12 April 1962, and this time the bachelor from Muddenahalli was ready, having made his mark in the world, and having said everything that needed to be said.

THE RESURRECTION OF BALAMANI

In 1903, one of Kerala's earliest advocates of the freedom of the press, K. Ramakrishna Pillai, issued a lamentation that suggests he was not necessarily as convinced an advocate for feminist thought. 'Oh ... the predicament you have reached!' he cried, with reference to his coastal homeland. 'You who were governed by noble ministers with high ideals ... what sin have you done to be trapped under the misgovernment of a wicked minister taken in by female charms!' His intention was to sharpen his attack on the local maharajah's controversial chief minister, but it was also an attack on an attractive woman—a public performer—who had evidently ensnared the old man with her treacherous charms. His proof? Her visit to Thiruvananthapuram drew sensational crowds, and the delighted minister had presented her a gold chain—by publicly placing it around her neck.

Pillai ascribed to the lady in question, the scholar Udaya Kumar notes, a 'destructive, seductive spell' that combined

The Courtesan, the Mahatma & the Italian Brahmin

'the perilous allure of theatrical exposure... manipulative charms and sexual promiscuity' to 'capture in her net the very authorities who [were] meant to protect the public' from everything she represented—female individuality, sexual autonomy, and the stage. As with all women performers of her time, scandal was firmly entangled with her appeal—an appeal that saw special trains organised to convey admirers to her shows. And it was not the first time she had provoked suspicion: The maharaja himself was 'much pleased with her' (which was interpreted as nocturnal pleasure), and so, as art historian Rupika Chawla records, when she sought to commission the court painter Ravi Varma for a portrait, his brother displayed 'intense disapproval', fearing it would affect the artist's own reputation and dignity.

But such pronounced scandal eclipsed much of what Balamani of Kumbakonam achieved, and the rich, albeit tragic accumulation of experience that is her story. Balamani, in the words of commentator Veejay Sai, was the first of many remarkable Indian women who challenged 'heteropatriarchy' in her day—and who, for her pains, mainly received, in return, ignominy and obscurity. Even though Balamani was 'fortressed amongst a thousand anecdotes', it 'is almost impossible to believe a character like her lived in the remote south', where today she is largely forgotten. But this was a talented woman who left fans ecstatic across the peninsula, even as she pursued an intellectual mission to reinvent on the modern stage, as she remarked herself to a French contemporary, 'the whole of the ancient Sanskrit plays'.

Balamani was a woman of ambition and resolve, determined to transport the art she had inherited as a devadasi to wider audiences in imaginative forms. Breaking out of the temple, she became among the earliest to establish a formal enterprise: the Balamani Drama Company. She was the first to introduce Petromax lighting onstage, just as she was the earliest to allot ladies-only spaces at her ticketed public performances. Her entire venture was female-run, and while others like the Kannamani and Danivambal companies in the same late nineteenth century period also followed this pattern, what distinguished Balamani was her preference for destitute women who were disenfranchised by anti-devadasi legislation. Her company, it has been noted, was in fact 'almost

an asylum for women who needed shelter and security'. Of course, none of this alleviated the stigma that came with being 'the dancing girl' of Kumbakonam, but Balamani flourished as a businesswoman and a patron of the arts, as much as an individual of singular personality.

As an artist too, she was inventive. She was, Sai points out, a pioneer in taking up 'social themes in Tamil theatre' and moving beyond mythology into fresher genres—a detective play she performed was later adapted for film. Infatuated poets and musicians composed pieces extolling her beauty and one such *javali* was later sung by the venerable M.S. Subbulakshmi for the gramophone. Instead of seeking approval from the orthodox by shoring up pious 'respectability', Balamani was what is pejoratively termed 'bold', cleverly executing even a nude scene in one play—naturally, the play was banned for this very reason by thin-skinned men of less 'bold' persuasions. Success also brought in its wake much wealth—Balamani drove in silver carriages and presided over a mansion staffed by fifty servitors (again, largely rehabilitated women). But it also wove through Balamani's life debates on censorship, the social challenge that came from the brahminisation of the arts, and of course, the anomaly of a successful working woman who had the capacity to claim that prized patriarchal prize: a legacy.

Patriarchy wouldn't be patriarchy if it allowed a challenge like that absolute success, though. 'History and fate turned cruel to Balamani,' Sai says, though her solitude in a world designed for men did its own damage. The years passed, and she aged. Her sense of charity, which included getting young girls married and settling them with handsome dowries, led to financial calamity. She, who lived in gardens, surrounded by peacocks and deer, moved impoverished to overcrowded

Madurai—when Balamani died in 1935, it took an old, loyal associate to collect money from well-wishers to pay for her cremation. But somewhere, the flame was kept alive. As the novelist Pierre Loti recorded in her heyday, 'The poor know the road to her house well enough.' And it was among those poor that Balamani's name survived, awaiting its resurrection as a story marked by many triumphs but also great tragedy.

THE GRAMOPHONE QUEEN OF INDIA

26 June 1873 is the birth anniversary of a remarkable Muslim woman. She wasn't born Muslim—this lady of decidedly imperious mien was in fact the daughter of an Armenian and his half-Hindu, half-British-Christian wife. Her mother was known as Victoria Hemmings, and the girl was named Eileen Angelina Yeoward. But when she was still a child, her identity was transformed forever after Victoria embraced Islam and became 'Badi' Malka Jaan. Her daughter followed suit and took the name Gauhar Jaan, a name that would deliver her to greatness as the 'first dancing girl of Calcutta', India's earliest recording sensation, and the foremost of this country's musical divas.

Gauhar and her mother were performers, both of them talented, impetuous women whose lives featured disappointing men or, at any rate, disappointments caused by men. Malka Jaan's marriage with her ice-factory-engineer husband ended when Gauhar was less than six years old. They moved from

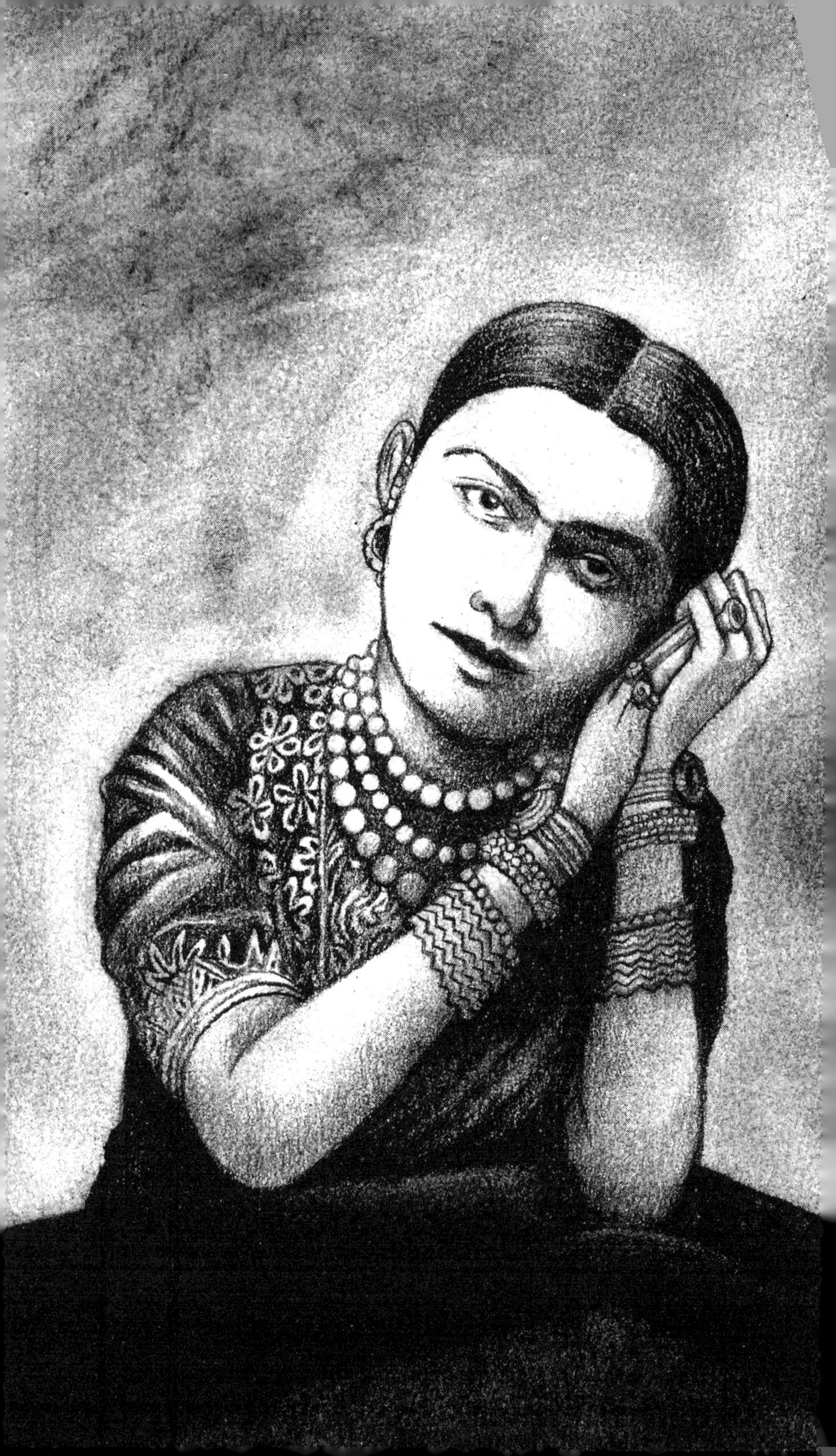

The Courtesan, the Mahatma & the Italian Brahmin

Azamgarh to Benares with Malka's paramour, and here the mother achieved considerable celebrity as a dancer and courtesan. By 1883, when the child was ten, they settled in Calcutta, and quickly grew accustomed to a life of luxury and success, even as Gauhar was trained in Kathak, to sing, and acquired a rich grasp of languages: Between 1902 and 1920, she would sing for around 600 gramophone records in tongues as diverse as Persian, Gujarati and Pashto, though at least occasionally, one presumes, she did not have a clue what she was actually singing.

Following in her mother's artistic footsteps, Gauhar's first public performance came in her teens at the court of the Rajah of Darbhanga in 1887. Though recognised immediately for her talent, she was not satisfied as a court musician in a second-grade principality, and chose, instead, to return to bustling Calcutta to cement her name. It was here that she began to attract the high and mighty, their wealth and riches collecting in proverbial mountains before her. Gauhar soon became something of a legend: the woman who drove around in splendid carriages and cars, the lady who disappeared to Bombay now and then for the races, the *tawaif* (courtesan) who demanded a whole train from a royal patron to convey her entourage to his capital and, most famously, as an eccentric who spent the then extravagant sum of ₹20,000 on a party to celebrate the advent of her beloved cat's kittens.

But what distinguished Gauhar from other wealthy tawaifs was the gramophone. In November 1902, at the Great Eastern Hotel in Calcutta, Gauhar arrived with her retinue to sing for Frederick Gaisberg of The Gramophone Company. Prolonged negotiations had preceded this meeting, and Gauhar was paid the princely sum of ₹3,000 for singing into a contraption rumoured to be the devil's own—something, people said, that might irreversibly seize her voice. She was undaunted, though perhaps somewhat irritated, by having to sing into the massive brass recording horn that was placed near her face. She had three minutes—and indeed, would master the technique of delivering an entire song in that duration—at the end of which, she spoke into the device, in English, signing off with what became her trademark: 'My name is Gauhar Jaan.'

Over the next two decades, and through hundreds of her recordings, Gauhar changed the way music was practised in India, and amplified its reach. Her voice travelled not only to faraway places in the country but also abroad, and as her biographer Vikram Sampath discovered, her unibrowed face appeared on picture postcards in Europe and even on matchboxes. Gaisberg knew he had a figure of great glamour here, noting that he never saw her repeat either her clothes or her jewellery, both of which she possessed in inexhaustible quantities, while rumour placed the price of a pass to her salon at anywhere between ₹1,000 and ₹3,000. Less than a decade after she first announced her name into that brass horn, Gauhar was at the height of her fame, performing at the famous Delhi Durbar of 1911 before the newly crowned British king, George V, and his royal consort.

But while professional successes were many, personal tragedy too forced its way into Gauhar's life through unfortunate romances. She fell in love with a famous stage actor and lived several happy years with him. When her mother died, it was he who consoled her, becoming a pillar of strength. His death by a sudden illness, however, terminated that relationship. What followed was a disastrous affair with her secretary, a man ten years her junior, who in the end proved to harbour more affection for Gauhar's possessions than Gauhar herself. Court cases had to be fought and at one time she was compelled to prove her paternity to a judge, pleading before her hostile, long-lost father to acknowledge her as his blood.

The ostentation that was as much a part of Gauhar's life as her talent, would, in the end, dissolve her life and career. Accustomed to a life of glitter and style, she made predictable mistakes where her finances were concerned. By the 1920s, she had passed her prime, and her legal battles and other woes had taken their toll on her bank balance. She moved, eventually, far away from the Calcutta where she once towered over her peers, and settled in Mysore, where the local maharajah granted her a modest pension. And here, in a cottage in the south of India, she who was born Eileen, knew fame as Gauhar, and whose voice thrilled a million admirers, died a forgotten woman in 1930.

A BRAHMIN WOMAN OF SCANDAL

At the dawn of the twentieth century, a scandal of horrific proportions reared its head before Kerala's brahminical elite. The year was 1905 and the setting was princely Cochin. Home to prominent Namboothiri families, this was also one of the seats of orthodoxy in India. The Namboothiris were fond of rules and ritual, perched though all of this was on extraordinary social privilege. As E.M.S. Namboothiripad put it, these brahmins 'occupied the highest position among all other communities … collected fabulous amounts as rent, enjoyed undisputed supremacy over the tillers of the soil, and maintained intimacy with the ruling monarchs'. The immortal Parasurama, they claimed, had bestowed Kerala upon them, this being the fount of their legitimacy. Every other group was to serve, and the Namboothiris would apportion caste status and privilege to those who subscribed to this world view. As late as 1875, the brahmin was officially cast as the common folk's 'royal liege and benefactor, their suzerain master, their household deity', and indeed, 'their very god on earth'.

The Courtesan, the Mahatma & the Italian Brahmin

While colonialism began to chip away at this cocoon of ritual and luxury, one of the earliest cracks in the order appeared not outside, but within—in the quarters of a woman. Namboothiri women, after all, saw little of the privilege that was so normal for their men. The only Malayali females in purdah, they had no freedom of movement, no ownership of property, and little education. Or as one of them put it, the *antharjanam* (literally, 'indoor person') was 'a jailed creature'. She was 'born crying, lives her life in tears, and dies weeping'. It was not an exaggeration. Even marriage—the only prospect for women in a patriarchal set-up—was denied to many of them. Among Namboothiris there was no rule decreeing early marriage for girls, while only the eldest male was permitted to take a brahmin wife. The result was that younger sons married non-brahmin women, while legions of Namboothiri females lived in sequestered spinsterhood. And if they did find husbands, it was often already married men, who used the opportunity to exchange their own sisters and daughters as though this were a transaction for chattel.

In 1905, however, the world of the elite was shattered by our protagonist, since enshrined in Malayali imagination as a *pratikaradevata*, goddess of revenge. Her name was Savitri, and she lived in Kuriyedathu house in Thrissur district. Married at eighteen to a man whose brother had sexually abused her at ten, she took it upon herself, it is said, to unleash fury upon her caste and its leaders. While Namboothiri men took wives and mistresses, the antharjanam was to be chaste and docile: it was this presumption that Savitri would demolish. In the words of the writer V.T. Bhattathiripad, she challenged male sexual entitlement 'with the same weapon'—she slept with men other than her husband. There were high-caste men, and there were lower-caste men; there was her brother-in-law, as there were other relations; there were Tamil brahmins and Nair aristocrats. There was even a Kathakali star, not to speak of an epileptic. By the time her deeds were revealed, occurring in her chamber as much as the temple grounds, Savitri, now twenty-three, had been with no less than sixty-six men.

It was a scandal unparalleled, partly because it was the first such to be disseminated widely through the newspaper press. There was a traditional round of interrogation by her caste-men, but the furore caused the local maharajah to order a second round in his palace. Various theories circulated: as scholar J. Devika records, one of these placed Savitri as the pivot of a cunning plot hatched by the ruler. She was apprehended with fewer lovers, but prevailed upon to name many more, to get rid of an emerging class of Namboothiri modernisers who were challenging the orthodox old guard. But what shocked all involved—and the public witnessing—was her reported coolness. As the *Malayala Manorama* put it, 'She replied like a barrister.' For she had evidence of her trysts. She knew what marks her lovers had on their persons, or if there were warts on their genitals. She remembered dates on the basis of festivals and events, and one by one she named them—great exemplars of contemporary society, all guilty of fornicating with a brahmin wife.

Cast as a victim seeking vengeance, Savitri has been reincarnated in fiction as well as film. Lalithambika Antharjanam retold her tale, and Matampu Kunhukuttan too describes this heroine who paid patriarchy back in its worst coin. But there are others who seek nuance. She was certainly a victim, many of her 'affairs' occurring when she was only an adolescent. But the emphasis on a calculated quest for revenge was perhaps exaggerated by voices championing reform, the scholar Rajeev Kumaramkandath suggests, seeking to use these unparalleled events to force change. Savitri herself had more complex experiences, as her testimony reveals. A mahout, for instance, had a bottle of rose water she wanted: he had heard of her relations with another mahout, and offered her the bottle if she would sleep with him. Savitri agreed. Another time, she slept with a man fearing he would divulge her involvement with a third person—it was fear of blackmail that motivated her, not necessarily a desire to ensnare more men in a web of revenge.

Still, there is in her meticulous recollection of each tryst something formidable. So too in the fact that when she was excommunicated, with her she took sixty-six men and their reputations. All of Kerala seemed to savour the blow she dealt her community, while champions of change rejoiced at the exposure. 'It is indeed a sight to watch the indomitability on their face when [the men named] go to question the woman,' it was reported, 'and the grief-stricken expression when they come back.' In the years that followed, Namboothiri women began to reject their seclusion; men began to breach custom. Savitri herself disappeared into Tamil country, never to be seen again. But in her wake she left horror and admiration both, casting the first stone at the house of orthodoxy. No longer was the brahmin a veritable god on earth—he had been tainted, his pretensions dismantled by a woman who was beyond shame and fear.

'I'M A NAGA FIRST, A NAGA SECOND, AND A NAGA LAST'

On 12 June 1960, puzzled immigration officials in London detained a traveller who had landed up without bothering about that small thing called a passport. His face was partially paralysed, but his tongue was defiant. 'When the British came to my country,' he declared, 'they did not bring any passport with them. Why should I now carry one to Britain?' It was a startling riposte but the visitor's identity clarified matters. Angami Zapu Phizo, one-time insurance salesman and proprietor of 'Gwiz Products', which offered a range of face creams and balms, was a dangerous separatist, sentenced to death by the Indian Union—a union over a decade old at the time but which was yet to fully reconcile with the people Phizo represented, and whose cause delivered him to his tragic destiny: exile and death in a foreign land.

The Nagas, descended from Mongoloid tribes and members of the Tibeto-Burman language family, occupied a vast hilly

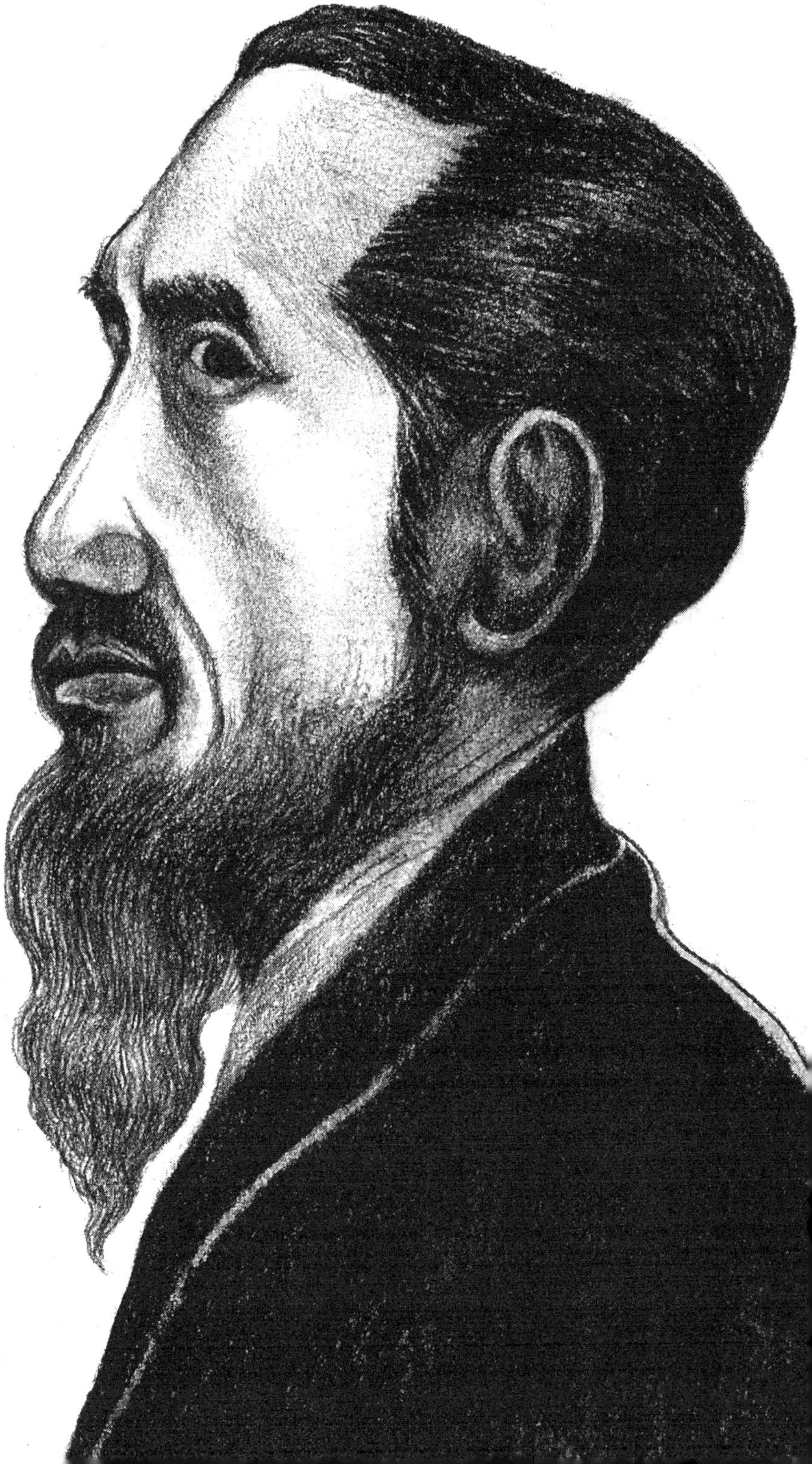

tract in the north-east of India for much of known history. Then, in 1832, an East India Company captain with 700 soldiers, 800 'coolies'—and no passport—decided to gun his way through their lands. Held loosely by rival clans, the advent of the British produced the tribes' first common enemy, transforming also into a catalyst for unity. For the captain, however, the motive was clear—the company had brought Manipur next door under its control and now sought a direct route into nearby Assam; a route that could only be had by bulldozing through what was later described as this 'savage tract lying in the midst of our settled districts'. A few patronising lines about 'civilising the hillmen' were also thrown in, and Naga territory was promptly justified as for the British to seize.

Despite the hysterical onslaught of propaganda about headhunting, the Nagas were not convinced of their so-called inferiority. On the contrary, 'We are all equal,' Phizo proudly noted. 'We have no caste distinctions, no high class or low class. There is no minority problem and we believe in that form of democratic government which permits the rule of the people as a whole. We talk freely, we live freely, and we often fight freely too. We have few inhibitions. Wild? Yes, but free. There is order in this chaos, law in this freedom.' It was not what the West defined as 'civilised' but it held many other cultural ingredients for nationhood. The Nagas of the time, naturally then, were alarmed to discover that an accident of history—and the construction of a highway—had transformed them into 'Indians' overnight.

Phizo, however, was an unlikely voice for Naga nationalism. Born in 1904, his was a family of converted Christians (and it should be remembered that after British arms, it was missionaries who followed into Naga territory). And yet their tribal background retained enough influence for his parents to delay his baptism till the age of eighteen. Selling insurance for a Canadian company in the bigger towns of the region, and the Bible in its villages, the man travelled extensively. Over time, he developed a sense of nationalism inspired by the past as well as by his peers. The time, though, was not ripe. He married and eventually moved to Burma, never, however, relinquishing his vision for a sovereign Nagaland. 'I am a Naga first, a Naga second, and a Naga last,' he announced, even as the British thought him 'as thoroughly a nasty piece of work as ever there was one'.

It was the Second World War that allowed Phizo an opportunity to realise his vision and rise above his middle-class existence. And this did not merely entail terminating British domination, but also aimed to challenge any Indian claims over Naga territory—he did not intend to watch a 'black government' replace the white. When in the 1940s Subhas Chandra Bose and the Japanese took Burma, Phizo cooperated more readily with the latter than with Bose, even as the campaign to invade India was ultimately defeated. The British, when they returned, locked him up in jail for his efforts. 'I was condemned a traitor,' he remembered without repentence. 'But I was certainly not a traitor to my own conscience.'

In 1946, Phizo came home to lead the Naga National Council. His opening sentiment was disappointment. In Burma, he 'had witnessed what patriotism could achieve'. In Nagaland, there 'was nothing—no unity, no ideas'. He decided to plant these ideas, therefore, meeting Mahatma Gandhi to negotiate a space outside India for his people. 'I will come to the Naga Hills,' Gandhi promised when the possibility of military coercion was raised, and 'I will ask them to shoot me before one Naga is shot.' But Jawaharlal Nehru after 1947 would not brook any talk of tribal autonomy—India was already in shock after partition, and the territories and borders that remained were not negotiable.

Phizo, who 'gave the impression of carrying, single-handed, in his little briefcase, the destiny of the entire Naga people', was prepared to fight. But when events turned violent under his direction, Nehru's determination was matched by the march of Indian troops. Phizo had no option but to live with the consequences. He went into exile, travelling via East Pakistan (now Bangladesh) on a fake El Salvadoran passport to Switzerland first. He made every effort to attract and win international support for his cause, but there was nothing tangible anybody could offer. After all, Nehru, despite a blood-curdling (though perhaps necessary) policy in Nagaland, was a towering post-colonial figure; Phizo, as London's newspapers announced, only a famous 'headhunter'.

By the time he died in 1990, thirty years later, Phizo was resigned to his fate. 'I made a mistake in over-estimating the will of those I had left behind in Nagaland to resist the pressures put on them,' he remarked gloomily to a journalist. 'I made another mistake in believing that in the West truth would conquer. That was not so. Having come here, I could see the world is too distracted, too divided. I thought of myself as a student of history, but I have discovered I have a lot to learn.' He had a dream that seduced many of his people. What he learnt painfully was that it was destined to remain just that: a dream.

THE MONK FOR EVERY INDIAN

It is tempting to wonder if Swami Vivekananda might have achieved his enduring fame and celebrity had he chosen to remain a 'Vividishananda' or even a 'Satchidananda' at the time of his sensational (and defining) visit to the United States. These were, after all, names he preferred at various points before finally confirming, in 1893, the label by which the world remembers him. 'Vivekananda' certainly rolls better off the tongue than the first of the other options, but more importantly, it is also the name by which this peerless Bengali monk has been appropriated by practically every political camp in India, to deploy in support of varied and sometimes antithetical motives. To those whose blood is not red but saffron, he was a champion of Hindu might and a beacon for resurgent pride. Those who abhor majoritarian claims also point to the very same man, in whose preachings may be found endorsements of a liberal order. This iconic thinker-saint has emerged as everybody's favourite precisely because he can be different things to different people—a feature in which resides both his strength and his fascinating longevity in the tug of war that is popular imagination.

His story is well established: birth as Narendranath into a *bhadralok* house in Calcutta, a promising academic career, his encounter with the spiritual master Ramakrishna, and his transformation as not only an architect of modern Hindu thought but also as a messenger for India itself. What firmly confirmed him as a force was his time abroad, beginning with his famous address at the Parliament of Religions in Chicago. As his Irish disciple, Sister Nivedita, remarked, 'it may be said that when he began to speak' at that 1893 gathering, 'it was of the religious ideas of the Hindus'. But by the time he had finished his monumental address, 'Hinduism had been created'. This modern rendition of ancient traditions entitled him to a place in history already, but some offer fantastical tales that heralded much earlier the certainty of distinction: he was Shiva incarnate, so that as a child the only way to calm his mischief was to pour 'cold water on his head and simultaneously [chant] the name of Shiva'. Other stories have him showing a tendency towards meditation—when a snake slithered into his room, so admiring was the reptile that it coiled up to study Narendranath, utterly transfixed. It can be safely concluded that these stories are entirely apocryphal, though they served their purpose in romanticising Vivekananda's work with the magic of god-ordained destiny.

The philosophy he upheld was a refashioned Advaita Vedanta, most famously associated with the eighth-century thinker Sankara. But esoteric concerns aside, what electrified contemporary nineteenth-century minds was his blending of a religious reawakening with national reinvigoration. After generations of an inferiority complex fed by a colonial state—

The Courtesan, the Mahatma & the Italian Brahmin

that India was rotten and devoid of civilisational value—Vivekananda refused to argue on conventional measures of progress. 'Let others,' he declared, 'talk of politics … of the immense wealth poured in by trade, of the power and spread of commercialisation, of the glorious fountain of physical liberty.' The 'Hindu mind' did not care—India's mission was not to count coins, focused as it was on 'the evolution of spiritual humanity', making it 'the blessed *punya bhumi*' of mankind itself. This formula was not original, but where Vivekananda differed from previous reformers in Bengal—who too sought to restore pride in Hinduism but whose message circulated within the elite—was in his conviction that the masses needed awakening, and religion was the medium for it. 'Before flooding India with socialistic or political ideas,' he argued, 'first deluge the land with spiritual ideas.' That he travelled the length of this vast country, and to places as distant as Nagasaki and New York, further energised his cause.

His spiritual ideas were derived from Sanskrit philosophy, even though its dissemination was not to remain in the language of philosophers. 'It is,' observed Vivekananda pithily, 'an insult to a starving man to teach him metaphysics.' Things would have to be simplified, translated into vernacular tongues, and 'fiery' missionaries were to transport the message. Old movements such as the Bhakti of popular worship had to be discarded. 'Look at this nation,' claimed Vivekananda, 'and see what has been the outcome.' While in Chicago he highlighted divine love, in India itself he saw Bhakti as making the nation 'effeminate—a race of women!' Orissa, for example, was 'a land of cowards; and Bengal, running after the Radha-*prema* … has almost lost all sense of manliness.' While not violent or muscular, Hinduism had to become a proactive faith, he thought, and eschew the complacency of disorganised variety. Vivekananda affirmed his belief that such a reinvention of Hinduism was the key to 'awaken the national consciousness', in a point that proponents of Hindutva cherish. Internal differences had to be weeded out because 'the whole secret lies in organisation, accumulation of power, coordination of wills', and all this through a common religious spirit pervading the land—a spirit firmly Hindu.

Reformers from below were not to act too aggressively against brahminism. An example Vivekananda cited was the case of America's blacks. 'Before the abolition, these poor negroes were the property of somebody, and ... [were] looked after... Today they are the property of nobody. Their lives are of no value.' So too, in India, despite injustices of caste, it was unwise to attempt too aggressively to push the elite out of the way, for it might cripple unity. Besides, 'To the non-Brahmin castes I say ... you are suffering from your own fault. Who told you to neglect spirituality and Sanskrit learning? What have you been doing all this time?...Why do you fret and fume because somebody else had more brains, more energy, more pluck and go than you?' Despite problematic pronouncements like this at home, to his global audience, Vivekananda's words were refreshingly open. 'I am proud to belong to a religion which has taught the world both tolerance and universal acceptance. We believe not only in universal toleration, but we accept all religions as true'—a message often highlighted by liberal Hindus to challenge the intellectual and often physical violence against minorities by right-wing groups in India now.

There were in Vivekananda's message contradictions, and indeed he may have had more than one message. In his own time, however, these did not seem like contradictions at all. He spoke to different people in different ways. When addressing

The Courtesan, the Mahatma & the Italian Brahmin

Indians struggling against caste, speaking multiple languages, and with regional identities, his purpose was to engender national unity through a common, reinvented Hinduism. To those abroad, his mission was to present Hinduism not as that tangled jungle of superstition the British deemed it, but as a highly mature and accomplished faith: 'a robust, modernist and universalist Hinduism, anchored in its own precepts, that could look the rest of the world's religions in the eye—and oblige them to blink', as Shashi Tharoor puts it. Consistency was not Vivekananda's strong point, but it was his inconsistency that made him such an appealing figure for large numbers of people. Besides, if he were to be consistent, why would he have ever even become a monk?

THE PHOTOGRAPHER–PRINCE OF JAIPUR

In 1857, when the great rebellion swept much of north India into a storm of gunpowder and rage, one of the consolations the embattled British possessed was the loyalty of numerous Indian princes. Even as several southern maharajahs issued proclamations of fidelity, a number of their northern counterparts mobilised actual armies in service of the East India Company (showing that, from the start, the rebellion was not a blanket uprising of Indians against their colonisers). Thus, leading princes of Punjab stood with the British, just as the reigning Scindia in Gwalior 'strove hard to keep his own subjects faithful to his liege lords'. In Rajputana, similarly, support came despite widespread public sympathy for the rebels. 'At every town through which we passed,' an officer wrote of Jaipur state, 'the inhabitants cursed and abused us ... In fact, we were really in an enemy's country.' But the local ruler himself pitched his flag with the British, lending them thousands of troops who not only served the Company gloriously but even punished those 'refractory villages' for flirting with mutiny.

From his position, it was a shrewd stand to take, for had it been otherwise, Sawai Ram Singh II of 'Jeypoor' himself might have been punished. Described subsequently as 'a ruler of singular intelligence and enlightenment', Ram Singh was only twenty-two at the time of the rebellion, and it was after some hesitation that he decided to endorse the cause of the British. He had spent his formative years in the guardianship of a regency council, which while ostensibly under Company supervision, was actually dominated by a coterie of noblemen. When in 1851 he succeeded to full powers, he had to balance both interests against each other—in order to actually exercise his authority, he proactively sought the 'constant counsels and active official support' of the British. His courtiers remained influential all the same, so that when they showed sympathy for the rebels in 1857, it took some time for Ram Singh to make up his mind about his own position—on whether he should raise swords in the name of the mutineers, or fight for a foreign power which bolstered his own princely authority.

Had he opted for the former, Ram Singh might later have been deposed and banished to the footnotes of history. Instead, he made a choice that not only ensured his survival, but also enabled him to become one of the nineteenth century's more remarkable Indians. That he had an interesting mind was clear early on in his life. When Prince Alexei Dmitrievich Saltykov of Russia (who travelled in India as far south as Kerala, sketching and diarising) met him a decade before the mutiny, the 'plain-looking' prince was still only old enough to play with wooden elephants and toy horses. But he left on his visitor a definite impression. 'Asking after my health,' recorded Saltykov, Ram Singh was quick to race on to other

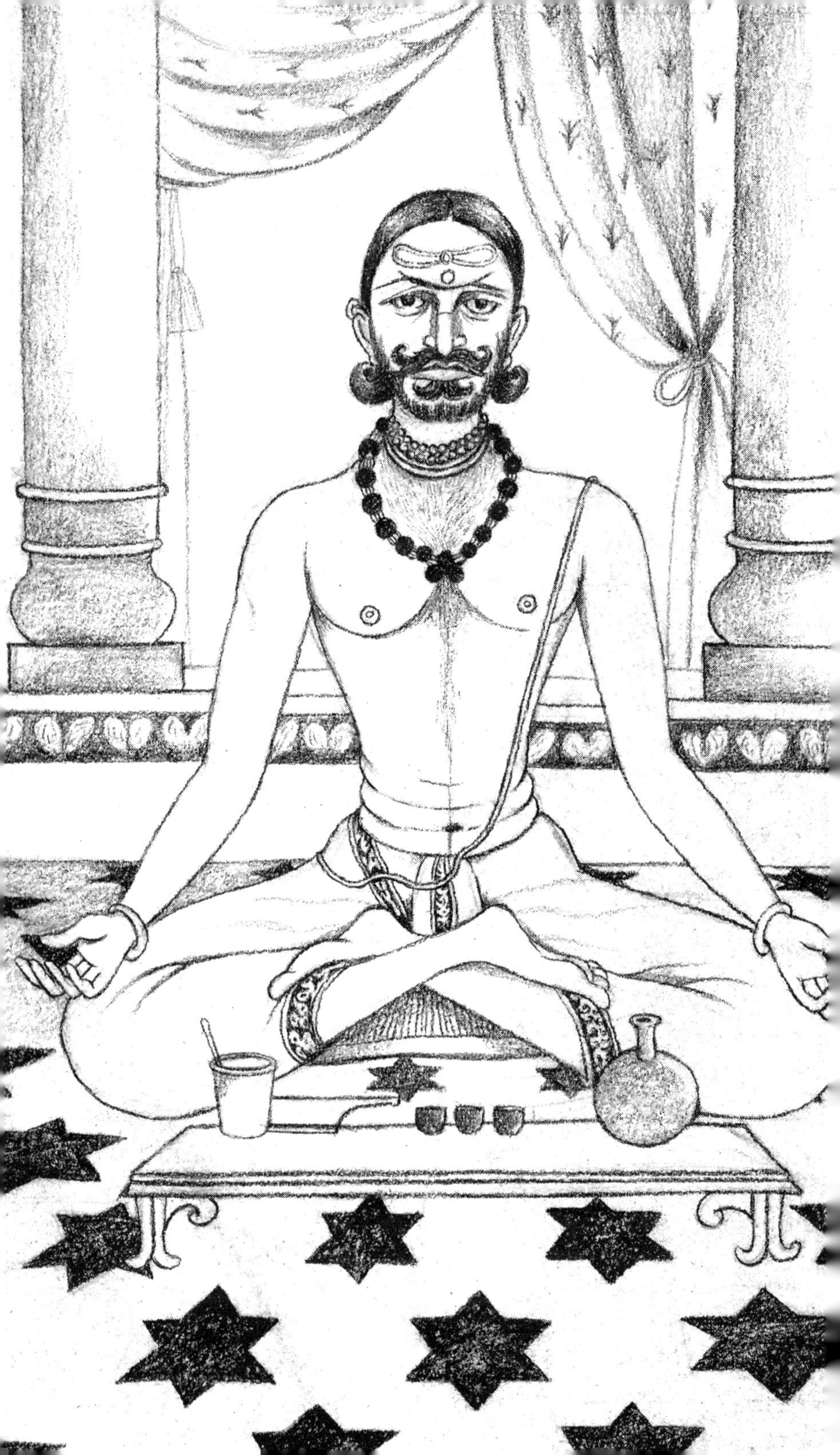

subjects. He wanted to know, for instance, 'where Russia is located and how long it would take to go there from Jaipur'. He then 'ordered his English language teacher to ask him a few words in that language', no doubt to dazzle the Russian dignitary. Finally, 'he got up from the throne, walked to the archery hall' and 'showed us his skill in archery'. Ram Singh, in other words, knew he had a captive audience—and he wanted to present an image that could not be easily forgotten.

As ruler of Jaipur, the lean and somewhat morose-looking Ram Singh was firmly a progressive. In 1867 he set up the first girls' school in his capital despite 'popular prejudice' against such innovations. He inaugurated the Maharaja's College, where English and Sanskrit were taught side by side, even as he established a school of art, a public library, and a hospital that commemorates the visit of a British viceroy, Lord Mayo. The main streets in Jaipur were paved in his reign, while highways were constructed to connect his seat to other towns in the principality. Kerosene and gas lights were installed along thoroughfares, just as other projects were launched, from waterworks and a drainage system to a postal network and a telegraph office. Changes in administration were also made, launching modern governance in the state through new instruments, public bodies and buildings. Meanwhile, fluent in English as well as in Western thought, Ram Singh became a bridge between two worlds, tuned into evolving times, but also married firmly to his roots and to Indian tradition.

What really distinguishes this collaborator of the Raj, though, is a royal pastime that quickly graduated into an enduring passion. When Louis Rousselet, the traveller, met Ram Singh in 1866, he was surprised that the maharajah's 'dress was handsome, but showed an indifference to ornament'; instead of jewels and a sword, as the stereotypical image of a native prince would depict, there was 'an immense revolver thrust into his belt'. Even more notable than the ruler's appearance, the Frenchman recalled, was how their conversation 'turned on photography'. And before long he realised that Ram Singh was not only 'an admirer of this art, but is himself a skilled photographer'. In fact, for about a decade, the maharajah had been a member of the Bengal Photographic Society, well before he acquired his first camera in 1862. And while princes across India developed a general fondness for photography, few mastered it in the way he did—or created a collection that wonderfully encapsulates the world in which the Victorian and the Indian met both constructively as well as to do ideological battle.

It was portraiture that most attracted the maharajah. In 1870, he photographed Queen Victoria's visiting son, just as he did his new palace doctor. But what marked Ram Singh for distinction even here were the portraits he made of his harem women. There were Hindu women, and there were Muslim women; there were superior concubines (*pardayats*) and there were junior mistresses (*paswans*). As the scholar Laura Weinstein notes, to photograph women ordinarily in purdah was 'completely without precedent'. Of course, Ram Singh never made portraits of his aristocratic wives—even he could not breach custom to that degree—but by bringing his establishment into view through the camera, he nevertheless dispelled multiple reigning stereotypes about the Indian harem. Where the British perceived the *zenana* as dark, sinister places, lacking in fresh air and guarded by scheming eunuchs (partly because this was the one cultural and political realm in India they could not penetrate despite their power), the women who appear in Ram Singh's photographs are powerful and dignified, far from Victorian cliché. 'The zenana portraits,'

The Courtesan, the Mahatma & the Italian Brahmin

concludes Weinstein, 'reveal no sickness or dirt, depraved or deviant faces, exposed bodies or sexually suggestive poses.' What they show, according to her, is a world where there is no pressing demand for Western 'light'—where there is nobody crying to be 'rescued' from despotic oriental hands.

Certainly, Ram Singh could have been making a conscious, deliberate statement in Indianising the gaze of the Western camera and he most definitely broke rules by immortalising in his album women of the Jaipur zenana. By photographing its inmates as exuding confidence and splendour, he was also challenging tropes about Indian women; about the self-righteous British claim to civilisation and the supposed Indian proclivity for debauched, unmanly sensuality. And yet, despite the scholarly approval he now enjoys, this is not the complete picture as far as this remarkable man is concerned—for Ram Singh was also able to employ the camera in ways that would have horrified the British, as is evident from another series of pictures he took, featuring himself in sexual congress with bemused ladies of his harem. In one of them, for example, a lady is on her back, smiling at the camera. Her ornaments are intact, as is the cloth that covers her head. But in the scene with her is also her ruler and prince, his hands on her breasts, and squatting as he penetrates her.

Perhaps, then, beyond his stately portraits of the high and the low, and over and above his desire to excel as a 'native' prince, Ram Singh was also a mischievous man whose curiosity took unconventional forms. But of all the achievements he lined up in his remarkable life, his love of photography remains the most memorable. Throughout the 1860s and 1870s, even as he carried out his programme of administrative reform in Jaipur, the maharajah honed his skill with the camera, leaving behind a collection now valued in the tens of millions. And by the time he went to the grave in 1880, aged only forty-five, Ram Singh had journeyed through a world of personal and political experience, going from the young prince of 1857, who gambled in favour of the British against the temptations of rebellion, to the photographer-maharajah, who created his own images and rejected what had till then been perpetuated by the Raj.

PERIYAR IN THE AGE OF 'ANTI-NATIONALS'

'There is no god. There is no god at all. He who created god is a fool. He who propagates god is a scoundrel. He who worships god is a barbarian.' In a time when scrutiny of even powerful mortals is deemed 'contrarian' and the simple application of common sense is seen as 'anti-national', Periyar's philosophy is a refreshingly blunt reminder of the freedom of thought and expression that existed in India in times gone by. As the Internet mobs and over-dramatic television anchors tell individuals off with alarming regularity for daring to possess a dissenting opinion 'while soldiers are dying on the border', for instance, one wonders what Periyar, born E.V. Ramasamy Naicker in 1879, would have said if someone asked him to swallow his voice because it was the fashion of the day to obey like good children and to think inside the box.

While over four decades have passed since Periyar died, one can't help but imagine him leading the ranks of 'anti-nationals' if he lived in contemporary India. He came close enough in the age of the Mahatma, against whom he maintained a catalogue of disagreements, declaring that Independence Day was really 'a day of mourning'. On another occasion, he thought the constitution deserved all the honour that came from being consigned to flames. 'Anti-national' was not the chosen term for those who refused to follow the herd in Periyar's time, but he was something perhaps even more unusual: He was the anti-Gandhi. Those who were privileged in caste could stomach Gandhi's message with its clear blunting of radicalism, while Periyar gave them a severe case of indigestion. And yet, many Indians of his day embraced him and millions celebrated his rationality instead of falling in line with what venerable elders chastely decided was 'proper'.

Where Gandhi was the embodiment of saintly piety, Periyar exemplified rebellion. Where Gandhi romanticised rural contentment, Periyar envisioned an ambitious age of aircrafts and heavy machinery. While Gandhi renounced sex in his thirties, Periyar married a thirty-year-old in his seventies. When Gandhi's satyagrahis in white stood up to British tyrants, Periyar excoriated the very Indian tyranny of caste by leading his Self-Respect Movement wearing black. Where the Mahatma's nationalism was immersed in Hindu morality, Periyar was an atheist who wrote op-eds titled 'Honeymoon in the Hindu Zoo'. Gandhi spent a lifetime seeking to tame the flesh while Periyar flaunted it (and had himself photographed) among like-minded nudists abroad. And where Gandhi was cremated like a good Hindu, Periyar was buried, flouting every dictum issued by his forefathers, who too were not beyond reproach or criticism.

Gandhi celebrated Sita as the embodiment of Indian womanhood with her purity and self-sacrifice, while Periyar

The Courtesan, the Mahatma & the Italian Brahmin

declared the Ramayana to be full of 'absurdities', with quite a controversial sequence of superlatives for its heroine. Gandhi painted visions of ideal women, while Periyar warned ordinary women to beware of deification. 'Have cats ever freed rats? Have foxes ever liberated goats or chickens?' he asked. 'Have whites ever enriched Indians? Have brahmins ever given non-brahmins justice? We can be confident that women will never be emancipated by men.' Gandhi thought motherhood was divine and spiritual; Periyar saw pregnancy and childbirth as 'impediments to liberty and independence', promoting birth control even if it came at the expense of maternal salvation. Against Gandhi's sage-like pronouncements on the female, Periyar was branded immoral. 'Morality,' he wryly retorted, 'cannot be one-way traffic.'

So too with nationalism (a word much misused in today's world) was Periyar irreverent. He viewed it as finely woven, brilliantly designed deception, diverting masses of people from the real state of affairs, sometimes through emotional blackmail and sometimes through the intoxications of pride, keeping them from checking the book of democratic accounts. He was suspicious of saints, arguing that Gandhi, with his 'religious guise, god-related discourse, constant mention of truth, non-violence, satyagraha, purifying of the heart, the power of the spirit, sacrifice and penance on the one hand, and the propaganda of his followers' had become a 'a political dictator'. Sure, there were many who 'consider him to be a rishi, a sage, Christ, the Prophet, a Mahatma', indeed even 'an avatar of Vishnu', but this was all, at the end of the day, plain politics.

Gandhi, so it seemed to Periyar, sought freedom from the British but feared social upheaval at home even if it offered greater justice—he preferred order over turbulent equality. 'A bhangi does for society what a mother does for a baby,' claimed Gandhi patronisingly, seeking 'the beauty of compromise' in social dynamics between the low, who had answers to seek, and the high, who had much to lose. Periyar ached for radical action to the extent that his remarks could seem patently hateful, once recommending that 'if you have to choose between killing a brahmin or a snake, spare the snake'. Gandhi thought 'life without religion is a life without principle' and that education must never lose sight of its moral responsibilities. Periyar believed that the 'worship of god, practice of religion, propitiation of rulers, which are all calculated to keep men in mental slavery, should never [even] enter the portals of education'.

Periyar was the enfant terrible of his time, puncturing with unafraid focus holy narratives of India's destiny at a time when the Mahatma was convinced of this destiny. He was a contrarian, and was branded worse, but many Indians of his time absorbed his philosophy even as they embraced Gandhi's vision. He was, in the larger scheme of things, handicapped by language, and besides, political incorrectness hardly makes for a great career. But as the ruckus around the world grows and even elementary expressions of reason provoke admonishments, one wishes we had a Periyar here again—not to set the cat among the mice but to hold up a mirror and to remind us that there is always another way, and that we must sometimes stop following and start thinking.

ANNIE BESANT
AN INCONVENIENT WOMAN

When Annie Besant arrived in India in 1893, she had already accumulated enough notoriety for a lifetime. This was a woman who had separated from her clergyman husband, losing custody of both her children. And given her 'wayward' conduct, his Victorian peers justified the raising of his hand against her, including, it appears, for her reluctance to share his bed. Her son was handed over to the father during the divorce, but she lost her daughter only after the man discovered the girl had forgotten her prayers—her mother had confidently told her there was nobody listening at the other end. Distraught though she was on losing her child, Besant remained defiant. 'It's a pity there isn't a God,' she declared as she exited the courtroom. 'It would do one so much good to hate him.'

The irony was that this Irishwoman who eventually found her way to India, began her life immersed in religiosity. She was born on 1 October 1847, a day and twenty-two years before Mahatma Gandhi, whose ascent would mark her eclipse. Her widowed mother enrolled her in an unconventional school where Besant obtained a good education, and where the boys too were made to sew. But it was a deeply Christian setting, and unquestioning service was the cornerstone of her existence. At eighteen, she met Frank Besant and accepted his proposal, hoping it would bring her closer to god—in reality, she found herself discussing laundry with other pious wives. Her restless mind, fear of domesticity, and a waning belief in Christ resulted in a meeting with a theologian to get closer to the 'truth'. 'It is not your duty to ascertain the truth,' he announced sharply, nearly accusing her of blasphemy.

After her marriage collapsed in 1873, Besant joined the National Secular Society. Alongside Charles Bradlaugh, leader of what was called the Freethought movement, she wrote on science and economics, becoming also a public advocate for women's rights. While her ex-husband appointed a detective to see if she was sleeping with Bradlaugh, Besant embraced atheism. 'Atheist is one of the grandest titles [one] can wear,' she explained in her autobiography. 'It was howled over the grave of Copernicus ... it was yelled ... at Voltaire ... [so that] where the cry of "Atheist" is raised... we [may] be sure that another step is being taken towards the redemption of humanity.' And if all this were not adequately scandalous, in 1877 Besant confirmed her status as a rebel by republishing Charles Knowlton's *Fruits of Philosophy*, an innocently titled work that was actually a forbidden handbook on birth control.

Unsurprisingly, given the times, Besant and her colleagues were charged with obscenity. 'I risk my name, I risk my liberty; and it is not without deep and earnest thought that I have entered this struggle,' she stated with determination, but the book was banned anyway to protect 'public morals'.

For Besant, what followed was social persecution. She had certificates from London University qualifying her to teach chemistry, botany and mathematics, but when she sought access to the Botanical Gardens, her request was denied—the curator's daughters went for their walks there, and the last thing he wanted was to expose them to this refractory divorcee. Others called her a deranged female, but Besant remained steely. 'The moment a man uses a woman's sex to discredit her arguments,' she pointed out, we know 'that he is unable to answer [her] arguments'.

Not everyone could gauge Besant comprehensively. The playwright Bernard Shaw thought her a 'born actress' who was 'successively a Puseyite Evangelical, an Atheist Bible-smasher, a Darwinian secularist, a Fabian Socialist, a Strike Leader, and finally a Theosophist', lacking both conviction and consistency. And indeed, Besant changed her political colours every decade—when she became a Theosophist after encountering the controversial Madame Blavatsky, she withdrew support for the Knowlton pamphlet she once had defended with so much passion. But at the end of the day, it was theosophy that brought her to India. On her very first trip, she gave 121 lectures, visited temples, began Sanskrit lessons, and understood that far from 'civilising' Indians, what the British presided over was an elaborate system of enslavement.

Besant won admiration from several local thinkers for her appreciation of Indian culture. 'Hindu polity is built up on its religion,' she argued somewhat romantically. 'You have not only the Vedas and the Upanishads showing a mighty intellect ... You find the very foundation of modern science laid down as part of the Hindu philosophy.' More problematically, while caste had to go, she felt it had had 'a glorious past'. Her strongest message, however, was that while 'the jewels of Western learning' must come to India, 'the diamonds of the Eastern faith' must also be given their due. In other words, Besant decided that her quest in life was to champion India and Hinduism, more important than all of the missions that had animated her journey thus far.

Besant was also, incidentally, one of the founders of the famous Banaras Hindu University (B.H.U.), her intention being to create an institution 'not to enable a man to earn forty or sixty rupees a month, but to raise [his] intellect'. In 1914, she joined the Congress party, and soon enough was elected its president. Her assumed Indian nationalism became a headache for the colonial authorities (who called her a 'great nuisance') while her Home Rule movement was deemed positively seditious. With the First World War raging, and Besant ceaseless in her newspaper activism and speeches, she was arrested and parked in Ooty for some time. The Indian public, however, saw in her a hero, and news of her eventual release was received with absolute jubilation.

The Courtesan, the Mahatma & the Italian Brahmin

In the end, Gandhi's rise coincided with Besant's exit from the limelight, for suddenly politics moved from the anglicised Indian's drawing room into the hands of the masses. Besant spoke no Indian languages, and could no longer lend initiative in the way the Mahatma could. 'All these forty years my white body has been an asset,' she wrote. 'It is no longer so.' Somewhat disappointed, she spent the rest of her years focused on the Theosophical Society's future, in Madras. By the time she died in 1933, she was respected as a kind of grand dame but was no longer relevant to India's political future. For all that, nobody could deny, as her biographer Rosemary Dinnage noted, however, that she was a lady with a 'powerful will' whose 'energy and courage were of an extraordinary order'—a woman whose life was a series of battles, and who faced them with fortitude as much as unbending conviction.

WHAT IF THE MAHATMA HAD LIVED?

The funeral of the man remembered as the apostle of peace was a scene of dramatic military display. Legions of policemen were deployed around New Delhi as the cortège wound its way through town, while the solemn procession itself featured not less than 4,000 trained men of war. The remains of Mahatma Gandhi, who saw even an indiscreet thought as violence to the soul, were placed on a gun carriage, a bed of flowers perhaps mitigating the strange irony of the spectacle. Flags were at half-mast, and crowds lined the roads, their unfeigned grief spilling over to the immaculate streets of Lutyens' zone. At the spot where Gandhi was killed, such was the clamour for handfuls of earth that a crater took form, one foot deep; where he was cremated, the authorities quickly plastered up a platform of cement. As the historian Yasmin Khan writes, it was concrete, 'the ultimate symbol of the modernizing and developmental aspirations of the postcolonial state', that was used to virtually 'seal' the memory of the Mahatma. In his

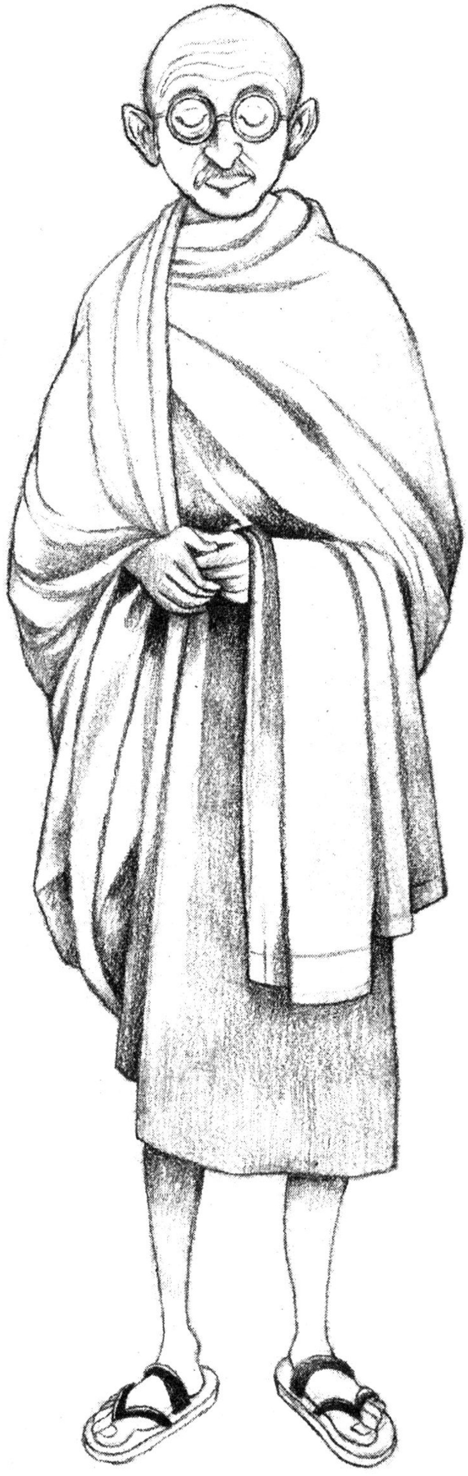

own lifetime, he viewed such conventional aspirations with a mixture of suspicion and dismay at best—in death, it was no longer for him to say what should or should not be the destiny of the land for which he had wholly spent himself.

The man born Mohandas would have rolled his eyes at the pageantry that accompanied his funeral proceedings, treating him less as a disenchanted sage and more as a powerful potentate. But if the ritual of his funeral went against every principle he upheld in life, the India that took shape in his wake became even more alien to the vision he had so carefully crafted in his mind. By dying when he did—and in the way he did—Gandhi could be quickly deified. Without embarrassment to his heirs, who were set on a course different from his own, he was consigned with due pomp to banknotes as well as the background; a totem, deployed one moment and ignored the next. His assassin, Nathuram Godse, claimed that the Mahatma, with his 'childish inanities and obstinacies', would have got in the way of tomorrow. With him, India would have had to handle his 'subjective morality under which he alone was to be the final judge of what was right or wrong'. Without him, Indian politics 'would be more practical'. It was a profoundly arrogant statement coming from an unrepentant killer. But even before the Mahatma fell to the ground, was Godse alone in fearing that the venerable old man might not fit too well in a changing world? Gandhi was a formidable instrument in the struggle for freedom—but freedom having come, all that was available for him was that special respect that the more honest know as pious lip service and soulless rhetoric.

But what if Gandhi had not died that winter morning in Birla House? What if Godse's revolver had been snatched from his hand before the trigger that changed history was pulled? Would India, on the cusp of its socialist embrace of modernity, have grown tired of its greatest elder, parking him on some variant of the present-day Margdarshak Mandal? Or would he have retired to his ashram, writing as much about his bowel movements as against the new dams and Jawaharlal Nehru's industrial 'temples'? Gandhi is to us a martyr, but might he have become, instead, a resigned old man with no place in the world? His legacy was certainly of value—when his ashes were conveyed to Prayag (Allahabad), atop the train fluttered flags both of the Indian people and the Indian National Congress—but Gandhi in the flesh had raised a formidable moral question to new leaders who replaced foreigners in the old seats of power. 'Will the hand of truth at any time reduce the vile myth of Gandhi to the putrid mass it deserves to be?' asked the writer Nirad C. Chaudhuri after the Mahatma was dead. If he lived longer, would he have had to suffer remarks such as this in person and in the press? Had he acted on his desire to live in Pakistan, would the old man have become, for Nehru and Muhammad Ali Jinnah, that inconvenient thing: 'an international problem'?

It is not impossible to conceive of relations between Nehru and his mentor crumbling into polite disrepair, especially on the question of India's governance. As early as 1938, the two had clashed, each as determined as the other; and in this lay the seeds of discord. Perhaps, at first, Nehru's affection might have let the Mahatma prevail, but eventually would they have parted ways? Gandhi, after all, as one scholar writes, sought 'legitimacy... not in the laws and the constitutions, not in parliaments and courts, but in the conscience of man' (which to him was his own conscience). Nehru, meanwhile, absorbed more lessons from history—institutions and courts married to the steel frame of bureaucracy alone offered stability to a diverse land which, even during the midnight tryst in 1947, saw bloodshed in the West and rebellion in the East. Gandhi thought economic planning 'a waste of effort' while Nehru was enamoured of the idea, infused as it was, he declared, with 'magic'. 'For me,' proclaimed Gandhi, 'India begins and ends in the villages.' Cities, a 'matter for sorrow rather than congratulation', argued the Mahatma, prospered by 'sucking the blood' of the rural poor. It was the village that thirsted for reinvention. No, disagreed Nehru, it was in the listless countryside that the 'physically and intellectually degenerate' feudal class preyed like 'vultures' on the weak. India could not wallow in romantic yearnings of the ideal village—cities were emblems of progress, and progress necessarily meant change, no matter the Mahatma's dreams.

Gandhi thought modernity a disease, albeit one that could be cured to pave the way for Ram Rajya. 'I entirely disagree with this viewpoint,' insisted his political heir, for 'I neither think the so-called Rama Raj was very good in the past, and nor do I want it back.' Where Gandhi thought machinery represented 'great sin'—even as he unironically embraced the munificence of titans of Indian industry—Nehru descended into ecstasies at visions of 'industrialisation and the big machine'. 'Independent India can only discharge her duty towards a groaning world by adopting a simple but ennobled life ... living at peace with the world,' stated Gandhi with conviction, seeking self-sufficient village republics that had no quarrels beyond their borders. But India's first prime minister knew that the 'world has become internationalised' and that, in a networked universe, such autonomy was wishful thinking.

In 1909, in his famous (and in some contexts, infamous) *Hind Swaraj*, Gandhi explained that freedom on a Western model was nothing but a curse. It meant, he announced, that

The Courtesan, the Mahatma & the Italian Brahmin

'we want English rule without the Englishman. You want the tiger's nature, but not the tiger; that is to say, you would make India... not Hindustan but Englistan.' Nehru, on the other hand, envisioned a 'socialist economy within a democratic structure', and codes of the British inherited alongside habits that went 'My Lord' and 'Your Honour'. If the Mahatma had not died in 1948, would he have turned his fingers towards Motilal's son and accused him of nurturing not Hindustan but a veritable Englistan, as many do today?

Who might have been Gandhi's friends? Most certainly, the Mahatma would have found an obdurate foe in B.R. Ambedkar, not only in matters of caste. 'I know Gandhi better than his disciples,' the dalit leader once proclaimed. 'They came to him as devotees and saw only the Mahatma. I was an opponent... He showed me his fangs.' The greater fight for freedom may have persuaded Ambedkar to sacrifice the political interests of his own people to satisfy the national interests Gandhi stood to represent. But after independence, would matters have stayed the same? 'He was never a Mahatma,' Ambedkar went on to say. If he was, how could he advocate his less-is-more philosophy, consigning those with the least to remain behind forever? Gandhism, to Ambedkar, 'with its call back to nature, means back to nakedness, back to squalor, back to poverty and back to ignorance for the vast mass of the people'. He disagreed with Nehru too, but as a constitutionalist and a builder of institutions himself, Ambedkar could meet halfway with the Pandit while parleying bitterly with his guru. So, when the time came to formulate a rulebook, would the Mahatma have blessed it, or seen in it Western weaknesses that could never be allowed to taint the Indian nation's soul? Would the man who won India its freedom have stood in the way of that document his people today proudly celebrate as sacred: the blessed constitution? Or would the former lawyer in him have returned to frame a charter of his own?

Though he was not himself a communalist, those ordinarily identified with rabid communalism might, ironically, have offered to champion the old man in his moment of decline. After all, a good deal of what Gandhi said could be deployed in favour of their own peculiar cause on the right. 'I have been long pledged to serve the cow,' he once said, hoping elsewhere to 'approach my Mohammedan brother and urge him for the sake of the country to join me in protecting her'—lines that might still find ready reception among those who despise Nehru and Ambedkar. So too, Gandhi found abhorrent a society divorced from religion. 'Religion is dear to me and my first complaint is that India is becoming irreligious,' he once proclaimed. It was a different matter that what he sought was ethical politics inspired by religion, not politics in the name of religion. Still, those in certain quarters might have revelled in such a view.

And, what of his position that the state must be absolutely secular? 'The question of the "protection of minorities",' he once said, 'is not good enough for me; it rests upon the recognition of religious groupings between citizens of the same state.' Would those who wish to change the constitution have seized on this and deployed the Mahatma's words to demand at once, perhaps, a uniform civil code? Gandhi said that we are 'Indians first and Hindus, Musalmans, Parsis and Christians after', but would they, instead, have chosen to lift his 'Nationalism is greater than sectarianism' to give legitimacy to their own brand of nationalism, infused with impulses that can only be called majoritarian at their core?

What would have come of Indian education had Gandhi lived? 'Of all the superstitions that affect India,' wrote the

The Courtesan, the Mahatma & the Italian Brahmin

Mahatma, 'none is so great as that a knowledge of the English language is necessary for imbibing ideas of liberty and developing accuracy of thought.' To him, Hindi ought to have been the language of the Indian nation, and diverse mother tongues the medium of learning for all children till they were fourteen. He was not, to be sure, averse to Western learning. 'I do not want,' he affirmed, 'my house to be walled on all sides and my windows to be stuffed. I want the cultures of all lands to be blown about my house as freely as possible.' However, he added, 'I refuse to be blown off my feet by any of them.' This too, ironically, would have appealed to those who for decades had little to do with Gandhi and his nationalist cause, but whose desire to cultivate uniformity is well known, and who see no reason to seek knowledge from the West when all of it is already, of course, available in ancient texts of the East. Would Gandhi, through his words, have breathed life into causes that were strange then and remain so to this day? Would the tallest Indian leader have gone down in the minds of many as a proponent of what we know as the imposition of Hindi?

'I have been known,' the Mahatma once said, 'as a crank, faddist, mad man. Evidently, the reputation is well deserved. For wherever I go, I draw to myself cranks, faddists and mad men.' It is reassuring that he did not live in the age of WhatsApp and the Internet; his work may have been subjected to lampooning and ridicule. He blamed the Bihar earthquake in 1934 on the Hindus' treatment of dalits—it was punishment from god for the evils of caste. In 1940, he wrote wishfully, 'I do not believe Herr Hitler to be as bad as he is portrayed.' He spoke with the certainty that even the worst could be shown the light, but would the courts of Indian television have forgiven the Mahatma for a remark such as this? On medicine, he was convinced that this too required a marriage with religion. 'A man who attends to his daily Namaz or his Gayatri mantras in the proper spirit need never get ill,' he once stated. In order to know the universe, all one needed to know was one's own body, he was convinced: 'That which cannot be found in the body,' he declared, 'is not found in the universe.'

For everything he said, Gandhi also said the opposite. 'I have never made a fetish of consistency. I am a votary of Truth and I must say what I feel and think at a given moment … without regard to what I may have said before.' What a gift this man would have been to satirists and humourists, with his remarks and idiosyncrasies, but would they have allowed him to remain that unique creation: a Mahatma towering over an entire nation?

There was a time when Gandhi expressed the opinion that a human life could span 125 years and that he would quite like to live that long. If he had had his way, he would have departed not in 1948 but around 1994. He would have seen the rise of the first communist government in Kerala, and its unholy dismissal a couple of years later—one is tempted to picture him preparing to fast unto death to preserve the legitimate right to govern of a party he may not have agreed with but would defend to uphold a greater principle. Might he, after Independence, have been quietly allowed to take his fast to a full success? The man, in his nineties, would have been witness to the war with China in 1962. Would he have made an effort to mediate at the frontier himself, requiring the Indian state to restrain him for his own protection? In the face of fascism, he was prepared to tolerate war, so would he have sided with Indira Gandhi to end genocide in East Pakistan and help birth Bangladesh? More importantly, would

The Courtesan, the Mahatma & the Italian Brahmin

Mrs Gandhi have thrown the man who meant everything to India in prison during the Emergency? As the Congress faced decline, what would the original Gandhi have said to those who borrowed his name? Would he have uttered that word 'karma' and suggested, yet again, that the answer to their problems lay in disbanding the whole vehicle and its teetering mission? Most importantly, if Godse's bullets had not killed him, would the tragedy that was Babri Masjid have pierced the Mahatma's heart as he approached his own deadline of a century and a quarter?

'It is generally foolhardy to write about Gandhi,' the philosopher Akeel Bilgrami once said, 'not only because you are never certain you've got him right, but because you are almost sure to have him wrong.' To venture on a journey of 'what ifs' is an even more foolish enterprise, with a man who said and did things with no parallels, and which are still open to endless interpretations. There is little that can be said with certainty, but many are the questions one must ask of the Mahatma and his message; of what he offered then, and what he might have offered later had he had the chance.

Never will we know what Gandhi might or might not have done. But a glance at the history of this nation can assure us of one fact—if the Mahatma had lived a full life, as he once desired, the obituary on his death would have sadly said: 'Mr Mohandas Karamchand Gandhi, one-time barrister at law, one-time freedom fighter, and neglected thinker of an orphaned philosophy, passed away yesterday. He was 125 years old and died of a shattered heart, in a country he no longer recognised.'

PART THREE

Afterword

AN ESSAY FOR OUR TIMES

A little after the inaugural meeting of the Indian National Congress on 28 December 1885, the *Bombay Gazette* carried a report on the event, expressing genuine wonder at the spectacle that had unfolded before its correspondent's eyes. To begin with, it was noted, the very fact that Indians 'representing the various races and communities, castes and sub-divisions of castes, religions and sub-divisions of religions, met together in one place to form themselves, if possible, into one political whole', was 'most unique and interesting'. Then there was fascination born from the sheer visual extravaganza that the opening meeting of the Congress appeared to be: 'There were men from Madras,' announced the *Gazette* (throwing political correctness to the wind) 'the blackness of whose complexion seemed to be made blacker by spotless white turbans.' Standing beside them was the cream of colonial Bengal society, many of whom 'appeared in entirely European costume'. There were 'bearded, bulky and large-limbed' Pathans from the north-west, just as there were 'Banyas from Gujarat' and 'Sindhees from Kurrachee'. The Marathi delegates came flaunting their 'cart-wheel' turbans while the fire-worshipping Parsis displayed, in the *Gazette*'s opinion, a 'not very elegant head-dress'. To add to this, there were many delegates from the south who appeared bare-chested, but for loose shawls, just as there were some who saw no reason to use footwear. 'All these men assembled in the same hall,' concluded the report, 'presented such a variety of costumes and complexions, that a similar scene can scarcely be witnessed anywhere'—except perhaps, it offered, 'at a fancy [dress] ball'.

To Indians today there is nothing particularly unusual about the multiplicity of languages and cultures their fellow countrymen uphold and celebrate—in a single urban classroom, for example, there may be children who speak English during their lessons, Malayalam or Meitei at home when with their parents, and Hindi with friends while playing *gully* cricket, added to which might well be extra lessons in Sanskrit or German or French. But a little over a century ago, the sight of so many diverse groups of people represented in one single room was nothing short of extraordinary. The proposition that these men—with their different colours, costumes, cuisines and castes—desired to assert a common political identity was even more revolutionary. After all, an almost chaotic sense of division seemed to be the guiding principle of life in India. There was language to begin with, so utterly complex that a dialect spoken in one district could be replete with peculiar inflections unfamiliar to fellow speakers of the same tongue in the next district. Beyond geography, there were the divisions of caste: while brahmins existed everywhere, there were 107 different types of them in the city of Varanasi alone, each variety claiming superiority over the rest, and each asserting the distinctness of its identity. Costume, again, revealed a great deal: where Tamil brahmins grew their tuft of hair at the back of the head, the Malayali brahmin wore it in the front; where Iyengar women saw white as the colour of widowhood, the Namboodiri bride, just across the Western Ghats, wore nothing but white to her bridal chamber. And while the Rajput lady moved around with a veil, wearing even a blouse was considered indecent in Malabar. Only the most tenuous of links seemed to run through these groups while the more solid ingredients essential to the birth of modern nationalism seemed, even to most Indians, worryingly absent.

What, then, united these people and brought them together on a common platform in 1885? To begin with, it helped that they were standing up to British inequity, which was an unpleasant experience they all suffered in common. As was once remarked, 'It is not so much sympathy with one's fellows as much as hostility towards the outsider that makes for nationalism.' It certainly did seem the case that while finding sturdy bonds between Indians was not an easy task, it was definitely possible to identify a common, oppressive enemy, in whose expulsion lay everybody's combined salvation. The irony that this nascent sense of national feeling was, in some respects, a byproduct of British rule was not lost on India's early freedom fighters. As we saw earlier, it was after all the English language—a colonial import, if ever there was one— that permitted India's nationalists to engage with one another. It was in English that Jyotirao Phule, one of India's most remarkable crusaders against caste, read Thomas Paine's *Rights of Man*, and it was also this very foreign language, among others, that delivered to the Maratha rajah Serfoji lessons in modern science in early nineteenth-century Thanjavur. Indeed, when that first meeting of the Indian National Congress was convened in 1885, the circular inviting participants insisted that while delegates 'from all parts' of India were welcome, they would need to be 'well acquainted with the English language' in order to be able to communicate with one another. In other words, to birth a new mood of nationalism, what was needed was not only a shared love for India, but also one of the most potent instruments of imperial rule: the coloniser's grammar book.

As late as 1947, the lack of a common language troubled the minds of India's leaders, for language could potentially unite or divide the land. The report of the Linguistic Provinces Commission, appointed in 1948 by the Constituent Assembly, is telling of the formidable challenges in welding together such a patchwork of cultures as existed in India. 'The work of 60 years of the Indian National Congress' with its vision of a united land, the Commission noted, confronted 'face to face' the 'centuries-old India of narrow loyalties, petty jealousies and ignorant prejudices engaged in a mortal conflict'. They were, furthermore, 'simply horrified to see how thin was the ice upon which we were skating'. After all, why should Naga tribes in the north-east of India feel any affinity with former subjects of the maharajah of Baroda in western India? What was to be done about the fact that though they were now people of one country, a Malayali's traditional links with Arabia were stronger than any that existed with northern India, just as Delhi's bonds with Kabul were richer than its relationship with Tamil Nadu? So, too, the Islam of the Mappila in Kozhikode had little to do with the faith as practiced in Bhopal, just as the daily worship of the Punjabi Hindu was vastly different from that of her co-religionists in Orissa or Telangana. It was no wonder, then, that while the Congress had, before 1947, established regional units

The Courtesan, the Mahatma & the Italian Brahmin

on linguistic lines, there was profound (though ultimately unsuccessful) resistance to permitting Indian states to be established on the basis of language. As the Linguistic Provinces Commission warned, 'Some of the ablest men in the country came before us and confidently and emphatically stated that language in this country stood for and represented culture, race, history, individuality, and finally a sub-nation.' If such sub-nations were given political expression, would that not jeopardise the larger vision of a united India? Was this not a recipe for the future disintegration of the India for which our freedom fighters had suffered and fought?

These questions had exercised India's best minds from the very start, with the result that more than one vision of nationalism was articulated across the political spectrum, from the poet Rabindranath Tagore to the proponent of Hindutva, V.D. Savarkar. As the scholar Sunil Khilnani notes, from the late nineteenth century the challenge, both philosophical and political, was always about 'How to discover or devise some coherent, shared norms—values and commitments—that could connect Indians together under modern conditions'. And whether or not India's diversity was an asset or a dangerous weakness depended on which of these visions was allowed to prevail and gain moral influence over the vast majority of the country's people.

To some thinkers, India was enriched and made strong by the breathtaking heterogeneity that had long been its hallmark; others argued that homogeneity was what made sturdy nation-states, and as far as possible, diversity ought to make way for a master narrative and a master culture, largely woven around a majoritarian religious principle. To some, as Shashi Tharoor puts it, India resembled a *thali* or a platter with 'a selection of sumptuous dishes in different bowls. Each tastes different, and does not necessarily mix with the next, but they belong together on the same plate, and they complement each other in making the meal a satisfying repast.' This vision of nationalism was focused on transcending difference by looking to a shared, modern future—whatever India's fragmented yesterdays may have been, everybody could now be an equal partner in shaping its tomorrow. On the other hand, to proponents of what would become Hindutva, this was, to quote Ashutosh Varshney, the 'opposite of nation building' for a 'salad bowl does not produce cohesion; a melting pot does'. And if India had to become a melting pot, as opposed to a thali or a salad bowl, its regional cultures and local identities would have to make sacrifices for a greater cause. Hindutva was the pot, and it was the smaller cultures that would have to endure the melting.

Given that the freedom fighters had to rally Indians behind them and stand up to imperial might, it is understandable that the first of these visions was more popular—to take everyone along in a working consensus was wiser than to succumb to quarrels about which culture would become national, and whose identities would need to be renounced. Instead of one kind of uniform appearance, a joint cooperative effort was what they envisioned. As early as 1884, the poet and champion of the modern Hindi language, Harishchandra, explained this vision of Indian nationalism. Referring to all residents of Hindustan as Hindus, he declared: 'Brother Hindus! You, too, should not insist any more on all details of religious faith and practice. Increase mutual love and chant this "mahamantra". Who lives in Hindustan, whatever his colour and whatever his caste, he is a Hindu. Help the Hindus. Bengalis, Marathis, Panjabis, Madrasis, Vaidiks, Jains, Brahmos, Mussalmans, all should join hands.'

The Courtesan, the Mahatma & the Italian Brahmin

The following year, the prominent Muslim reformer Sir Syed Ahmed Khan added his weight to this conception of Indian nationalism: 'Remember,' he pointed out, that 'the words "Hindu" and "Muhammadan" are only meant for religious distinction, otherwise all persons whether Hindu, Muhammadan, or Christian, who reside in this country belong to one and the same nation.' By 1909, Madan Mohan Malaviya too, in an address to the Indian National Congress, reaffirmed this position. 'How ennobling it is,' he pronounced, 'to even think of that high ideal of patriotism where Hindus, Mohammedans, Parsees and Christians stand shoulder to shoulder as brothers and work for the common good of all ... we cannot build up in separation a national life such as would be worth living; we must rise and fall together.'

Perhaps the greatest support for this vision of modern Indian nationalism came from Mahatma Gandhi and the country's future prime minister, Jawaharlal Nehru. Though they disagreed on many things, the Father of the Nation and his protégé were more or less in agreement on the broad idea of what made the Indian people one. Ethnic nationalism would not work here because the subcontinent was bursting with ethnic diversity, and forcing any kind of rigid, overpowering uniformity over its peoples would break the nation before it was even born. Religion, as far as Gandhi saw it, could mobilise people but could not serve as a sufficient or enduring basis for nationalism. It had value, admittedly, and there was civilisational unity among the people despite numerous differences—why else would men and women from across the subcontinent crisscross the land on pilgrim routes that encompassed Rameswaram and Benares, Jagannath and Haridwar? But this did not make India a land of Hindus alone—everyone who had adopted India as their home had a place in the nation. As the Mahatma wrote, 'Hindustan belongs to all those who are born and bred here and who have no other country to look to. Therefore, it belongs to Parsis, Beni Israels, to Indian Christians, Muslims and other non-Hindus as much as to Hindus. Free India will not be a Hindu *raj*; it will be an Indian *raj* based not on the majority of any religious sect or community, but on the representatives of the whole people without distinction of religion...' 'Religion,' he believed, 'is a personal matter which should have no place in politics.' Naturally, the idea of nationalism as a commodity designed only for Hindus was as abhorrent to him as the notion that Muslims constituted a separate nation and could seek, for that reason, an exclusive territory on which to live.

Nehru, too, articulated nationalism in similar terms where diversity was not an impediment to love for one's country, and inclusiveness and tolerance were, in fact, an ancestral principle once again elevated to the forefront as India reclaimed its destiny in modern times. He, too, pointed to a certain civilisational unity. 'Some kind of a dream of unity,' he argued in *The Discovery of India*, 'has occupied the mind of India since the dawn of civilisation. That unity,' however, 'was not conceived as something imposed from outside', as the British had done. 'It was something deeper, and within its fold the widest tolerance of belief and custom was practiced, and every variety acknowledged and even encouraged.' Various races, religions and ethnicities had co-existed from the dawn of time in India, and difference was accommodated within a larger tradition rather than subjugated or rejected. There was, in other words, room for everyone in India in the past, and the India of the future would reinforce such inclusive national ideals in order to make its way in the twentieth century and beyond. To quote Tharoor again in this context,

The Courtesan, the Mahatma & the Italian Brahmin

'The singular thing about India is that you can only speak of it in the plural. This pluralism emerged from the very nature of the country; it was made inevitable by India's geography and affirmed by its history. There was simply too much of both to permit a single exclusionist nationalism' that was based on narrow parameters. Instead, Indian nationalism was birthed consciously by its leaders, in whose mind democracy, a liberal order, and enough space for coexistence would forge a unique nation in which everyone could thrive, and disagree, in liberty and peace. If a nation was, as Marcel Mauss noted in *L'Anee Sociologique*, a society 'where there is a relative moral, mental, and cultural unity between the inhabitants', in India that unity was exemplified in the mature understanding among its peoples to preserve and cherish diversity.

This vision of nationalism was not without its challengers. V.D. Savarkar articulated in what is now a founding text of the Hindutva vision of India an ideology where 'Hinduness' rather than a celebration of unity in diversity becomes the cornerstone of the nation. This was not originally a religious argument, offering instead several political criteria. After all, Hindus themselves were hardly a united force. The 1911 census of India found, for example, that 'a quarter of the persons classed as Hindus deny the supremacy of Brahmans, a quarter do not worship the great Hindu gods... a half do not regard cremation as obligatory, and two-fifths eat beef'. There was, in other words, no perfect way to define who was a Hindu and who was not on account of the sheer divergence of custom and practice within Hindu communities—i.e. Hindus, too, could only be understood in the plural rather than the singular.

Savarkar offered an explanation for this state of affairs. The Hindus, soon after the Aryans arrived, had formed themselves into a nation. Over time, however, this was 'first overshadowed and then almost forgotten' as culture and identity became fragmented. Lord Rama, who is treated by Savarkar as a historical figure, rejuvenated the nation, only for its unity to be crushed by the advent of Muslim invaders. Leaving aside the lack of historicity in this argument, the point ultimately made was that what bound together the Hindu nation was the 'blood of the mighty race' of the Aryans, so that 'no people in the world can more justly claim to get recognised as a racial unit than the Hindus and perhaps the Jews.' That is why, he claimed, 'the Nayars of Malabar weep over the sufferings of the brahmins of Kashmir' (when in fact the Nairs had little knowledge of where precisely Kashmir was or what its brahmins were doing). Meanwhile, though Muslims and Christians in India were converts from Hindus of yore, they were, nonetheless, disqualified from membership of the nation.

Why was this so? Hindus, according to Savarkar, were members of a single nation because no matter the countless diversities they counted within their ranks, no matter how fragmented they were, they saw India not only as their motherland (*mathrubhumi*) and fatherland (*pitrubhumi*, the land of their ancestors), but also as their holy land (*punyabhumi*). Muslim and Christian converts might fulfil the first two criteria but they did not envision the subcontinent, defined since antiquity as the land between the Himalayas and the Indian Ocean, as sacred—it was in Mecca and Rome and other foreign lands that their sacred sites were located. The Buddhists, Sikhs, Jains, and others whose religions were born in India were all eligible to be members of the Hindu nation, but Christians and Muslims, whose faiths emerged in lands beyond India's historical limits, were at best second-class citizens.

The Courtesan, the Mahatma & the Italian Brahmin

Savarkar's heir, M.S. Golwalkar, built on this idea and rejected the notion of territorial nationalism, as promoted by Gandhi, Nehru and the freedom fighters from the very start. 'In this land,' he declared, 'Hindus have been the owners, Parsis and Jews the guests, and Muslims and Christian the dacoits.' Religious resentment was pronounced in Golwalkar, who was suspicious of minorities. 'They are born in this land, no doubt,' he wrote. 'But are they true to its salt? Are they grateful …? Do they feel that they are the children of this land … Do they feel it a duty to serve her? No! Together with the change in faith, gone are the spirit of love and devotion for the nation.' In essence, then, the Hindutva vision of the nation was perched on the twin notions of Hindu pride as well as an antagonism towards the ominous, disloyal 'other'—nationalism, according to Golwalkar, was not 'a mere bundle of political and economic rights', it was a cultural idea in which some were included and some had necessarily to be left out.

But this predictably controversial Hindutva vision existed largely on the fringes of society. While the inclusive nationalism of Gandhi, Nehru and assorted political leaders came from direct experience of fighting for freedom, from a personal interaction with the people, Hindutva was constructed by thinkers who were not active participants in the struggle against imperialism and therefore could fabricate theories divorced from the lived experience and reality of the masses. In actual fact, most Hindus hardly saw themselves as a fixed, united group who could transform that identity into a rock-solid sense of nationalism. Even the question of who exactly a Hindu was, in practical terms, remained frustratingly unresolved. In 1871, for example, a 'committee of native gentlemen' defined as Hindu all those who believed in caste. But caste appeared among Muslims and Christians also. In the 1891 census, then, the Hindu was defined by exclusion, as 'the large residuum that is not Sikh, or Jain, or Buddhist, or professedly Animistic, or included in one of the foreign religions, such as Islam, Mazdaism, Christianity, or Hebraism'. Sir M. Monier-Williams felt that the notion of a pan-Indian Hindu identity was 'wholly arbitrary and confessedly unsatisfactory' for the simple reason that in practice, Hinduism was amorphous. Some, such as a census commissioner in princely Travancore, argued that Hindus were those who accepted the faith of the brahmins, which, however, ran into trouble when one considers the words of J.W. Massie, who as early as 1840 pointed out that to consider the brahmin as representative of all Hindus was as bewildering a statement as saying that the Italians represented all Europeans—there was too much diversity for simplistic statements to be true.

The issue of diversity and nationalism and whether they complement or oppose each other, then, as stated earlier, boils down quite simply to which vision of the nation is embraced. The constitution India adopted in 1950 enshrines the former idea, creating a space for Indians to love the country without having to surrender any other equally legitimate identity—to repeat a cliché, one can be simultaneously a proud Santhal or Kashmiri, a devout Muslim or Parsi, a determined atheist or rationalist, a straight majority or a gay minority, and yet love one's country. One can assert proudly a patriotism that rises over and above other feelings, without clashing with individual and group identities. In this vision of the nation, nationalism is not a zero-sum game; it can coexist with a variety of other valid sentiments. It draws wisdom from the past, but is oriented towards a progressive future. As Nehru saw it, it was predicated on a national philosophy featuring the seven goals of unity, parliamentary democracy, scientific temper, non-alignment, socialism, industrialisation and secularism. Some of these values may change with time, as Indians evolve as a people, but the nation is not threatened if a group voices sharp concerns, or if raucous debate and disagreement take place routinely, so long as they occur within established institutions and in keeping with certain ground rules by which everybody agrees to play. Indeed, it creates checks and balances that prevents any one group from dominating the rest; any one region from engulfing others; and one version of a religion from enforcing its principles on even the last rationalist who denies god, or believes in a different definition of the same religion. The principle was that everyone could continue to embrace their differences while staying wedded to the national consensus that is India.

The other vision of nationalism, meanwhile, has mutated into a one-size-fits-all variant, which is at odds with the history and tradition of the country, and denies consensus as the guiding principle of the Indian nation. 'Such identity,' the historian Romila Thapar notes, 'tends to iron out diversity and insists on conformity'—in other words, pluralism is weakness. Leaving aside the treatment it proposes for religious minorities, this means radical changes even for Hindus themselves, as a tradition that has been described as a fascinating 'mosaic of distinct cults, deities, sects and ideas' (including contradictory ideas) is regimented to address various anxieties. This is a nationalism that follows one definition, one form, one loyalty, and one narrow ideology. Naturally, this calls for a new structure and a new vocabulary of Hindu identity, featuring certain sacred books but not others; fewer gods, at the cost of others; and a standardisation of practice that sometimes goes against India's own manifest heritage in its quest to service an overarching, synthetic cultural identity. So, for instance, all Hindus must avoid eating beef (though several castes happily did in the past) and should avoid meat in general (though a number of brahmin communities too were not vegetarian). Nationalism must have a fixed language—Sanskrit is ideal but in the interim, Hindi will do—a language that to large numbers of Indians is hardly less alien than English, with which the country has made its peace. And then dress codes, social behaviour and much else must also fall in line, creating more a sharp machine to nurse narrow-minded insecurities than an organic people who live, breathe, prosper and preserve their diverse traditions and personalities.

One-size-fits-all rules, however, have a tendency to backfire in India. And decades and generations of officially promoting diversity means that attempting to reverse the flow and manufacture a narrow brand of nationalism will provoke challenges, if not long-term disaster—where, for instance, Hindi nationalism was force-fed from Delhi, the powers in Karnataka responded in 2018 with a Kannada-oriented sub-nationalism that even flew its own flag. If the idea is to create an 'us or them' with the 'majority' on one side, and the minority as the enemy within, the instigators of this scheme will discover too many 'thems' sown into the fabric of the majority itself. The historical lesson is clear—there was a reason why in 1947 India prevented nationalism from distorting into a rigid political beast and envisioned it as a more malleable reflection of the land's multiple realities. To re-engineer this mature, long-standing policy in black and white today will only prove calamitous, showing that far from making India great again, what one will end up doing is breaking India.

SOURCES AND FURTHER READING

PART I

THE ITALIAN BRAHMIN OF MADURAI
Ines G. Zupanov, *Disputed Mission: Jesuit Experiments and Brahmanical Knowledge in Seventeenth-Century India* (1999) (New Delhi: Oxford University Press)

Kyoko Matsukawa, *European Images of India before the Rise of Orientalism in the Late Eighteenth Century* (Thesis submitted to the London School of Economics, London, 2000)

C.C. Lorance, 'Cultural Relevance and Doctrinal Soundness: The Mission of Roberto de Nobili' in *Missiology*, Vol. 33, No. 4 (2005), pp. 415–424

Eileen Burke-Sullivan and Kevin F. Burke, *The Ignatian Tradition*, (2009) (The Liturgical Press)

Julius Richter, Sydney H. Moore (trans.), *A History of Missions in India* (1908) (New York: Fleming H. Revell Company)

Unknown, 'Robert De Nobili', *The Irish Monthly*, Vol. 9, No. 102 (1881), pp. 643–662

A MARATHA PRINCE'S MORALITY PLAY
Translation of the *Sati Dana Suramu* taken from Velcheru Narayana Rao and David Shulman (eds.), *Classical Telugu Poetry: An Anthology* (2002) (Berkeley: University of California Press)

Sanjay Subrahmanyam, *Penumbral Visions: Making Polities in Early Modern South India* (2001) (Ann Arbor: University of Michigan Press)

K.R. Subramanian, *The Maratha Rajas of Tanjore* (1928) (K.R. Subramanian: Madras)

A MUSLIM DEITY IN A HINDU TEMPLE
Richard H. Davis, *Lives of Indian Images* (1997) (Princeton: Princeton University Press)

K.R. Sundararajan and Bithika Mukerji (eds.), *Hindu Spirituality: Postclassical and Modern*, Vol. 2 (2003) (New Delhi: Motilal Banarsidass Publishers)

T.S. Parthasarathy, *The Koyil Olugu: History of The Srirangam Temple* (1954) (Tirupati: Tirumalai Tirupati Devasthanams)

THE TALE OF TWO SHAKUNTALAS

M.B. Emeneau, 'Kalidasa's Sakuntala and the Mahabharata' in *Journal of the American Oriental Society*, Vol. 82, No. 1 (1962), pp. 41–44

P.P. Sharma, 'Kalidasa's Shakuntala: Some Sidelights' in *Indian Literature*, Vol. 22, No. 3 (1979), pp. 75–85

Mirella Schino and Leo Sykes, 'Shakuntala among the Olive Trees' in *Asian Theatre Journal*, Vol. 13, No. 1 (1996), pp. 92–111

Wendy Doniger, 'Rings of Rejection and Recognition in Ancient India' in *Journal of Indian Philosophy*, Vol. 26, No. 5 (1998), pp. 435–453

Romila Thapar, *Sakuntala: Texts, Readings, Histories* (2002) (London: Anthem Press)

A DALIT AT THE TEMPLE DOOR

Hirozhi Fukazawa, 'State and Caste System in the Eighteenth Century Maratha Kingdom' in the *Hitotsubhasi Journal of Economics*, Vol. 9, No. 1 (1968), pp. 32–44

Jayant Lele (ed.), *Tradition and Modernity in Bhakti Movements* (1981) (Leiden: E.J. Brill)

Eleanor Zelliot and Rohini Mokashi-Punekar (eds.), *Untouchable Saints: An Indian Phenomenon* (2005) (New Delhi: Manohar Publishers and Distributors)

Patton Burchett, 'Bhakti Rhetoric in the Hagiography of 'Untouchable' Saints: Discerning Bhakti's Ambivalence on Caste and Brahminhood' in *International Journal of Hindu Studies*, Vol. 13, No. 2 (2009), pp. 115–141

Philip Constable, 'Early Dalit Literature and Culture in Late Nineteenth- and Early Twentieth-Century Western India' in *Modern Asian Studies*, Vol. 31, No. 2 (1997), pp. 317–338

Justin E. Abbott and N.R. Godbole (trans.), *Stories of Indian Saints: Translation of Mahipati's Marathi Bhaktavijaya* (1999) (New Delhi: Motilal Banarsidass Publishers)

THE WORLD OF SHIVAJI MAHARAJ

Manu S. Pillai, *Rebel Sultans: The Deccan from Khilji to Shivaji* (2018) (New Delhi: Juggernaut Books)

James Laine with S.S. Bahulkar, *The Epic of Shivaji: Kavindra Paramananda's Sivabharata* (2001) (New Delhi: Orient Longman)

James Laine, 'The Dharma of Islam and the Din of Hinduism' in *International Journal of Hindu Studies*, Vol. 3, No. 3 (1999), pp. 299–318

Jadunath Sarkar, *Shivaji and His Times* (1952) (Calcutta: M.C. Sarkar & Sons Pvt. Ltd.)

George Michell and Sugandha Johar, 'The Maratha Complex at Ellore' in *South Asian Studies*, Vol. 28, No. 1 (2012), pp. 69–88

A.R. Kulkarni, *The Marathas* (2008) (Pune: Diamond Publications)

G.S. Sardesai, *New History of the Marathas*, Vol. 1 (1946) (Bombay: Phoenix Publications)

Stewart Gordon, *The New Cambridge History of India: The Marathas, 1600-1818* (1993) (Cambridge: Cambridge University Press)

Gijs Kruijtzer, *Xenophobia in Seventeenth-Century India* (2009) (Leiden: Leiden University Press)

BASAVA, WOMEN AND THE LINGAYAT TRADITION

P.B. Desai, *Basavesvara and His Times* (1968) (Dharwar: Kannada Research Institute)

S.A. Palekar, *Basaveshwara's Political Philosophy* (2006) (New Delhi: Serials Publications Pvt. Ltd.)

K. Ishwaran, *Speaking of Basava: Lingayat Religion and Culture in South Asia* (1992) (Boulder: Westview Press)

S.A. Palekar, *Concept of Equality and Ideal Society: Basaveshwara's Model* (1997) (New Delhi: Rawat Publications)

Sheldon Pollock, *Literary Cultures in History: Reconstructions from South Asia* (2003) (Berkeley: University of California Press)

William McCormack, 'Lingayats as a Sect' in *The Journal of the Royal Anthropological Institute of Great Britain and Ireland*, Vol. 93, No. 1 (1963), pp. 59–71

Julia Leslie, 'Understanding Basava: History, Hagiography and a Modern Kannada Drama' in *Bulletin of the School of Oriental and African Studies*, Vol. 61, No. 2 (1998), pp. 228–261

Vijaya Ramaswamy, 'Rebels-Conformists? Women Saints in Medieval South India' in *Anthropos*, Vol. 87, No. 1/3 (1992), pp. 133–146

Vijaya Ramaswamy, 'Mystics or Housewives? Women in Virasaivism' in *India International Centre Quarterly*, Vol. 23, No. 3/4 (1996), pp. 190–203

H.S. Shivaprakash, 'Journeying to Kalyana' in *India International Centre Quarterly*, Vol. 30, No. 3/4 (2004), pp. 215–223

H.S. Shivaprakash, 'Vachanas of Akkamahadevi' in *India International Centre Quarterly*, Vol. 30, No. 3/4 (2003–04), pp. 32–37

C.N. Venugopal, 'Factor of Anti-Pollution in the Ideology of Lingayat Movement' in *Sociological Bulletin*, Vol. 26, No. 2 (1977), pp. 227–241

'JODHABAI': MORE THAN AKBAR'S WIFE

Ellison B. Findly, 'The Capture of Maryam-uz-Zamani's Ship: Mughal Women and European Traders' in the *Journal of the American Oriental Society*, Vol. 108, No. 2 (1988), pp. 227–238

Ellison Banks Findly, *Nur Jahan: Empress of Mughal India* (1993) (New York: Oxford University Press)

Soma Mukherjee, *Royal Mughal Ladies and Their Contributions* (2001) (New Delhi: Gyan Publishing House)

Abraham Eraly, *Emperors of the Peacock Throne: The Saga of the Great Moghuls* (2014) (New Delhi: Penguin Random House)

A WEAVER AND HIS MESSAGE

Charlotte Vaudeville, *Kabir: Volume One* (1974) (London: Oxford University Press)

V.K. Sethu, *Kabir: The Weaver of God's Name* (1984) (Amritsar: Radha Soami Satsang Beas)

The Courtesan, the Mahatma & the Italian Brahmin

Arvind Krishna Mehrotra (trans.), *Songs of Kabir* (2011) (New York: New York Review of Books)

William J. Dwyer, *Bhakti in Kabir* (1981) (Patna: Associated Book Agency)

David Lorenzen, *Kabir Legends and Ananta-Das's Kabir Parichai* (1991) (New York: SUNY Press)

Ahmad Shah (trans.), *The Bijak of Kabir* (1917) (Hamirpur: Ahmad Shah)

Shraddha Upadhyay, 'Seeking Femininity in Kabir's Poetry' at https://feminisminindia.com/2018/07/11/seeking-femininity-kabir-poetry/;

https://karmabhumi.org/kabir-women/, accessed on 27 April 2019

A CITY FOR A COURTESAN?

Manu S. Pillai, *Rebel Sultans: The Deccan from Khilji to Shivaji* (2018) (New Delhi: Juggernaut Books)

WHAT IF VIJAYANAGAR HAD SURVIVED?

Manu S. Pillai, *Rebel Sultans: The Deccan from Khilji to Shivaji* (2018) (New Delhi: Juggernaut Books)

SULTANS AND RAJAHS: TEXTS AND TRADITION

Phillip B. Wagoner, *Tidings of the King: A Translation and Ethnohistorical Analysis of the Rayavacakamu* (1993) (Honolulu: University of Hawaii Press)

Manu S. Pillai, *Rebel Sultans: The Deccan from Khilji to Shivaji* (2018) (New Delhi: Juggernaut Books)

Lidia Sudyka, *Vijayanagara: A Forgotten Empire of Poetesses: Part 1: The Voice of Gangadevi* (2013) (Krakow: Ksiegarnia Akademicka

DARA SHUKOH: POET AMONG WARRIORS

Abraham Eraly, *The Mughal World: Life in India's Last Golden Age* (2007) (New Delhi: Penguin Books)

Abraham Eraly, *Emperors of the Peacock Throne: The Saga of the Great Moghuls* (2014) (New Delhi: Penguin Random House)

Rakshat Puri and Kuldip Akhtar, 'Sarmad: The Naked Faqir'

in *India International Centre Quarterly*, Vol. 20, No. 3 (1993), pp. 65–78

Rakshat Puri, 'The Mystic Prince' in *India International Centre Quarterly*, Vol. 21, No. 4 (1994), pp. 149–152

Tasadduq Husain, 'The Spiritual Journey of Dara Shukoh' in *Social Scientist*, Vol. 30, No. 7/8 (2002), pp. 54–66

Francois Bernier, *Travels in the Mogul Empire* (translated by Irving Brock) (1826) (London: William Pickering)

John Phillips (trans.), *Tavernier's Travels in India* (1905) (Calcutta: N. Roy)

THE LOST BEGUM OF AHMEDNAGAR

Manu S. Pillai, *Rebel Sultans: The Deccan from Khilji to Shivaji* (2018) (New Delhi: Juggernaut Books)

Sanjay Subrahmanyam, *Courtly Encounters: Translating Courtliness and Violence in Early Modern Eurasia* (2012) (Cambridge: Harvard University Press)

J.D.B. Gribble, *A History of the Deccan*, Vol. I (1896) (London: Luzac & Co.)

H.K. Sherwani and P.M. Joshi (eds.), *History of the Medieval Deccan* (1973) (Hyderabad: Government of Andhra Pradesh)

THE STORY OF THE *KAMASUTRA*

A.N.D. Haksar (trans.), *The Kamasutra* (2012) (London: Penguin Books)

Jyoti Puri, 'Concerning Kamasutras: Challenging Narratives of History and Sexuality' in *Signs*, Vol. 27, No. 3 (2002), pp. 603–639

Shailaja Sharma, 'Kamasutra' in *Counterpoints*, Vol. 169 (2002), pp. 103–107

Wendy Doniger, 'On the Kamasutra' in *Daedalus*, Vol. 131, No. 2 (2002), pp. 126–129

Wendy Doniger, 'The 'Kamasutra': It Isn't All About Sex' in *The Kenyon Review*, Vol. 25, No. 1 (2003), pp. 18–37

The Courtesan, the Mahatma & the Italian Brahmin

SULTANS AND PADSHAHS: FOREIGNNESS IN INDIANNESS

Manu S. Pillai, *Rebel Sultans: The Deccan from Khilji to Shivaji* (2018) (New Delhi: Juggernaut Books)

Surendranath Sen, *Siva Chhatrapati: Being a Translation of Sabhasad Bakhar with Extracts from Chitnis and Sivadigvijaya, with Notes* (1920) (Calcutta: University of Calcutta)

A.R. Kulkarni, *Explorations in Deccan History* (2006) (Delhi: Pragati and the Indian Council of Historical Research

Brajadulal Chattopadhyaya, *Representing the Other? Sanskrit Sources and the Muslims* (1998) (New Delhi: Manohar Publishers and Distributors)

Appendix to *Epigraphia Indica*, Vol. XIX to XXIII (1983) (New Delhi: Archaeological Survey of India)

Prachi Deshpande, *Creative Pasts: Historical Memory and Identity in Western India, 1700–1960* (2007) (New York: Columbia University Press)

Sumit Guha, 'Transitions and Translations: Regional Power and Vernacular Identity in the Dakhan, 1500–1800' in *Comparative Studies of South Asia, Africa and the Middle East*, Vol. 24, No. 2 (2004), pp. 23–31

MEENAKSHI: FIRST A WARRIOR

Elisabeth Benard and Beverly Moon (eds.), *Goddesses Who Rule* (2000) (Oxford: Oxford University Press)

Vijaya Ramaswamy, *Re-searching Indian Women* (2003) (New Delhi: Manohar Publishers and Distributors)

THE WOMAN WHO HAD NO REASON FOR SHAME

A.K. Ramanujan, Velcheru Narayana Rao, and David Shulam (eds.), *When God is a Customer: Telugu Courtesan Songs by Ksetrayya and Others* (1994) (Berkeley: University of California Press)

Velcheru Narayana Rao, David Shulman and Sanjay Subrahmanyam, *Symbols of Substance: Court and State in Nayaka Period Tamilnadu* (1992) (New Delhi: Oxford University Press)

Susie J. Tharu and K. Lalita (eds.), *Women Writing in India: Vol. 1: 600 BC to the early twentieth century* (1991) (New York: The Feminist Press)

Sandhya Mulchandani (trans.), *Muddupalani: The Appeasement of Radhika: Radhika Santawanam* (2011) (New Delhi: Penguin Books)

I. Lakshmi, 'Perception of Prostitution: A Study of Two Medieval Telugu Literary Texts' in *Proceedings of the Indian History Congress*, Vol. 64 (2003), pp. 583–590

Davesh Soneji, 'Siva's Courtesans: Religion, Rhetoric and Self-Representation in Early Twentieth-Century Writing by Devadasis' in *International Journal of Hindu Studies*, Vol. 14, No. 1 (2010), pp. 31–70

Uttara Asha Coorlawala, 'The Sanskritized Body' in *Dance Research Journal*, Vol. 36, No. 2 (2004), pp. 50–63

ALAUDDIN KHILJI: RULING BY THE SWORD

R.S. Chaurasia, *History of Medieval India: From 1000 AD to 1707 AD* (2002) (New Delhi: Atlantic)

Sultan Hameed Warsi, *History of Ala-Ud-Din Khilji* (1930) (Allahabad: Rama Dayal Agarwala)

Syama Prasad Basu, *Rise and Fall of Khilji Imperialism* (1963) (Calcutta: U.N. Dhur & Sons Pvt Ltd.)

Ghulam Sarwar Khan, *The Life and Works of Sultan Alauddin Khalji* (1992) (Delhi: Atlantic)

Manu S. Pillai, *Rebel Sultans: The Deccan from Khilji to Shivaji* (2018) (New Delhi: Juggernaut Books)

Abraham Eraly, *The Age of Wrath: A History of the Delhi Sultanate* (2014) (New Delhi: Penguin Random House)

THE COURTESAN WHO BECAME A PRINCESS

Julia Keay, *Farzana: The Tempestuous Life and Times of Begum Samru* (2013) (New Delhi: HarperCollins Publishers India)

Alka Hingorani, 'Artful Agency: Imagining and Imaging Begum Samru' in *Archives of Asian Art*, Vol. 53 (2002–03), pp. 54–70

David James, 'The "Rajah of Tipperary" and the Begum of Sardhana' in *The GPA Irish Arts Review Yearbook* (1988), pp. 49–55

Brijraj Singh, 'The Enigma of Begum Samru: Differing Approaches to Her Life' in the *India International Centre Quarterly*, Vol. 24, No. 4 (1997), pp. 33–43

Farha Khan, 'Begum Samru of Sardhana: Socio-Political Interventions and Continuing Legacy' in *Proceedings of the Indian History Congress*, Vol. 73 (2012), pp. 707–718

Amy Marshall, 'Unconventional Subjects: A Very British Approach to Dealing with Extraordinary People considered through a Portrait of the Begum Samry, by Jiwan Ram, and The History of Zeb-ul-Nissa the Begum Samru of Sardhana, a poem by Lalla Gokul Chand' at https://open.conted.ox.ac.uk/sites/open.conted.ox.ac.uk/files/resources/Create%20Document/Unconventional%20Subjects_Amy%20Marshall.pdf, accessed on 27 April 2019

MEERABAI: A DIFFERENT KIND OF VALOUR

S.M. Pandey and Norman Zide, 'Mirabai and her Contributions to the Bhakti Movement' in *History of Religions*, Vol. 5, No. 1 (1965), pp. 54–73

Kanu Desai, *Mirabai: Ten Pictures from the Life of India's Greatest Poetess of the Past* (1950) (Bombay: Taraporevala and Sons)

Robert Bly and Jane Hirshfield, *Mirabai: Ecstatic Poems* (2004) (Boston: Beacon Press)

A.J. Alston, *The Devotional Poems of Mirabai* (1980) (New Delhi: Motilal Banarsidass Publishers)

John Stratton Hawley, *Three Bhakti Voices: Mirabai, Surdas and Kabir in Their Times and Ours* (2005) (New Delhi: Oxford University Press)

Akshaya Kumar, 'Latter-day Meeras: From Nationalist Icon to Subaltern Subject' in *Indian Literature*, Vol. 51, No. 2 (2007), pp. 176–195

THE AKBAR OF THE DECCAN

Manu S. Pillai, *Rebel Sultans: The Deccan from Khilji to Shivaji* (2018) (New Delhi: Juggernaut Books)

JAHANGIR: THE ENDEARING ECCENTRIC

Parvati Sharma, *Jahangir: An Intimate Portrait of a Great Mughal* (2018) (New Delhi: Juggernaut Books)

Wheeler M. Thackston trans., *The Jahangirnama: Memoirs of Jahangir, Emperor of India* (1999) (Oxford: Oxford University Press)

VARARUCHI'S CHILDREN AND THE MAPPILAS OF MALABAR

Stephen F. Dale and M. Gangadhara Menon, 'Nerccas': Saint Worship among the Muslims of Kerala' in *Bulletin of the School of Oriental and African Studies*, Vol. 41, No. 3 (1978), pp. 523–538

Stephen F. Dale, 'Conversion and the Growth of the Islamic Community of Kerala, South India' in *Studia Islamica*, No. 71 (1990), pp. 155–175

Stephen F. Dale, *Islamic Society on the South Asian Frontier: The Mappilas of Malabar, 1498–1922* (1980) (Oxford: Clarendon Press)

Stephen F. Dale, 'The Mappila Outbreaks: Ideology and Social Conflict in Nineteenth-Century Kerala' in *The Journal of Asian Studies*, Vol. 35, No. 1 (1975), pp. 85–97

Conrad Wood, 'The First Moplah Rebellion against British Rule in Malabar' in *Modern Asian Studies*, Vol. 10, No. 4 (1976), pp. 543–556

Conrad Wood, 'Historical Background of the Moplah Rebellion: Outbreaks, 1836–1919' in *Social Scientist*, Vol. 3, No. 1 (1974), pp. 5–33

Roland E. Miller, *Mappila Muslim Culture: How a Historic Muslim Community in India has Blended Tradition and Modernity* (2015) (Albani: SUNY Press)

V. Kunhali, 'The Marakkar Legacy and Mappila Community' in *Proceedings of the Indian History Congress*, Vol. 61 (2003), pp. 369–374

M.H. Ilias, 'Mappila Muslims and the Cultural Content of Trading Arab Diaspora on the Malabar Coast' in *Asian Journal of Social Science*, Vol. 35, No. 4/5 (2007), pp. 434–456

K.V. Krishna Ayyar, 'Islam in Malabar or One Thousand Years of Hindu-Muslim Unity' in *Proceedings of the Indian History Congress*, Vol. 5 (1941), pp. 271–274

A.P. Ibrahim Kunju, 'The Kunjali Marakkars of Kottakkal' in *Proceedings of the Indian History Congress*, Vol. 21 (1958), pp. 607–617

D.N. Dhanagare, 'Agrarian Conflict, Religion and Politics: The Moplah Rebellions in Malabar in the Nineteenth and Early Twentieth Centuries' in *Past & Present*, No. 74 (1977), pp. 112–141

The Courtesan, the Mahatma & the Italian Brahmin

Robert L. Hardgrave, 'The Mappila Rebellion, 1921: Peasant Revolt in Malabar' in *Modern Asian Studies*, Vol. 11, No. 1 (1977), pp. 57–99

Sukumar Sakar, 'The British Attitude towards the Moplah Uprising of 1921' in *Proceedings of the Indian History Congress*, Vol. 33 (1971), pp. 494–498

THE WOMAN WITH NO BREASTS

Manu S. Pillai, *The Ivory Throne: Chronicles of the House of Travancore* (2015) (New Delhi: HarperCollins Publishers India)

Note: Nangeli exists in Ezhava folklore, and there is a parallel tale featuring a tribal couple, recorded in another part of Kerala. Lately there has been debate on the absence of 'real' documentation on Nangeli. Documentation, however, in India largely revolves around high-caste groups, while low-caste heroes and heroines often exist only in song and lore, much of which has not been catalogued. Given the paucity of written material where marginalised communities are concerned, such folklore cannot be written off simply because there is no paper to back the stories they tell—on the contrary, when it comes to marginalised groups, these songs and tales are often the only sources of information we have, leaving historians to work with these to the extent possible.

PART II

WHAT IF THERE WAS NO BRITISH RAJ?

Roy Moxham, *The Theft of India: The European Conquests of India*, 1498–1765 (2016) (New Delhi: HarperCollins Publishers India)

Irfan Habib (ed.), *Confronting Colonialism: Resistance and Modernization under Haidar Ali and Tipu Sultan* (2002) (London: Anthem Press)

Julia Keay, *Farzana: The Tempestuous Life and Times of Begum Samru* (2013) (New Delhi: HarperCollins Publishers India)

Rachel Fell McDermott, Leonard A. Gordon, Ainslie T. Embree, Frances W. Pritchett, and Dennis Dalton (eds.), *Sources of Indian Traditions*, Vol. 2 (2014) (New York: Columbia University Press)

J. Marsham in *Fourth Report from the Select Committee on Colonization and Settlement (India) Together with Proceedings of the Committee, Minutes of Evidence, and Appendix* (1858) (London: The House of Commons)

ROWDY BOB: THE VICTOR OF PLASSEY

Robert Harvey, *Clive: The Life and Death of a British Emperor* (1998) (London: Hoddern and Stoughton)

Thomas Babington Macaulay, *Essays: Critical and Miscellaneous* (1844) (Philadelphia: Carey and Hart)

Evgenia Sifaki, 'Masculinity, Heroism, and the Empire: Robert Browning's "Clive" and other Victorian Re-constructions of the Story of Robert Clive' in *Victorian Literature and Culture*, Vol. 37, No. 1 (2009), pp. 141–156

John Malcolm, *The Life of Robert, Lord Clive*, Vols. I, II, III (London: John Murray)

THE BLOODY MONSOON OF VELLORE

Letters and documents pertaining to the Vellore Mutiny in Parliamentary Papers:

Papers Relating to East India Affairs (1813) (London: House of Commons)

Papers Relating to East India Affairs (1811) (London: House of Commons)

C.Y. Bayly, *Empire and Information: Intelligence Gathering and Social Communication in India*, 1780–1870 (1996) (Cambridge: Cambridge University Press)

Bunny Gupta and Jaya Chaliha, 'Exiles in Calcutta: The Descendants of Tipu Sultan' in *India International Centre Quarterly*, Vol. 18, No. 1 (1991), pp. 181–188

WILLIAM JONES: INDIA'S BRIDGE TO THE WEST

Abu Taher Mojumder, *Sir William Jones: The Romantics and The Victorians* (1976) (Dacca: University Press)

Abu Taher Mojumder, *Sir William Jones and the East* (1978) (Dacca: Begum Zakia Sultana)

Satya S. Pachori, *Sir William Jones: A Reader* (1993) (Delhi: Oxford University Press)

S.N. Mukherjee, *Sir William Jones: A Study in Eighteenth-Century British Attitudes to India* (1987) (London: Sangam Books)

Garland Cannon, *Sir William Jones' Founding and Directing of the Asiatic Society* (Offprinted from the India Office Library and Records Report for 1984–85)

P.J. Marshall (ed.), *The British Discovery of Hinduism in the Eighteenth Century* (1970) (London: Cambridge University Press)

L.S.R. Krishna Sastry, *Sir William Jones: Interpreter of India to the West* (1998) (Hyderabad: Booklinks Corporation)

Michael J. Franklin, *Orientalist Jones: Sir William Jones, Poet, Lawyer, and Linguist* (2011) (New York: Oxford University Press)

THE GENTLEMAN REFORMER OF BENGAL

B.N. Dasgupta, *The Life and Times of Rajah Rammohun Roy* (1980) (New Delhi: Ambika)

B.M. Sankhdher, *Rammohan Roy: The Apostle of Indian Awakening: Some Contemporary Estimates* (1989) (New Delhi: Navrang)

Bruce Carlisle Roberts on *Raja Rammohan Ray: The Father of Modern India* (2001) (New Delhi: Oxford University Press)

Lynn Zastoupil, *Rammohun Roy and the Making of Victorian Britain* (2010) (New York: Macmillan)

Upendra Nath Ball, *Rammohun Roy: A Study of His Life, Works, and Thoughts* (2009) (Kolkata: Bibliophile)

Manas Chakraborty and Tapan Kumar Mohanta, 'Assessing Radicalism in Early Nineteenth Century Bengal' in *The Indian Journal of Political Science*, Vol. 66, No. 1 (205), pp. 153–174

Brian A. Hatcher, 'Remember Rammohan: An Essay on the (Re-)Emergence of Modern Hinduism' in *History of Religions*, Vol. 46, No. 1 (2006), pp. 50–80

Ulysses Young, 'Rammohan Roy and the Modern World' in *East and West*, Vol. 5, No. 4 (1955), pp. 300–303

Manu S. Pillai

THE COLONIAL STATE AND INDIA'S GODS

T.K. Velu Pillai, *The Travancore State Manual*, Vol. IV (1940) (Trivandrum: Government of Travancore)

Devaswoms in Travancore (Trivandrum: Sri Vilas Press), https://archive.org/details/in.ernet.dli.2015.128204, accessed on 27 April 2019

Chandra Mudaliar, *State and Religious Endowments in Madras* (1976) (Madras: University of Madras)

Arjun Appadurai, *Worship and Conflict under Colonial Rule: A South Indian Case* (2007) (Cambridge: Cambridge University Press)

WHEN A TEMPLE WAS BESIEGED IN AYODHYA

Peter van der Veer, 'God must be Liberated!': A Hindu Liberation Movement in Ayodhya' in *Modern Asian Studies*, Vol. 21, No. 2 (1987), pp. 283–301

Peter van der Veer, 'Ayodhya and Somnath: Eternal Shrines, Contested Histories' in *Social Research*, Vol. 59, No. 1 (1992), pp. 85–109

Peter van der Veer, *Religious Nationalism: Hindus and Muslims in India* (1994) (Berkeley: University of California Press)

Mushrul Hasan, 'Traditional Rites and Contested Meanings: Sectarian Strife in Colonial Lucknow' in *Rivista degli studi orientali*, Vol. 69, No. 1/2 (1995), pp. 151–171

John Pemble, *The Raj, the Indian Mutiny and the Kingdom of Oudh*, 1810-1859 (1977) (Hassocks: The Harvester Press)

Sarvepalli Gopal (ed.), *Anatomy of a Confrontation: Ayodhya and the Rise of Communal Politics in India* (1993) (London: Zed Books)

Jan Platvoet and Karel van der Toorn (eds.), *Pluralism and Identity: Studies in Ritual Behaviour* (1995) (Leiden: E.J. Brill)

Sarvepalli Gopal, Romila Thapar, Bipan Chandra and Others, 'The Political Abuse of History: Babri-Masjid-Rama Janmnabhumi Dispute' in *Social Scientist*, Vol. 18, No. 1/2 (1990), pp. 76–81

Hans Bakker, 'Ayodhya: A Hindu Jerusalem: An Investigation of 'Holy War' as a Religious Idea in the Light of Communal Unrest in India' in *Numen*, Vol. 38, No. 1 (1991), pp. 80–109

Juan Richard Cole, *Sacred Space and Holy War: The Politics, Culture and History of Shi'ite Islam* (2005) (London: IB Tauris)

Paul R. Brass (ed.), *Riots and Pogroms* (1996) (London: Palgrave Macmillan)

A FORGOTTEN INDIAN QUEEN IN PARIS

Rosie Llewellyn-Jones, *The Last King in India: Wajid Ali Shah* (2014) (London: Hurst and Company)

THE STORY OF WAJID ALI SHAH

Rosie Llewellyn-Jones, *The Last King in India: Wajid Ali Shah* (2014) (London: Hurst and Company)

Sudipta Mitra, *Pearl by the River: Nawab Wajid Ali Shah's Kingdom in Exile* (2017) (New Delhi: Rupa Publications)

William Knighton, *The Private Life of an Eastern King* (1921) (London: Oxford University Press)

John Pemble, *The Raj, the Indian Mutiny, and the Kingdom of Oudh*, 1801–1859 (1960) (New Delhi: Oxford University Press)

VICTORIA MAHARANI AND INDIA

Miles Taylor, *The English Maharani: Queen Victoria and India* (2018) (New Delhi: Penguin Random House)

Shrabani Basu, *Victoria and Abdul: The True Story of the Queen's Closest Confidant* (2011) (Stroud: History Press)

THE ABSENT QUEEN OF LAKSHADWEEP

S.M. Mohamed Koya, 'British Relations with Arakkal Royal House' in *Proceedings of the Indian History Congress*, Vol. 33 (1971), pp. 432–438

R.H. Ellis, *A Short Account of Laccadive Islands and Minicoy* (1924) (Madras: Government Press)

S.M. Mohamed Koya, 'Matriliny and Malabar Muslims' in *Proceedings of the Indian History Congress*, Vol. 40 (1979), pp. 419–431

M.O. Koshy, *The Dutch Power in Kerala* (1729–58) (1989) (New Delhi: Mittal Publications)

Abraham Eraly, *Tales Once Told: Legends of Kerala adapted from Kottarathil Sankunni's Ithihyamala* (2006) (New Delhi: Penguin Books)

T.J. Joseph Mathew, *Lakshadweep in the Maritime History of India: A Study of the Original Correspondence between the British and the Arakkal Family of Malabar* (1992) (Pondicherry: Pondicherry University)

THE ENGINEER AND HIS RICE BOWL

Jon Wilson, *India Conquered: Britain's Raj and the Chaos of Empire* (2016) (New Delhi: Simon & Schuster India)

Lady Hope, *General Sir Arthur Cotton: His Life and Work* (1900) (London: Hodder & Stoughton)

Arthur Cotton, *Public Works in India* (1854) (London: Richardson Brothers)

THE MAN BEHIND MODERN HINDI

Sheldon Pollock (ed.), *Literary Cultures in History: Reconstructions from South Asia* (2003) (Berkeley: University of California Press)

Mohinder Singh, 'Temporalization of Concepts: Reflections on the Concept of Unnati (Progress) in Hindi (1870–1900)' in *Contributions to the History of Concepts*, Vol. 7, No. 1 (2012), pp. 51–71

Madan Gopal, 'Remembering Bharatendu Harishchandra' in *Indian Literature*, Vol. 28, No. 2 (1985), pp. 101–109

Vasudha Dalmia, *The Nationalization of Hindu Tradition: Bharatendu Harischandra and Nineteenth-Century Banaras* (1997) (Delhi: Oxford University Press)

Ramesh Rawat, '1857 and the 'Renaissance' in Hindi Literature' in *Social Scientist*, Vol. 26, No. 1/4 (1998), pp. 95–112

Babu Sivaprasad, *Memorandum: Court Characters in the Upper Provinces of India* (1868) (Benares: Medical Hall Press)

THE RAILWAYS AND INDIA

Anthony J. Parel (ed.), *Gandhi: Hind Swaraj and Other Writings* (1997) (Cambridge: Cambridge University Press)

Anonymous ('An Old Post Master'), *Indian Railways and Their Probable Results* (1848) (London: T.C. Newby and Others)

Bibek Debroy, Sanjay Chadha and Vidya Krishnamurthi, *Indian Railways: The Weaving of a National Tapestry* (2017) (New Delhi: Penguin Random House)

Arup K. Chatterjee, *The Purveyors of Destiny: A Cultural Biography of the Indian Railways* (2017) (New Delhi: Bloomsbury Publishing India)

THE PHULES AND THEIR FIGHT

Sudhakar Marathe (trans.), Bhaskar Lakshmi Bhole, *Mahatma Jotirao Phule* (2011) (New Delhi: Sahitya Akademi)

Gail Omvedt, *Jyotirao Phule and the Ideology of Social Revolution in India* (2004) (New Delhi: Critical Quest)

J.R. Shinde, *Dynamics of Cultural Revolution: 19th Century Maharashtra* (1985) (New Delhi: Ajanta Publishers)

P.G. Patil (trans.), Jotirao Phule, *Slavery* (1991) (Bombay: Government of Maharashtra)

Rosalind O'Hanlon, *Caste, Conflict and Ideology: Mahatma Phule and Low-Caste Protest in Nineteenth-Century Western India* (1985) (London: Cambridge University Press)

Ramachandra Guha, *Makers of Modern India* (2011) (Cambridge: Harvard University Press)

Hari Narake, 'Dnyanajyoti Savitribai Phule', http://roundtableindia.co.in/index.php?option=com_content&view=article&id=5681:dnyanajyoti-savitribai-phule-i&catid=115&Itemid=127 and http://roundtableindia.co.in/index.php?option=com_content&view=article&id=5784:dnyanajyoti-savitribai-phule-ii&catid=115:dalitbahujan-renaissance&Itemid=127, accessed on 27 April 2019

THE AMMACHIES OF TRAVANCORE

Manu S. Pillai, *The Ivory Throne: Chronicles of the House of Travancore* (2015) (New Delhi: HarperCollins Publishers India)

Samuel Mateer, *Native Life in Travancore* (1883) (London: WH Allen & Co.)

Journal of the National Indian Association in Aid of Social Progress and Education in India (1885) (London: C Kegan Paul, Trench & Co.)

Charles Allen and Sharada Dwivedi, *Lives of the Indian Princes* (1984) (London: Century Publishing)

MACAULAY: THE IMPERIALIST WE LOVE TO HATE

Zareer Masani, *Macaulay: Pioneer of India's Modernization* (2012) (New Delhi: Random House Books)

Arthur Bryant, *Macaulay* (1938) (London: Thomas Nelson & Sons)

J. Cotter Morison, *Macaulay* (1909) (London: Macmillan & Co.)

George Otto Trevelyan, *Selections from the Writings of Lord Macaulay* (1920) (Bombay: Longmans, Green & Co.)

William H. Pritchard, 'Macaulay Reconsidered' in *The Hudson Review*, Vol. 63, No. 1 (2010), pp. 91–99

FOOTBALL AND NATIONALISM IN INDIA

Ronojoy Sen, *Nation at Play: A History of Sport in India* (2015) (New York: Columbia University Press)

Paul Dimeo, 'With Pakistan in the Offing...': Football and Communal Politics in South Asia, 1887-1947' in *Journal of Contemporary History*, Vol. 38, No. 3 (2003), pp. 377–394

Moti Nandy and Shampa Banerjee, 'Football and Nationalism' in *India International Centre Quarterly*, Vol. 17, No. 3/4 (1990–91), pp. 240–254

Christian Koller and Fabian Brandle, *Goal!: A Cultural and Social History of Modern Football* (2015) (Washington DC: The Catholic University of America Press)

Partha Chatterjee, *The Black Hole of Empire: History of a Global Practice of Power* (2012) (Princeton: Princeton University Press)

MANUBAI: THE RANI BEFORE THE BATTLE

C.A. Kincaid, 'Lakshmibai Rani of Jhansi' in the *Journal of the Royal Asiatic Society*, Vol. 75, Nos. 1–2 (1943), pp. 100–104

Joyce Lebra-Chapman, *The Rani of Jhansi: A Study in Female Heroism in India* (1986) (Honolulu: University of Hawaii Press)

Alexander Rogers, *The Rani of Jhansi or The Widowed Queen: A Play* (1895) (Westminster: Constable & Co.)

M.S. Renickk, *A New Light Upon the History of Rani Laxmibai of Jhansi* (2004) (New Delhi: Agamala Prakashan)

POWER, PREJUDICE AND CURZON

Nayana Goradia, *Lord Curzon: The Last of the British Moghuls* (1993) (New Delhi: Oxford University Press)

The Earl of Ronaldshay, *The Life of Lord Curzon: Being the Authorized Biography of George Nathanial Marquess Curzon of Kedleston*, Vols. I, II, III (1928) (London: Ernest Benn)

H. Caldwell, *Lord Curzon in India* (1903) (London: R.A. Everett)

G.H. Bennett and Marion Gibson, *The Later Life of Lord Curzon of Kedleston: Aristocrat, Writer, Politician, Statesman* (2000) (New York: Edwin Mellen Press)

Peter King (ed.), *A Viceroy's India: Leaves from Lord Curzon's Note Book* (1984) (London: Sidgwick & Jackson)

Syed Sirdar Ali Khan, *Lord Curzon's Administration of India: What He Promised, What He Performed* (1905) (Bombay: The Times Press)

WHEN SAVARKAR JUMPED SHIP

Indian Office Records, London:

IOR/L/PJ/6/994: 'VD Savarkar; arrest and extradition; escape and recapture and Marseilles' (1910)

IOR/L/PJ/6/1060: 'Savarkar Case; Cases, counter-cases & replies &c' (1910–11)

SAVARKAR'S THWARTED 'RACIAL DREAM'

Indian Office Records, London:

IOR/L/PS/12/484: 'Future Emperor of India by VD Savarkar'

V.D. Savarkar, *Hindu Sanghatan: Its Ideology and Immediate Programme: A Collection of His Three Presidential Speeches at Karnavati (Ahmedabad), Nagpur & Calcutta* (1940) (Bombay: NV Damle)

Manu Bhagavan, 'Princely States and the Hindu Imaginary: Exploring the Cartography of Hindu Nationalism in Colonial India' in *The Journal of Asian Studies*, Vol. 67, No. 3 (2008), pp. 881–915

THE CHAMPION OF TUTICORIN

R.A. Padmanabhan, *VO Chidambaram Pillai* (1977) (New Delhi: National Book Trust)

R.N. Sampath and P.S. Mani, *VO Chidambaram Pillai* (1992) (New Delhi: Government of India)

Frank Broeze, 'Underdevelopment and Dependency: Maritime India during the Raj' in *Modern Asian Studies*, Vol. 18, No. 3 (1984), pp. 429–457

A.R. Venkatachalapathy, 'In Search of Ashe' in the *Economic and Political Weekly*, Vol. 45, No. 2 (2010), pp. 37–44

THE COMPLICATED V.K. KRISHNA MENON

V.K. Krishna Menon, *Unity with India Against Fascism* (1943) (London: The India League)

Janaki Ram, *V.K. Krishna Menon: A Personal Memoir* (1997) (New Delhi: Oxford University Press)

Michael Brecher, *India and World Politics: Krishna Menon's View of the World* (1968) (London: Oxford University Press)

Paul M. McGarr, 'India's Rasputin'?: VK Krishna Menon and Anglo-American Misperceptions of Indian Foreign Policymaking, 1947–1964' in *Diplomacy and Statecraft*, Vol. 22, No. 2 (2011), pp. 239–260

Paul M. McGarr, 'A Serious Menace to Security': British Intelligence, VK Krishna Menon, and the Indian High Commission in London, 1947–52' in *The Journal of Imperial and Commonwealth History*, Vol. 38, No. 3 (2010), pp. 441–469

T.J.S. George, *Krishna Menon: A Biography* (1964) (London: Jonathan Cape)

Ian Hall (ed.), *Radicals and Reactionaries in Twentieth-Century International Thought* (2015) (New York: Palgrave Macmillan)

Eminent Parliamentarians Monograph Series, *VK Krishna Menon* (1991) (New Delhi: Lok Sabha Secretariat)

THE SEAMSTRESS AND THE MATHEMATICIAN

Robert Kanigel, *The Man who Knew Infinity: A Life of the Genius Ramanujan* (1991) (New York: Charles Scribner's Sons)

Suresh Ram, *Srinivasa Ramanujan* (1972) (New Delhi: National Book Trust)

Bruce C. Berndt and Robert A. Rankin, *Ramanujan: Letters and Commentary* (1991) (American Mathematical Society)

Bruce C. Berndt and Robert A. Rankin, *Ramanujan: Essays and Surveys* (2001) (American Mathematical Society)

G.H. Hardy, 'The Indian Mathematician Ramanujan' in *The American Mathematical Monthly*, Vol. 44, No. 3 (1937), pp. 137–155

AN UNSENTIMENTAL MAN OF ACTION

M. Visvesvaraya, *Memoirs of My Working Life* (1951) (Bangalore: Mokshagundam Visvesvaraya)

M. Visvesvaraya, *Reconstructing India* (1920) (London: P.S. King & Son)

'*MV*' *Birth Centenary Commemoration Volume* (1960) (Bangalore: Visveswaraya Centenary Celebration Committee)

T. Rangadasappa, *Sir M Visvesvaraya: A Biography* (1985) (Bombay: All Indian Manufacturers' Association)

Pandri Nath, *Mokshagundam Visvesvaraya: Life and Work* (1987) (Bombay: Bharatiya Vidya Bhavan)

A.P. Srinivasa Murthy, *Sir M Visvesvaraya: His Economic Thought and Achievements* (1995) (Bangalore: Shiny Publications)

Vinod Vyasulu, 'Nehru and the Visvesvaraya Legacy' in the *Economic and Political Weekly*, Vol. 24, No. 30 (1989), pp. 1700–1704

THE RESURRECTION OF BALAMANI

Divya Dwivedi and Sanil V (eds.), *The Public Sphere from Outside the West* (2015) (London: Bloomsbury Publishing)

Veejay Sai, *Drama Queens: Women who Created History on Stage* (2017) (New Delhi: Roli Books)

Pierre Loti, *India* (1906) (London: T. Werner Laurie)

Rupika Chawla, *Raja Ravi Varma: Painter of Colonial India* (2010) (Ahmedabad: Mapin Publishing)

Manu S. Pillai

THE GRAMOPHONE QUEEN OF INDIA

Vikram Sampath, *My Name is Gauhar Jaan* (2010) (New Delhi: Rupa Publications)

Arvind Rajagopal and Anupama Rao (eds.), *Media and Utopia: History, Imagination and Technology* (2016) (Abingdon: Routledge)

Mekhala Sengupta, 'Courtesan Culture in India: The Transition from the Devadasi to the Tawaif or Boijee' in *India International Centre Quarterly*, Vol. 41, No. 1 (2014), pp. 124–140

A BRAHMIN WOMAN OF SCANDAL

Rajeev Kumaramkandath, 'The Discursive Formation of Sexual Subjects: Sexual Morality and Homosexuality in Keralam', Unpublished thesis, (2013) (Manipal University)

A.M.N. Chakiar, *The Last Smartha Vicharam: A Victim's Reminiscences* (1998) (Tripunithura: Padma C Menon)

Devaki Nilayamgode, *Antharjanam: Memoirs of a Namboodiri Woman* (translated by Indira Menon and Radhika P. Menon) (New Delhi: Oxford University Press)

Susie J. Tharu and K. Lalita (eds.), *Women Writing in India: Vol. 1: 600 BC to the early twentieth century* (1991) (New York: The Feminist Press)

Bina Agarwal, *A Field of One's Own: Gender and Land Rights in South Asia* (1994) (Cambridge: Cambridge University Press)

'I'M A NAGA FIRST, A NAGA SECOND, AND A NAGA LAST'

Pieter Steyn, *Zapuphizo: Voice of the Nagas* (2002) (London: Kegan Paul)

A.S. Atai Shimray, *Let Freedom Ring: Story of Naga Nationalism* (2005) (New Delhi: Promilla & Co.)

A. Lanunungsang Ao, *From Phizo to Muivah: The Naga National Question in North East India* (2002) (New Delhi: Mittal Publications)

V.R. Krishna Iyer, 'Saga of the Nagas' in *Economic and Political Weekly*, Vol. 29, No. 12 (1994), pp. 674–678

Kamarupee, 'Passing of Phizo' in *Economic and Political Weekly*, Vol. 25, No. 18/19 (1990), pp. 983–984

THE MONK FOR EVERY INDIAN

Gautam Ghosh, *The Prophet of Modern India* (2003) (New Delhi: Rupa Publications)

Gautam Sen, *The Mind of Swami Vivekananda* (2012) (Mumbai: Jaico Publishing House)

Chaitanya Singhania, 'From the Hindu Man to Indian Nationalism: Vivekananda's Political Realism' in *The Yale Historical Review*, Vol. 3, No. 2 (2014), pp. 7–29

B.G. Gokhale, 'Swami Vivekananda and Indian Nationalism' in the *Journal of Bible and Religion*, Vol. 32, No. 1 (1964), pp. 35–42

Swami Nikhilananda, 'Swami Vivekananda Centenary' in *Philosophy East and West*, Vol. 14, No. 1 (1964), pp. 73–75

N.K. Kumar, 'The Swami and the Mahatma: The Socio-Political Relevance' in *The Indian Journal of Political Science*, Vol. 53, No. 2 (1992), pp. 297–313

Rajgopal Chattopadhyaya, *Swami Vivekananda in India: A Corrective Biography* (1999) (New Delhi: Motilal Banarsidass Publishers)

Tomoko Masuzawa, *The Invention of World Religions: Or How European Universalism was Preserved in the Language of Pluralism* (2005) (Chicago: University of Chicago Press)

The Complete Works of Swami Vivekananda, Vol. 3 (2016) (Kolkata: The Adhyakha Advaita Ashrama)

Makarand R. Paranjape (ed.), *Swami Vivekananda: A Contemporary Reader* (2015) (New Delhi: Routledge)

THE PHOTOGRAPHER–PRINCE OF JAIPUR

Robert W. Stern, *The Cat and the Lion: Jaipur State in the British Raj* (1998) (Leiden: E.J. Brill)

R.P. Singh & Kanwar Rajpal Singh, *Sawai Man Singh of Jaipur: Life and Legend* (2014) (New Delhi: Roli Books)

Jadunath Sarkar, *A History of Jaipur, c. 1503-1938* (1984) (Hyderabad: Orient Longman)

Laura Weinstein, 'Exposing the Zenana: Maharaja Sawai Ram Singh II's Photographs of Women in Purdah' in *History of Photography*, Vol. 34, No. 1 (2010), pp. 2–16

Mrinalini Venkateswaran, 'Cameras at Court', http://www.indiaseminar.com/2014/660/660_mrinalini_venkateswaran.htm, accessed on 27 April 2019

Vibhuti Sachdev, 'Negotiating Modernity in Princely Jaipur' in *South Asian Studies*, Vol. 28, No. 2 (2012), pp. 171–181

Vidya Dehejia, *India Through the Lens: Photography, 1840-1911* (2000) (Ahmedabad: Mapin Publishing)

R.A.E. Benn, *Notes on Jaipur* (1916) (Jaipur: Printed by the Jaipur Central Jail)

PERIYAR IN THE AGE OF 'ANTI-NATIONALS'

E.S. Viswanathan, *The Political Career of EV Ramasami Naicker* (1983) (Madras: Ravi and Vasanth Publishers)

Anita Diehl, *EV Ramaswami Naicker: Periyar: A Study of the Influence of a Personality in Contemporary South India* (1977) (Stockholm: Esselte Studium)

K. Veeramani (ed.), *Periyar Feminism* (2010) (Thanjavur: Periyar Maniammai University)

Debi Chatterjee, *Up Against Caste: Comparative Study of Ambedkar and Periyar* (2004) (New Delhi: Rawat Publications)

S. Saraswathi, *Towards Self Respect: Periyar EVR on A New World* (1994) (Madras: Institute of South Indian Studies)

The Editor, 'Passing of the Periyar' in *Economic and Political Weekly*, Vol. 9, No. 1/2 (1974), pp. 13–15

N. Ram, 'Dravidian Movement in its Pre-Independence Phases' in *Economic and Political Weekly*, Vol. 14, No. 7/8 (1979), pp. 377–402

V. Geetha, 'Periyar, Women and an Ethic of Citizenship' in *Economic and Political Weekly*, Vol. 33, No. 17 (1998), pp. WS-9–WS-15

A.P.S. Chouhan and Niraj Kumar Jha, 'Periyar Persona, Principles, Praxis' in *The Indian Journal of Political Science*, Vol. 66, No. 3 (2005), pp. 667–692

ANNIE BESANT: AN INCONVENIENT WOMAN

Rosemary Dinnage, *Annie Besant* (1986) (London: Penguin Books)

Jyoti Chandra, *Annie Besant: From Theosophy to Nationalism* (2001) (Delhi: K.K. Publications)

The Courtesan, the Mahatma & the Italian Brahmin

Annie Besant, *Wake Up India: A Plea for Social Reform* (1913) (Madras: Theosophical Publishing House)

Arthur H. Nethercot, *The Last Four Lives of Annie Besant* (1963) (London: Rupert Hart-Davis)

Anne Taylor, *Annie Besant: A Biography* (1992) (New York: Oxford University Press)

Olivia Bennett, *Annie Besant* (1988) (London: Hamish Hamilton)

Theodore Besterman, *Mrs Annie Besant: A Modern Prophet* (1934) (London: Kegan Paul)

WHAT IF THE MAHATMA HAD LIVED?

Tridip Suhrud, 'Gandhi's Absence' in *India International Centre Quarterly*, Vol. 37, No 2 (2010), pp. 16–25

Aakash Singh, 'Gandhi and Ambedkar: Irreconcilable Differences?' in *International Journal of Hindu Studies*, Vol. 18, No. 3 (2014), pp. 413–449

Parvis Ghassem-Fachandi, *Pogrom in Gujarat: Hindu Nationalism and Anti-Muslim Violence in India* (2012) (Princeton: Princeton University Press)

Yasmin Khan, 'Performing Peace: Gandhi's Assassination as a Critical Moment in the Consolidation of the Nehruvian State' in *Modern Asian Studies*, Vol. 45, No. 1 (2011), p. 57–80

Joseph S. Alter, *Gandhi's Body: Sex, Diet, and the Politics of Nationalism* (2000) (Philadelphia: University of Pennsylvania Press)

William Mazzarella, 'Branding the Mahatma: The Untimely Provocation of Gandhian Publicity' in *Cultural Anthropology*, Vol. 25, No. 1 (2010), pp. 1–39

Manujila Koshal and Rajindar Koshal, 'Gandhi's Influence on Indian Economic Planning: A Critical Analysis' in *The American Journal of Economics and Sociology*, Vol. 32, No. 3 (1973), pp. 311–330

Vinay Lal, 'The Gandhi Everyone Loves to Hate' in *Economic and Political Weekly*, Vol. 43, No. 40 (2008), pp. 55–64

Koilpillai J Charles, 'Gandhi's Views on Health' in *Journal of Religion and Health*, Vol. 18, No. 1 (1979), pp. 60–73

Mahesh Gavaskar, 'Gandhi's Hind Swaraj: Retrieving the Sacred in the Time of Modernity' in *Economic and Political Weekly*, Vol. 44, No. 36 (2009), pp. 14–18

Manu Bhagavan, 'The Hindutva Underground: Hindu Nationalism and the Indian National Congress in Late Colonial and Early Post-Colonial India' in *Economic and Political Weekly*, Vol. 43, No. 37 (2008), pp. 39–48

Meghnad Desai, 'Gandhi & Gandhi' in *India International Centre Quarterly*, Vol. 34, No. 2 (2007), pp. 46–61

Irfan Habib, 'Gandhi and the National Movement' in *Social Scientist*, Vol. 23, No. 4/6 (1995), pp. 3–15

Bidyut Chakraborty, 'Jawaharlal Nehru and Planning, 1938–41: India at the Crossroads' in *Modern Asian Studies*, Vol. 26, No. 2 (1992), pp. 275–287

Kumkum Sangari, 'A Narrative of Restoration: Gandhi's Last Years and Nehruvian Secularism' in *Social Scientist*, Vol. 30, No. 3/4 (2002), pp. 3–33

Nicholas Dirks, *Castes of Mind: Colonialism and the Making of Modern India* (2001) (Princeton: Princeton University Press)

Akeel Bilgrami, 'Gandhi, the Philosopher' in *Economic and Political Weekly*, Vol. 38, No. 39 (2003), pp. 4159–4165

Rajmohan Gandhi, 'The Gandhi You May Not Know' in *India International Centre Quarterly*, Vol. 34, No. 2 (2007), pp. 1–17

A.B. Mathur, 'Mahatma Gandhi's Relevance Today' in *The Indian Journal of Political Science*, Vol. 50, No. 2 (1989), pp. 145–156

Rudolf Heredia, 'Gandhi's Hinduism and Savarkar's Hindutva' in *Economic and Political Weekly*, Vol. 44, No. 29 (2009), pp. 62–67

Kazuya Ishii, 'The Socioeconomic Thoughts of Mahatma Gandhi: As an Origin of Alternative Development' in *Review of Social Economy*, Vol. 59, No. 3 (2001), pp. 297–312

Poromesh Acharya, 'Educational Ideals of Tagore and Gandhi: A Comparative Study' in *Economic and Political Weekly*, Vol. 32, No. 12 (1997), pp. 601–606

B.G. Bhosale, 'Indian Nationalism: Gandhi vis-à-vis Tilak and Savarkar' in *The Indian Journal of Political Science*, Vol. 70, No. 2 (2009), pp. 419–427

Vinay Lal, 'Gandhi's West, the West's Gandhi' in *New Literary History*, Vol. 40, No. 2 (2009), pp. 281–313

The Courtesan, the Mahatma & the Italian Brahmin

AFTERWORD

Proceedings of the First Indian National Congress: Held at Bombay on the 28th, 29th and 30th of December, 1885

Maria Misra, *Vishnu's Crowded Temple: India Since the Great Rebellion* (2007) (London: Allen Lane Books)

Linguistic Provinces Commission, *Report of the Linguistic Provinces Commission* (1948) (New Delhi: Government of India Press)

Sunil Khilnani, 'Nehru's Faith' in *Outlook* Magazine (09 December 2002): https://www.outlookindia.com/website/story/nehrus-faith/218248, accessed on 27 April 2019

Shashi Tharoor, *India: From Midnight to the Millennium* (2012) (New Delhi: Penguin Books)

Ashutosh Varshney, *Battles Half Won: India's Improbable Democracy* (2013) (New Delhi: Penguin Books)

Michael Gottlob, 'India's Unity in Diversity as a Question of Historical Perspective' in the *Economic and Political Weekly*, Vol. 42, No. 9 (2007), pp. 779–789

Proshanta Nandi, 'Visions of Nationhood and Religiosity Among Early Freedom Fighters in India' in *Sociological Bulletin*, Vol. 48, No. 1/2 (1999), pp. 135–149

Jawaharlal Nehru, *The Discovery of India* (1946) (Calcutta: The Signet Press)

E.A. Gait, *The Census of India, 1911*, Vol. I (1913) (Calcutta: Superintendent, Government Printing)

V.D. Savarkar, *Who is a Hindu?* (1949) (Poona: S.P. Gokhale)

M.S. Golwalkar, *Bunch of Thoughts* (1966) (Bangalore: Vikrama Prakshan)

Monier Monier-Williams, *Religious Thought and Life in India: An Account of the Religions of the Indian Peoples* (Part I: Vedism, Brahmanism, and Hinduism) (1885) (London: John Murray)

Lewis McIver, *Imperial Census of India 1881: Operations and Results in the Presidency of Madras*, Vol. I (1883) (Madras: Government Press)

J.A. Baines, *Census of India 1891: General Report* (1893) (London: Eyre and Spottiswoode)

J.W. Massie, *Continental India: Travelling Sketches and Historical Recollections...* (1840) (London: Thomas Ward & Co.)

AUTHOR'S NOTE & ACKNOWLEDGEMENTS

It was a newspaper column that inspired the chapters in this book. In September 2016 the then editor of *Mint Lounge*, Sanjukta Sharma, asked me to commence a weekly column for her. We called it 'Medium Rare', and though I was meant to cover a series of themes, it was only a little while before my focus came to be firmly anchored in my principal interest: history.

That turn has proved rewarding in multiple ways, and the generous acceptance the column received led Karthika V.K. of Context, who also edited and published my first book, *The Ivory Throne* (2015), to suggest compiling the essays in book form. I must confess that as someone whose books so far have been not only voluminous but also heavily annotated and footnoted, I had reservations about writing in a new format and putting together such a collection.

And yet, the idea did also appeal. The original drafts of my *Mint Lounge* articles were often much longer, pruned down afterwards to fit the allocated space in print. These long versions could sit well, I reasoned, in a book, allowing an enthusiast of history to dip in and out more freely, unlike my previous work which requires a more sustained immersion. They were also a way for me to present episodes from Indian history which so appealed to me that week after week I looked forward to retelling them for readers of my column.

I do, however, recognise that there may be flaws in such a format covering so many subjects. Some contents of this book are sourced from primary archival material—the Savarkar and the Vellore Mutiny essays for instance. Others are from secondary sources—books, old and new, that I found compelling. But I have taken care to ensure that they are almost all rooted in material verified in peer-reviewed journals and not neglectful of the latest academic research. Many established names will therefore be visible in the notes: names such as Sanjay Subrahmanyam, Arjun Appadurai, Sunil Khilnani, Ashutosh Varshney, A.R. Venkatachalapathy, Richard Eaton, David Shulman, A.K. Ramanujan and others.

There may yet be weaknesses. For these I am solely responsible.

My thanks, however, I owe to many people: Anindita Ghose of *Mint Lounge* and Somak Ghoshal who have been my editors over the last two years, and the wider team involved in the process, including Vikram Shah, Anindita Satpathy, Anandi Mishra, Tanushree Ghosh, Rohit Ranjan, Chandrika Mago, Nipa Charagi and Anindita D. I have never ceased to be amazed by the stringent fact-checking at *Mint Lounge*, and their insistence on sources for even passing remarks has ensured the maintenance of high standards.

Thanks are due also to Sukumar Ranganathan, formerly editor of *Mint* proper, Vaishna Roy of *The Hindu*, Poonam

Saxena of *Hindustan Times*, Nandini Nair of *Open*, Dhanya Rajendran and Anna Isaac of *The News Minute* and Soumya Bhushan of *Mathrubhumi*.

So too am I grateful to friends who have often joined me as I set out to explore places or discuss history: Uzair Siddiqui, who accompanied me in the quest to locate the tombs of Awadh's begums in London and Paris, Sidharth Gokhale, off whom I bounced ideas in Pune, Sharat Sunder Rajeev, a repository of knowledge in Thiruvananthapuram, and my esteemed friends, Prof P. Vijayakumar and the writer, Khyrunnisa A., whose advice and sincere interest in my welfare has been most gratifying. Thanks are also owed to Colonel Balasubramanian in Pune, and Rukmini Varma, Jay Gopal Varma and Sandeep and Gitanjali Maini in Bengaluru for their unfailing support. In New Delhi, the untiring and prolific Shashi Tharoor has never tired of encouraging me, for which I remain immensely grateful.

At Context/Westland, besides my wonderful editor, V.K. Karthika, I am thankful to Vishwajyoti Ghosh, Shrutika Mathur, Ajitha G.S., Karthik Venkatesh, and the rest of the team, as well as to Shyama Warner who brought her patience and fine eye to bear on the text. Priya Kuriyan has not only demonstrated her prodigious talent through the illustrations in this book but has also been exceedingly kind and patient with me. My friend Satyajit V. Patil took it upon himself to take a series of pictures for the author page, a challenge that can ordinarily frustrate even a seasoned photographer.

This book is dedicated to my father, M.S. Pillai, whom I lost in January this year. What is owed to him cannot be easily condensed into words. He never fully read my previous books, but he did follow—and send me regular feedback on—my columns in *Mint Lounge*. In that sense, I am glad that it is this collection that serves as my tribute to him and his memory.

Finally, my thanks to Pushpa and Indrani. Without them I would neither have read a book nor picked up the pen, let alone waded into the fascinating world of Indian history.

Manu S. Pillai
May 2019